Unit Testing in Java

Johannes Link

With Contributions by Peter Fröhlich

Unit Testing in Java

How Tests Drive the Code

Johannes Link

With Contributions by Peter Fröhlich

MORGAN KAUFMANN PUBLISHERS

AN IMPRINT OF ELSEVIER

AMSTERDAM BOSTON LONDON NEW YORK
OXFORD PARIS SAN DIEGO SAN FRANCISCO
SINGAPORE SYDNEY TOKYO

Senior Editor	Tim Cox
Publishing Services Manager	Edward Wade
Editorial Coordinator	Stacie Pierce, Richard Camp
English translation	Angelika Shafir
Project Management	Matrix Productions, Inc.
Cover Design	Frances Baca
Cover Image	Photodisc Collection/Getty Images
Text Design	Rebecca Evans
Composition	Nancy Logan
Illustration	Dartmouth Publishing, Inc.
Copy Editor	Yoni Overton
Proofreader	Dan Young
Indexer	Edwin Durbin
Interior printer	The Maple-Vail Book Manufacturing Group
Cover printer	Phoenix Color Corporation

Designations used by companies to distinguish their products are often claimed as trademarks or registered trademarks. In all instances in which Morgan Kaufmann Publishers is aware of a claim, the product names appear in initial capital or all capital letters. Readers, however, should contact the appropriate companies for more complete information regarding trademarks and registration.

Morgan Kaufmann Publishers
An Imprint of Elsevier
340 Pine Street, Sixth Floor
San Francisco, CA 94104-3205
www.mkp.com

Library of Congress Cataloging-in-Publication Data
Link, Johannes.
    Unit testing in Java : how tests drive the code / by Johannes Link ; with contributions by Peter Fröhlich.
        p. cm.
    Includes bibliographical references and index.
    ISBN 1-55860-868-0
        1. Computer software—Testing. 2. Java (Computer program language)
    I. Fröhlich, Peter. II. Title.
    QA76.76.T48L55 2003
    005.1'4—dc21
Morgan Kaufmann ISBN: 1-55860-868-0
dPunkt ISBN: 3-89864-150-3

Foreword

Erich Gamma

As a professional software developer, I want to develop software as fast as possible, as well as possible, and as stress-free as possible. Automated unit tests help to bring me closer to this goal. They are a small investment, which help me get confidence in the code I produce and maintain later on. When I don't have automated tests, I have to fall back on manual testing. However, manual tests cannot be automatically repeated. Consequently, the stress increases, particularly when they have to be done under time pressure, which isn't, of course, the exception. At the push of a button you can determine at any given time whether or not the last change impacts the fitness of your software. You can do this today, tomorrow, or any time in the future, regardless of whether or not a deadline is knocking at your door.

This book by Johannes Link and contributor Peter Fröhlich is a practical introduction to using automated unit tests and the test-first approach in your day-to-day software development. The automation framework used in the book is JUnit. It is a small and simple framework for creating and managing tests. However, more is needed for successful development with unit tests. In fact, a developer has to be familiar with many different testing techniques, in particular when unit tests have to be created in the context of databases or distributed applications based on application servers. This book sheds light on these problems and is a highly welcome contribution to the field of automated unit testing.

JUnit itself was also developed with automated unit tests and the test-first approach, as explained in this book. In fact, the techniques were even used under challenging conditions, such as while fighting jet lag or during electric power failures in alpine cabins. Still, the techniques have proven themselves every time. I hope that, thanks to this book, you will become test infected and that in the future you will always be able to give a positive answer to the classical unit test control question, "Where are the unit tests?"

Erich Gamma
Co-author of JUnit
Technical Director, Object Technology International

Foreword

Frank Westphal

Do you remember your first programming experience? I don't mean the details of the computer or language used; I mean how did you feel?

I remember typing in a few statements from the programming handbook, eager to see the program run. It was amazing to watch how the code sprang to life. Within a few hours I had grown the book example into what seemed an impressive program. I had made additions here and there and after every change I would rerun the program to see how it was doing. In the evening I showed it to my parents. They could tell by the look in my eyes how proud I was.

How things have changed. I enjoy programming more than ever, but now and then I realize that some of the original fun is gone. It's in these moments that I reflect back on my first experience. Why can't programming always be like that?

Actually, it was in one of those moments that I came across the techniques described in this book. Automated tests and continuous refactoring applied in tandem brought me a bit closer to the beginning of my programming career. More often than not since then, I have been able to act like the only thing I have to do is write a few lines of code. But don't be fooled; these techniques are not only applicable to small programs. The larger the scale, the more valuable these techniques became to me.

I was glad when Johannes asked me to write a second foreword for two reasons. First, this book brings together the knowledge that a number of pioneering extreme programmers wish they had when they started applying test-first programming five years ago. If you follow down that route, you will invariably run into testing problems. Even though you are writing your tests first, you will come to halt because you won't see how to test your code. That's natural. Actually, that's the perfect time to reflect. Or to pick up this book and read what Johannes tells us.

Second, I was going to write a book just like this one. However, when Johannes shared with me the first few chapters for review, I could see that it was well written and even covering a large suite of tools to support testing code that is usually hard, if not impossible, to test. I wish I had written this book. Therefore, writing an accompanying foreword is a great pleasure.

There is but one danger in reading this book. You might come away with the impression that it's all about techniques and tools. When in fact, it's all about you.

Test-infected programmers will tell you how the tests changed their relationship to the code. There is a certain fascination in seeing a few hundred tests passing and checking all the innards of your software. Indeed, sometimes you will find yourself pressing the run button a few more times, just for the extra kick that everything's working fine.

Frank Westphal
Independent trainer and consultant

Contents

Part II
Advanced Topics

| Chapter 15 | **Loose Ends and Opportunities** | **313** |

Part III

Appendices

| Appendix A | **Notes to JUnit** | **325** |

Appendix B   Unit Tests with Other Programming Languages   335

Glossary   345

Bibliography and List of References   353

Index   **365**

Preface

When my German publisher told me that my book was going to be translated into English I was delighted: no work for lots of fame. This view was more than naive. Despite the translator's excellent job, the number of errors and omissions uncovered by the reviewers was quite a revelation.

So I had to take the challenge and rewrite parts of a book that I had already deemed finished and of high quality. What you hold in your hands now is maybe 70% translation and 30% new, updated, and improved material. And still I feel guilty for not having been able to seize all of the reviewers' suggestions.

As the book changed shape and went through heavy restructurings, my life did as well. Thanks to all who supported me in one process or another. These include the reviewers of both the German and the English versions: Frank Adler, Achim Bangert, Markus Barchfeld, Ekard Burger, Frank Cohen, Herbert Ehrlich, Eitan Farchi, Tammo Freese, Dierk König, Andreas Leidig, Erik Meade, Steve Metsker, Rainer Neumann, Christian Popp, Ilja Preuß, Stefan Roock, Michael Ruppert, Roland Sand, Martin Schneider, Thomas Singer, Andreas Schoolmann, Robert Wenner, Timothy Wall, and Frank Westphal; Angelika Shafir, who succeeded in translating not only the facts but also the spirit of the original text; Tim Cox and Stacie Pierce of Morgan Kaufmann Publishers, who value quality much higher than publication speed; Peter Fröhlich, co-author of the German version, who persevered through our discussions about language and style; all the people forming andrena objects, a more than suitable place to develop new ideas and to confront these ideas with reality; and Bettina and Jannek, who will hopefully help me fill many pages of our shared personal "book" with happiness and sadness.

Part I

Basic Techniques

Chapter 1

Introduction

Testing is important. All software developers know it, but (hardly) anyone does it.[1] Luckily, you have bought this book and therefore don't belong to this ignorant crowd ;-)

There are many reasons for the poor interest of programmers in the quality of their own products. Education plays an important role. Academically educated computer scientists hear of the fact that software has to be tested mostly as a theoretical topic within their two-semester software course. The autodidacts among programmers normally find nothing in their textbooks and programming books, except a note that programs should "of course" be thoroughly tested. Only you won't find how and why in these books, with a few praiseworthy exceptions, like those by Hunt and McManus [98] and Larman and Gutherie [00].

Eventually, developers build their own stock of prejudices and reasons reinforcing their dislike for testing. Here a few examples.

"I have no time for testing."

This frequently heard sentence assumes that testing takes a great deal of time. If you believe this, you will be caught in a vicious circle. The greater the time pressure, the fewer tests; the fewer tests, the more unstable your code. The more unstable your code, the more error reports will fly

---

1. In my experience this is a sad truth in the field of plain business application development but—as one reviewer remarked—not in other areas like telecommunications, where intensive unit testing is an absolute must to provide software with the required reliability.

in from customers. The more error reports, the more debugging time will be required. The more debugging time, the greater the time pressure. . . .

On the other hand, if you believe that *tests stabilize your code,* then this vicious circle will turn into an open spiral. The more stable your code, the less debugging time will be required. The less debugging time, the more time left for development (and tests). This is what this book is about.

"Software testing is boring and mindless."

Common literature about software testing [Binder99, McGregor01] is rather dry and theoretical, scaring off more practically oriented program-mers. However, a closer look reveals that **the discovery and thus avoid-ance of software errors is a demanding and creative activity,** just like pro-gramming itself, more so. Early testing can even help to control the programming process and make it more satisfactory because we gain more confidence in the results of our work. This is what this book is about.

"My code is virtually faultless, good enough in any event."

We as developers like to believe in our own intellectual brilliance. After all, we have read all the books about the issue, have fallen in all the traps, and know all published design patterns plus the details of 363 classes of our own frameworks by heart. Still, sudden doubts creep up at the slightest change to class 276, leaving us wondering what impact that new line of code may have on other parts of the system. Wouldn't it be great if we could use **a set of proven and automated tests to check whether an improvement at one end won't inadvertently disturb a function at the other end**? This is what this book is about.

"The test department does the testing; they do this much better anyway."

Anti-decomposition axiom

After all, there are exactly the type of pedantic and fussy people in our test department needed for a job like running the same test scripts over and over again. What a pity that test theory provides a few massive indica-tions and proofs that the test department **cannot,** in fact, do our job, which leads us to the statement of the *anti-decomposition axiom.*[2] This axiom states that testing a composite system is not sufficient to discover errors in

---

2. The three test axioms [Weyuker88] will be discussed more closely in Chapter 7.

its components. This means that the programmer is responsible for additional testing of his or her components in an isolated environment. Also, **errors found at an earlier stage can be removed much faster and at less cost**. And this is what this book is about.

| 1.1 | **Important Terms** |

Different
test types

Now we (hopefully) agree that *developer tests* are indispensable for high-quality software. But, then, even developers test different things in different ways. For example, *performance* and *load tests* concentrate on the fulfillment of certain nonfunctional requirements, like required response times and the expected number of users. A programmer's central test tasks are, however, the so-called *unit tests*. This term originates from the pre-object-oriented era and tells us that individual tests concentrate on single *units* of the system rather than on the entire system. Today, we also often speak of *component tests.*

Unit tests

Component tests

What is a
unit test?

Back then, it was pretty easy to recognize such a unit as a procedure or function. In object-oriented systems, this "unit to be tested" can take different shapes. The span reaches from a single method over a class and subsystem to the entire system. Mostly (but not always) this unit concerns the "natural" abstraction unit of an object-oriented system: the class or its instantiated form, the object. To avoid the somewhat clumsy phrase *unit to be tested,* I will also be using the terms *class under test (CUT)* and *object under test (OUT)* from the relevant literature in the further course of this book. The difference between the two terms lies in one's perspective: in the middle of a test, I'm interested in the object itself; when talking about several tests, then the class is my point of reference.

Class under test
(CUT)

Object under test
(OUT)

Integration tests

Interaction tests

Developers also have to grapple with *integration tests.* These are tests concentrating on the interplay of several previously tested components. For this reason, McGregor [01] also calls these tests *interaction tests.* However, considering that, in object-oriented systems, each integration is also represented by one or more objects, it is often impossible to strictly separate between component tests and integration tests. We will deal with this issue wherever a differentiation appears meaningful in the further course of this book. However, we should generally not pay too much attention to this issue. What's important is the result of our test efforts and not a perfect terminological classification.

Static tests
Dynamic tests

Unit tests are the central topic of this book, but it takes much more to achieve a high-quality software that is well accepted by the customer. For example, we distinguish between *static* and *dynamic* tests. Static tests can be applied without actually running the program and comprise such things as automated code analyzers as well as code inspections performed by other developers [Gilb93]. Dynamic tests require the code to be executed and are found again as *functional tests, acceptance tests, regression tests,* and other variants. Often, these tests are specified and conducted by a dedicated test team or even by the customers themselves. In this book, we will mainly focus on developer-side tests, until Chapter 14, where we describe the role of our unit tests from an overall view, i.e., *software process* and *quality assurance.*

Test coverage

To many testers and testing developers the key problem is, When are my tests adequate? When have I tested enough? In classic unit testing these questions are usually answered by the notion of *test coverage:* how much of the code and how much of the requirements specification is being covered by my tests? In that respect a suite of tests is considered adequate when it just covers everything; more tests would be a waste of effort. To decide what a term like *full coverage* means, numerous coverage metrics can be defined (see Chapter 8, Section 8.3, Test Coverage).

1.2 | XP Testing

Component tests in XP

Although their importance is stressed in the test literature, unit tests have played a subordinate role for most developers. This situation changed (at least slightly) when *Extreme Programming (XP)* promoted the execution of component tests to a central activity within the XP development cycle. XP [Beck00a, Jeffries00] is a lightweight development process returning full control over the direction and change of direction in a project to the customer. The actual code writing moves to the center of the development activity. With this provocative shift of focus, XP scares off the advocates of detailed and sophisticated analysis and design methodologies. On the other hand, it wins over those many software developers who had felt bossed around by rather inappropriate and bureaucratic development processes.

Those interested in Extreme Programming as an overall complex and its relationship to heavyweight development processes will have to study the relevant literature and Web sites (see Bibliography and List of References, Further Reading). At this point, we will limit our discussion to a few central issues important for testing as described in this book.

Communication, Simplicity, Feedback, and Courage

XP values   Communication, simplicity, feedback, and courage are central values of XP and thus reflect in every piece of program code: in XP, code should be written so that it communicates all the things it contains. This requires particular care when naming classes and methods. Also, short methods with meaningful and expressive names can often replace long program comments and are less prone to becoming inconsistent in future changes to the program.

In addition, the program should be only as complex as required by the *current functionality*. This means in particular that we should do without considering any presumed future functionality. This is because XP assumes that if all central practices are observed, later changes will cost less than weaving presumed requirements into the design in advance, particularly because the majority of presumptions turn out to be wrong later on in every project.

Automated tests on several levels (discussed shortly) serve for quick *feedback* on whether or not our code does what it should do. *Courage* is needed by a team whenever changes have to be made to the system. Extensive tests will ensure that the task calls for courage rather than recklessness.

Pair Programming

Pair programming   XP requires that each piece of code to be taken to production be created jointly by two developers on a single computer. Ideally, one programmer focuses closely on the lines he or she currently types, while the other one focuses on the larger picture, and both change their roles constantly. *Pair programming* or programming in pairs is a kind of constant review, ensuring fewer errors, more consistency with the coding guidelines, and knowledge sharing across the entire team. The tests ensure that the pair will not lose focus.

While many managers have a feeling that this approach wastes resources, this fear is disproved in studies on the productivity of pair programming [Cockburn00a]. These studies have shown that a slightly smaller output of code is more than compensated for by better design and a clearly lower error rate.

Incremental and Iterative Development

Software development in XP does not occur *en bloc,* but in small steps. The entire system is created in *iterations* taking from one to three weeks. Each iteration is aimed at implementing one set of small *user stories* selected by the customer. The development team decomposes these user stories into *tasks,* small parts that can be completed by a developer pair within a few days. Again, these tasks are not implemented en bloc, but in small steps. Such a micro step includes both the implementation code and the test proving that the implementation does indeed do what it should do. Note that the implementation is not deemed to exist without this test.

Refactoring

Refactoring describes the constant restructuring of code all the way to the simplest design. The word *simplest* is based on the following criteria, and the order is important.

Simplest design
1. All unit tests are running.

2. The code communicates all of its design concepts.

3. The code does not contain redundancy (duplicated code or logic).

4. Under the above rules, the code contains the smallest possible number of classes and methods.

XP demands for constant refactoring, in particular after successful completion of a task. Frequent refactoring is hardly possible without automated unit tests, or there would be too big a risk of interfering with functioning components at one end when refactoring something at the other. This fear of unwanted side effects is a major reason why many developers seem to shrink from "cleaning up" apparently functioning components. In the long run, this leads to the unmanageable systems that all of us dread and have come across. It's not surprising then that the need for disciplined refactoring to control software evolution has long been recognized [Lehman85].

Martin Fowler [99] describes the most common refactoring measures, how to discover their necessity,[3] how to execute them step by step, and how unit tests facilitate refactoring. Nowadays many Java development environments (e.g., Eclipse and IntelliJ) provide built-in support for some automated basic refactorings. However, the correctness of a refactoring—signified by no change in the program's functional behavior—generally cannot be proven for more complex restructuring tasks.

Test Types in XP

Extreme Programming proclaims two types of software tests: *acceptance tests* and the previously introduced unit tests. While the same techniques and tools can basically be used for both types, they differ in their purposes and responsibilities.

Unit tests in XP

- **Unit tests** secure the developer's confidence in his or her own software and that of their colleagues. They are created together with the development code and then modified and completed as needed. Unit tests **always** have to be 100% successful. The word *always* means that, when integrating new code into the system, all tests created to this point will be executed. If only one single test fails, then we first have to fix this error before continuing with the integration. This is very important in XP, because *continuous integration* means that all edited code has to be incorporated into the overall system several times daily (see also Chapter 14, Section 14.2, Process Types and Testing Strategies).

Acceptance tests in XP

- **Acceptance tests** serve both the customer and the management team as a measurement for the progress of the entire project. Acceptance tests are specified by the customer; after all, it's the customer who has to believe in the test result. Acceptance tests normally specify the

---

3. Or better, how to smell it. By the way, a sign of code in need of improvement is called "code smell."

functionality of the overall system from the user's perspective. It is important to specify the majority of all test cases for a given run before an iteration begins. The percentage share of successful tests is determined at least once per day and is available to all interested parties.

The job of turning a specification into automated executable test cases is normally assumed by developers. However, it would be conceivable to assign this job to a dedicated test team who would advise the customer during the specification phase and implement the tests [Crispin01]. In some cases it is possible to automate the acceptance tests similarly to the unit tests. Also, commercial test tools may be a meaningful approach. However, it is often recommended to develop a small framework that can form a basis to use the customer's specifications, for example in tabular form, directly as control files for the test runs [URL:WakeAT].

Test automation   Both for unit tests and for acceptance tests, there is a requirement for full automation. The higher initial investment, compared to manual tests, will pay off after only a few runs. Unit tests are started innumerable times per day, so it would be unthinkable in practice not to automate them. On the other hand, when automating some types of acceptance tests, such as the user interface, we often find ourselves in all sorts of troubles. Before giving up and falling back into manual testing, however, consider that this would not only be more expensive over the long run but also more error-prone, because errors could sneak in during execution and verification. Literature dealing with test automation [Dustin99] may help in difficult cases.

XP or Not XP?

Agile processes   XP belongs to the group of *agile* software processes.[4] This means, among other things, that as few steps as possible are prescribed, but as many as necessary exist.

Evolutionary design   One thing is most important for the type of unit testing introduced in this book: there is no big, previously executed, detailed design phase, or *Big Design Up Front (BDUF)*. The detailed software design, particularly the

---

4. *Agile* replaced the word *lightweight* with regard to software processes some time ago (see also [URL:AgileAlliance] and Chapter 14, Section 14.2).

establishment of interfaces of single classes and their relationships to other classes, is part of the coding or test creation. This *evolutionary design* [Fowler00] approach largely contradicts the design and test methods described in the literature, where models and specifications of all components are prepared "up front" and used to derive test cases. XP's intentional renunciation of a dedicated design phase before implementation is probably the biggest shooting target for its critics. Meanwhile, there exists a considerable body of anecdotal evidence that evolutionary design can work [Little01] and some well founded arguments that the constant focus on design improvement is more important than a thorough, initial *planned design* [Fowler00]. Robert Martin [02a] even argues that continuous care will correct a poor initial design whereas lack of continuous care allows a good design to degrade over time.

Complementary practices In addition, there are certain standard practices in XP facilitating (pair programming, incremental development) and validating (acceptance tests) unit tests and in building on them (refactoring). This means that XP is not a prerequisite for unit testing, but it is worthwhile for every developer and project manager to think about it and see whether or not some aspect of XP could improve their test efforts and thus the quality of their software. In particular the combination of unit tests, pair programming, and refactoring recommends itself to that end and integrates well in almost every development process.

1.3 Classic Testing

One particularity of the XP approach was briefly mentioned above: the *test-first approach*, a.k.a. *test-driven development*. *"Test-first"* means that the test is written before the actual implementation code. Before jumping into explaining what test-first means exactly (which we do in the next section), we use the following example of a small programming job to first look at the drawbacks of classic, subsequent testing.

> We want to program a dictionary to translate a German text into a language of our choice, say English. This dictionary, in the form of a class, *Dictionary*, is initialized with a word file and allows us to query the translation of a German word. The program should allow several translation alternatives.

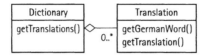

Figure 1.1 Class diagram of the dictionary.

This description of requirements is sufficiently clear and compact for us to write the program code in one iteration. We will define missing details, like the exact format of the word file, while programming. The "classic" iteration includes (at least) the following steps: detailed design, implementation, and subsequent tests.

We use a UML class diagram as our initial design (Figure 1.1).

Our Java implementation of the class Translation consists only of the constructor and two get methods:

```java
/**
 * Represents a possible translation of a
 * German word
 */
public class Translation {
    private String germanWord;
    private String translation;
    public Translation(String germanWord,
                       String translation) {
        this.germanWord = germanWord;
        this.translation = translation;
    }
    public String getGermanWord() {
        return germanWord;
    }
    public String getTranslation() {
        return translation;
    }
}
```

During their initialization, objects of the Dictionary class generate Translation objects and add them to an internal list. When querying the translation in the getTranslations() method, this list is iterated and the output string is built:

```java
import java.io.*;
import java.util.List;
import java.util.ArrayList;
import java.util.Iterator;
/**
 * Dictionary for translation of German words into
 * another language.
 * The dictionary is initialized with a word file.
 */
public class Dictionary {
    private List entries = new ArrayList();
    public Dictionary(String filename) throws IOException {
        this.initializeFromReader(new BufferedReader(
            new FileReader(filename)));
}

    /**
     * Supplies a translation of the German word.
     * If there are several alternatives, then these
     * are appended, separated by a comma.
     */
    public String getTranslations(String germanWord) {
        StringBuffer translations = new StringBuffer();
        Iterator i = entries.iterator();
        while (i.hasNext()) {
            Translation each = (Translation) i.next();
            if (each.getGermanWord().equals(germanWord)) {
                if (translations.length() > 0) {
                    translations.append(", ");
                }
                translations.append(each.getTransaltion());
            }
        }
        return translations.toString();
    }

    /**
     * The word file to be read consists of
     * 0 - n lines.
```

```
 * Each line contains an entry in the following form:
 * '<germanWord>=<translation>'
 */
private final void initializeFromReader(
    BufferedReader aReader) throws IOException {
    String line = aReader.readLine();
    while (line != null) {
        int index = line.indexOf('=');
        if (index != -1) {
            String germanWord = line.substring(0, index);
            String translation = line.substring(
                index + 1, line.length());
            Translation entry =
                new Translation(germanWord, translation);
            entries.add(entry);
        }
        line = aReader.readLine();
    }
}
```

So far, all of this looks quite easy; *only* the tests are missing yet. For example, we could accommodate the tests in a separate class, Dictionary-Tester, with all single test cases in its main() method:

```
public class DictionaryTester {
    /**
     * Start all test cases for the Dictionary class
     */
    public static void main(String[] args) {
        testCase1();
        testCase2();
        /*...*/
    }
}
```

The test cases are then programmed roughly in the following steps:

1. Create a word file.

2. Use this file to create an instance of the Dictionary class.

3. Query specific translations and check the results.

The simplest case of a word file with one word would look like this:

```
public static void testcase1() {
    String filename = "C:\\temp\\dictionary.txt";
    try {
        PrintWriter writer = new PrintWriter(
            new FileOutputStream(filename));
        writer.println("Wort=word");
        writer.close();
        Dictionary dictionary = new Dictionary(filename);
        String translation =
            dictionary.getTranslations("Wort");
        if (!translation.equals("word")) {
            System.out.println("Test case 1 failed." +
                               " Word found: " + translation);
        } else {
            System.out.println("Test case 1 successful.");
        }
    } catch (Exception ex) {
        System.out.println("Test case 1 failed." +
                           " Unexpected exception.");
        System.out.println(ex.toString());
    }
}
```

It would now be useful to have several test cases with a different number of entries in the file (0, 1, 2, and many), with identical entries, with several translations of the same word, to search for words that begin with uppercase or lowercase letters, and so on.

Unfortunately, this approach has a significant drawback: each single test case has to make a detour over a word file. This situation is not only complicated, it can also lead to nasty problems when creating and overwriting files. This problem would be avoided if we could add Translation objects to the Dictionary object without going a long way over a file. But is it really worth changing the implementation and giving up our hard earned encapsulation just for the test?

The same question comes up when we want to test the behavior while reading faulty word files. If an error occurs in the middle of a file, we would like to know how many translations have already been read. But there is no method available for this query yet. Also, we haven't thought about how the dictionary should generally react in case of errors. Should it ignore errors? Throw an exception? Output errors?

We would not have had to deal with a number of problems had we written the tests first and turned to the implementation after.

- We would have had to think about error behavior and clarify any specification that may have been missing in advance.

- Methods we need for test purposes would automatically have reached the (public or protected) interface, because a test is treated like any other "client" of our class.

- A closer look would have lead us to the question of whether or not our Translation class is really necessary or whether it would have been sufficient to use a hash map.

Chapter 3 will further elaborate the above example by use of the test-first approach and arrive at a different design, which simplifies not only the tests but also the program itself.

1.4 | Test-First Development—A Brief Definition

Test-first development is an approach to code software systems. More than that, it's the approach I use in my daily programming work and that I advocate in this book. Test-first is much more than a quality-assurance activity; it drives the software design towards easy testing and simplicity. That's why test-first development is also called *test-driven development* or even *test-driven design* [Beck02]. The following points describe the most important aspects of the test-first approach.

- Before writing a line of production code, you first build an automated-failing test, which motivates this code.

- You write only as much production code as required for the test to arrive at working code as fast as you can.

- As soon as the code works, you refactor it in order to make it as clean as possible, which basically means to *remove all duplication.*

- The development progresses in small steps, where testing and coding alternate. Such a "micro-iteration" does not take more than 10 minutes.

- When you integrate production code into the overall system, all unit tests have to run successfully.

This small set of rules may appear arbitrary to some programmers and contradict their personal experiences. Kent Beck [02] does an excellent job at showing the obvious and not so obvious reasons why test-driven development is a sound idea. The goal of this book is to show how test-driven development looks in practice and to convince you that it actually works. Some of its benefits are obvious.

- Each single piece of code gets tested. This means changes that could destroy existing functionality are discovered immediately. It plays a decisive role, particularly at the time of software integration, and thus serves as a form of continuous *regression testing.*

- The tests document the code because, in the ideal case, they show both the normal use and the expected reaction in case of errors.

- The micro-iterations are very short, which means very quick feedback. Within 10 minutes at most, you cannot program a lot, so you cannot make many mistakes.

- The design of a program is essentially determined by the tests (see also the subsection, Evolutionary design, in Section 1.2). In many cases, this leads to simpler design as compared to one devised on the drawing board, because it is hard to write simple tests for complex structures. This is the reason why many consider test-driven development to be much more of a design approach than a testing approach [URL:WikiTFD].

Don't get me wrong, though: test-driven programming can be difficult and trying; it is no silver bullet either. That's why another goal of this book is to show typical test-first problems and to explain when it is acceptable or even necessary to depart from the rules.

Healthy skepticism

Many experienced and successful software developers who have been engaged mainly in *design-first programming* during their professional careers are sceptical about the idea of a design that develops gradually in small steps. All these skeptics are encouraged to temporarily forget about their doubts, experiment with the approach (for not too short) a while, and then judge. For one phenomenon can only be experienced when you try it yourself: in contrast to subsequent testing, creating test cases before the application code is really fun!

1.5 Java Only—Or Other Coffee?

Other programming languages

So far we have hardly mentioned Java in this chapter. If, despite the word *Java* in the book title, this book has fallen into the hands of developers who use other object-oriented programming languages, they will surely ask themselves whether or not it will be worth their while to continue reading. Our answer is, Yes, under certain conditions:

- You read Java code and are willing to learn the basic terms of its syntax and the standard libraries in advance or when needed.

- You know how to abstract special Java constructs (e.g., interface) and to translate them into your development language.

- The 20% (or so) of this book really of interest only to Java developers doesn't bother you.

In this book we use *JUnit* as a framework for test automation. JUnit is the Java variant of a family of unit test tools, but it is also available for most of the other programming languages. Polyglot non-Java developers will eventually be rewarded for their endurance: Appendix B includes notes for unit tests in other programming languages.

1.6 Objectives of This Book

This book represents a practical introduction to unit testing for software developers. More specifically, it introduces test-driven development and suggests it as a general approach for system development. A large number of special fields and problem cases of this approach are discussed. Some of the questions addressed are, Which are the central tests to start with? How should I organize my tests? How many tests are enough? What about testing at the system boundary? and How can I test in the presence of inheritance and polymorphism?

However, many of the techniques introduced in this book can also be used for subsequent unit testing; in fact, some are meaningful for that purpose only. Other test types—mainly system and acceptance tests—will be explained whenever there does not appear to be a clear distinction to unit tests. In the ideal case, this book should instruct developers during the first, second, and third steps, and motivate them to further explore the numerous references given.

This book is not an introduction to Java or general software development; knowledge and experience in both areas are assumed. It also does not represent a systematic introduction to the testing of object-oriented systems, but the required theory will be examined and references for further reading will be given. Moreover, Extreme Programming will be discussed only to the extent that it offers us assistance and reasons for unit tests.

This book includes operating instructions for JUnit only to a limited extent. Many problems of practical operation, such as installation, integration into your own development environment, and other special issues, will be dealt with very briefly (see also Appendix A). However, JUnit serves as a basis for the automation of our unit tests (see Chapter 2).

1.7 Organization of This Book

In contrast to the majority of current software development literature, this book does not employ a single case example used throughout the entire book for two reasons. First, it is my personal preference to pick out specific sections in random order when reading textbooks; continual examples would make it difficult to recapitulate the details. Second, doing without one continual example allowed me to directly include authentic code examples from practice.

This book is organized in three main parts. Part I, Basic Techniques, supplies the fundamentals for the rest of the book and reading in sequential order best meets its purpose as a textbook. Readers already working with JUnit can skim Chapter 2, Automating Unit Tests.

Part II, Advanced Topics, is composed of independent chapters, which can be consulted according to the reader's personal need or interest. These topics include persistent objects, concurrent and distributed systems, Web applications, graphical user interfaces (GUIs), and unit testing in different development processes.

Part III consists of appendices, which include JUnit-specific material, useful tips for unit testing in other programming languages, a glossary of terms, and a bibliography with references for further reading.

1.8 Conventions in This Book

New terms introduced in the main text throughout the book are printed in *italics* and phrases of particular importance are printed in **bold**.

The book includes a large amount of source code. Code examples are set in monofont and organized as follows:

```
/** Source code beginning
 */
public class anExample {}
```

Modified or added code will additionally be highlighted in **bold**. References to code in the main text are set in monofont.

Compatible with Java SDK 1.2–1.4

Most code examples are compatible with Java SDK 1.2–SDK 1.4. Where a special SDK version is required, this will be noted in the margin in addition to the text.

Coding guidelines

All code examples are based on the following guidelines to keep them short:

- *Import statements* use the *asterisk* form where more than one class of a package is needed. This guideline is also useful for production code [Larman00].

- The examples do not include *comments*, unless needed for better understanding. In particular, there are no *JavaDoc comments*.

- The examples do not include `package` instructions, unless needed to avoid confusion.

These guidelines serve mainly to compress the printed code examples. In the real world, each team has to agree on the coding guidelines and observe them. Their consistent use is an important part of these guidelines.

Some readers may find the explicit use of `"this"` in messages to an object unusual. I use this convention because it emphasizes the semantic difference between sending messages and calling functions, namely, static methods.

1.9 Web Site to This Book

The companion Web site to this book is at

www.mkp.com/companions/1558608680

which includes further information, including the source code from all chapters, a collection of useful Web links, and selected sections from this book in PDF format.

Chapter 2

Automating Unit Tests

Let's assume for the time being that the arguments in favor of unit tests and the test-first approach outlined in the introduction are true. One important prerequisite for this approach is the complete automation of the test process. The counter argument most frequently heard concerns the presumably higher initial cost, compared to manual tests. Is there something to this argument?

Costs and benefits of test automation

In conventional test approaches it is assumed that the *break-even* point between costs and benefits is reached after about 10 test runs ([Kaner93, p. 196]). This means that automation pays at the latest when you run the automated test more than 10 times in unchanged condition. A rough estimate of our test-first approach looks like this:

Estimating costs and benefits for test-first development

With an average program size of 500 classes and a development time of one week per class, we have a total development time of 20,000 (500 x 5 x 8) hours. With an average integration frequency of hours and the rule that all unit tests have to be executed in each integration (see Section 1.4), we have 5000 runs for the entire test suite. This means that a test from the middle of the development time is executed approximately 2500 times—provided it survives development to the end—not including that it may be executed every five to ten minutes during the initial focus of development. This automation definitely pays.

Naturally, this estimate does not include several factors: many tests have to be changed in the course of their lifetime, especially under constant refactoring (see Chapter 4, Section 4.9); some tests will even disappear totally; and the cost for initial creation of a specific test can vary a lot.[1] It also does not include additional effects of unit tests with regard to design and documentation. Still, our estimate is good enough to show that unit tests following the test-first approach would be much more expensive without automation (as measured in developer time), provided that the rules described in Chapter 1, Section 1.4, are meaningfully applied. In addition, humans produce many more errors than machines when doing recurring tasks over and over again, which is the case with the execution of most existing tests.

In summary, we cannot do without automation. The questions are now: What do we want to automate? How do we automate? How do we make sure we won't lose track?

2.1 What Do We Want to Automate?

Different automation types   Automation is different depending on the test type, the test level, and the system type. For example, if we want to test the behavior of a server-based system under high load, we need some specific sort of tool. The ideal tool would allow us to send a certain number of jobs from several clients to that server and then to poll a number of parameters, such as response times, number of failed queries, storage consumption, and CPU load. In contrast, so-called *capture/playback tools* are often used to test graphic applications, allowing the recording and playback of interactions on user level, such as mouse movements, clicks, and keyboard inputs.

We are interested mainly in the automation of object-oriented unit tests. Such a test consists normally of the creation of one or more objects, bringing these objects into a specific initial state, feeding them with a number of messages, and finally checking for changes within the objects or impact on the environment (e.g., files). In other words, we are interested in creating a *test driver*.

Different test levels   While we have agreed on the test type we are interested in, we still have to think about different levels to which our test cases can refer:

- **Testing single methods.** The side conditions here are mainly pre- and post-conditions of the methods (see Chapter 4, Section 4.7, Design by Contract).

---

1. A critical analysis of the economics of automated tests can be found in Marick [00].

- **Testing the protocol of a class.** Typical scenarios for the use of instances play the most important role here (see Chapter 4, Section 4.3, Testing the Typical Functionality).

- **Testing the interaction between two or more objects** (see Chapter 4, Section 4.6, Object Interactions).

Our hope is to be able to complete all these types of test levels with one single approach and one single tool. This time our hope will not be unwarranted.

2.2 Requirements for an Automation Framework

While the tools available in the market include some that allow the creation of drivers by use of proprietary script languages, such tools are less suitable for the "developer as a tester" role. First, learning a new language represents a barrier and, second, the concurrent use of two languages demands constant mental "switching." For this reason, our first requirement for an automation environment states:

The language used to specify tests is the programming language itself.

Java as the test specification language

In our case, the programming language is Java. This means that we can use the same tools (e.g., version management) to handle both the test code and the application code. One drawback is that the test specification is contained in the code only implicitly: neither input data nor output data is marked as such but is distributed all over the program code.

A frequently used approach for class-based test drivers provides a *static method* that runs our tests for each class [Hunt98]. Another approach is to page out the tests into a dedicated *tester class*. We opted for this variant earlier in Section 1.3. The benefits and drawbacks of these two approaches are shown in Table 2.1 [McGregor01, p. 185].

Our main argument is the separation of application code and test code, which is important mainly for software shipping. For this reason, our second requirement states:

We need to separate application code from test code.

Table 2.1   *Benefits and drawbacks of test drivers.*

	Benefits	*Drawbacks*
Static method in CUT (class under test)	Allows access to private parts of the class	Does not separate application code and test code
	Easy reuse of the test code in subclasses	More code is in the application
Separate tester class	Separates application and test code	Requires an additional class
	Test code can be organized independently of the class structure	Private parts of the class cannot be accessed for white-box tests

What is a test case?   The granularity used to specify, run, and verify tests is normally a *test case*. Pol et al. [00, p. 528] define a test case as such: "A test case describes a test to be executed, which is oriented to a specific test objective." This description has to include the target object, input and output parameters, the context, and side effects. In the case of executable tests, all points reflect also in the program code. The decisive aspect is that the execution of a test case does not have any impact on subsequent test cases. Otherwise, dependencies between tests can cause single errors to have a non-local impact. In other words, if we rely on a specific order of the test run, then the failure of one test will cause a false alarm in a subsequent test. For this reason, we establish another requirement:

Test cases have to be executed and verified separately from one another.

What is a test suite?   The independence of single test case conflicts with the fact that we need a means to organize related tests to be able to handle them jointly. Such a group of test cases is called a *test suite*. Our next requirement states:

We need a way to arbitrarily group test cases into test suites.

When taking a closer look at our first attempt to obtain a test driver in Section 1.3, we can see that the success or failure of a test was communicated only by a text output, for example:

```
if (!translation.equals("word")) {
    System.out.println("Test case 1 failed...");
} else {
    System.out.println("Test case 1 successful.");
}
```

Although this may be acceptable for a single test case, for 20 or 100 or 5000 tests on hand, we would have to search several pages of text for "successful" and "failed" to find the number of successful and failed test cases. For this reason, our last requirement for a test automation environment states:

The success or failure of a test run should be visible at a glance.

This set of requirements will serve us as a basis to evaluate frameworks for unit test automation. Note that no tool is perfect. The tester or developer will have to ensure that the rules and "best practices" are observed wherever the selected framework may fail to enforce these rules.

| 2.3 | **JUnit** |

History and meaning

JUnit is the basis for most of the code examples contained in this book. This Open Source framework for the automation of unit tests under Java was originally written by Kent Beck and Erich Gamma, and is available through [URL:JUnit]. Historically, JUnit is an offspring of a similar framework for Smalltalk [Beck94]; its current variant is *SUnit,* which will be described in detail in Appendix B. There is no doubt that JUnit has become a quasi-standard tool for Java unit testing, which shows both in the large number of introductory and advanced articles (see Bibliography and List of References, Further Reading), and in the choice of enhancements available for JUnit (see Appendix A, Section A.2, JUnit Expansions). It has been widely accepted in a large number of Open-Source projects.[2] In addition, JUnit meets most of the testing requirements we've established thus far. Now, what does the creation and running of test cases look like in JUnit?

---

2. For example, in Apache's Tomcat and Avalon projects [URL:Apache].

Installing and Running Tests

Let's start from the beginning—the installation. The most recent JUnit version can be downloaded from [URL:JUnit].[3] To use the framework in your own projects, you have only to include the `junit.jar` file into the class path of the JDK version you are using, load the sources into your project, or just use the built-in JUnit support of your favourite IDE.[4] In its archive, `junit3.8.1.zip`, JUnit supplies examples (in the folder `junit/samples/`) and tests for the framework itself (in the folder `junit/tests/`) in addition to the Jar file. We will now use these to get an idea about the different types of test runs. JUnit offers three different `TestRunner` classes:

- `junit.textui.TestRunner` writes the test results to `stdout`.

- `junit.awtui.TestRunner` is a simple AWT-based graphic tool.

- `junit.swingui.TestRunner` is a complex Swing-based graphic tool.

All three classes have a `main()` method so they can be accessed from the command line. As a parameter, they require the fully qualified name of a test class, which includes the class' package name. We will further explain how this looks in the sections that follow.

Let's use the example tests included in the JUnit archive to have a look at the different set of test runners. First, we type the following in the command line to change to the folder JUnit used to unpack the files:

```
> cd wherever/junit3.8.1
```

Textual test runner　　Provided that a JDK is available in the current path, we first call the textual test runner:

```
> java -cp junit.jar;. junit.textui.TestRunner junit.
    samples.AllTests
```

And after a few seconds . . .

3.　We use JUnit Version 3.8.1 in this book.

4.　You find support at [URL:JUnit] for integration into various IDEs.

```
........................................
........................................
.....................................
Time: 1.462
OK (119 tests)
```

The result is rather sober: each dot of the output shows us a successfully completed test. In addition, we are informed about the test runtime, the total result (OK), and the number of tests. Failed tests would have reflected in an F or E text output and led to a different total result.

Graphic test runner   This picture looks slightly different when using the AWT tool. The lines

```
> java -cp junit.jar;. junit.awtui.TestRunner junit.
  samples.AllTests
```

open a window and start our tests (Figure 2.1).

And yet another window appears when using the Swing test runner (Figure 2.2). Note that Figures 2.1 and 2.2 do not show that the bar above the Runs/Errors statistic is bright green—a sign that the test run was

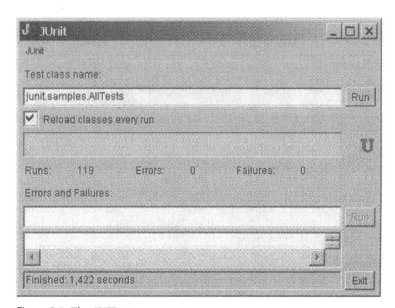

Figure 2.1 The AWT test runner.

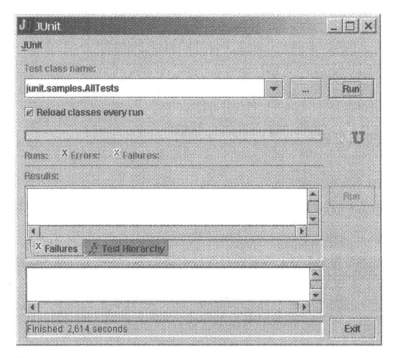

Figure 2.2 The Swing test runner.

successful. If just one test goes wrong, then the color in this progress bar changes to red.

Red bar–
green bar

Having a *green bar* or a *red bar* is commonly accepted JUnit wording to describe if your tests are currently working or failing.

In the further course of this book, we will mainly use the AWT–based TestRunner class, because it works for all JDK versions from 1.1 up, and its set of functions is sufficient for our purposes. Which test runner you will use in productive operation is mainly a question of taste. Nowadays some Java IDEs (e.g., Eclipse) come with tightly integrated JUnit test runners of their own. All of them meet an important criterion from our set of requirements: the success or failure of a test run can be seen at a glance.

Creating Test Classes

junit.
framework.
TestCase

JUnit defines test cases in separate classes. These classes are derived from junit.framework.TestCase or from a subclass. This separation between test class and class under test means that JUnit meets another requirement from our requirements catalog.

To keep things simple at the beginning, we will test a piece from the Java library, the class StringBuffer. First, consider our empty test class:

```
import junit.framework.*;
public class StringBufferTest extends TestCase {
}
```

The import of junit.framework.* will haunt us across the entire book, because it represents the central JUnit package.[5] Here the name of the test class is composed of the name of the target class and the ending *Test*. This is pure convention, facilitating the automatic detection and removal, if necessary, of test classes. Before Version 3.8 we needed a constructor with a String parameter for the framework to work; this constructor is now optional.

Next, we compile and call the test runner with the test class' name as its argument:

```
> java junit.awttui.TestRunner StringBufferTest
```

Obviously, nothing good happens now; the TestRunner shows its brightest red and produces an error message (Figure 2.3).

The only surprising thing is this: How does the runner know that we have not written any test yet? The answer lies in a convention which makes our lives (and future testing) easier: unless otherwise specified, JUnit considers all *public, non-static,* and *parameterless* methods whose names start with *test* as test methods. This mechanism works with Java's *Reflection* mechanism and saves us the trouble of having to explicitly register each single test case somewhere.

Creating a
test case
We are now ready to add the first test case, which we want to use to test for correct initialization of an empty StringBuffer. We do that by declaring the following method within the StringBufferTest class:

```
public void testEmptyBuffer() {
    StringBuffer buffer = new StringBuffer();
    assertTrue(buffer.toString().equals(""));
    assertTrue(buffer.length() == 0);
}
```

---

5. So please understand that we sometimes leave out the import line to save space.

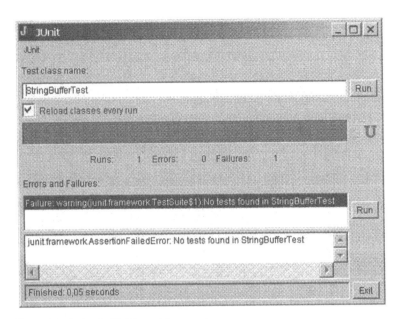

Figure 2.3 StringBufferTest without tests.

Although this example is very simple, we can see a few basic things. For instance, the second part of the name describes what we are testing—in our example, the behavior of an empty buffer.

assertTrue() Another typical structure is the method body, which first creates an object and then checks certain properties as to their compliance with our expectations. Those little one-line tests are usually called *assertions*. The method assertTrue(),[6] for example, takes a boolean expression as a parameter, and the expression's result is verified at runtime. If it is true, then the program continues. It if is false, then the test case terminates at this point, a *failure* is registered, and the next test case—if there is one—will be started.

What is a failure?

To run modified and added tests, we will no longer use the command line from now on, but the test runner's *Run* button. Note the tick next to "Reload classes every run"; this is important because it ensures that we can start all tests of a modified class without having to start up the tool every time. The very first test brings us back to a green bar—reason enough for another try:

---

6. assertTrue() was assert() before JUnit Version 3.7. Since *assert* rose to a reserved key word in JDK 1.4, assert() became *deprecated* in JUnit.

```
public void testAppendString() {
    StringBuffer buffer = new StringBuffer();
    buffer.append("A string");
    assertEquals("A string", buffer.toString());
    assertEquals(9, buffer.length());
}
```

assertEquals()   Here we see a variant of the Assert command—assertEquals(expected, actual)—that tests two returned objects for equality. JUnit lets us use this command in variations for most primitive types and also for real objects. The equals operator (==) is used to compare primitive types, while the equals() method is used to compare objects. We will see more varieties of this central JUnit method as we progress in this book.

Unfortunately, running the test results in yet another red bar (Figure 2.4). This time, the test runner reports a *failure,* namely, an assertion that failed. The use of assertEquals() ensures that the error message is unique: expected: <9> but was: <10>. We made a mistake when creating the test, and correcting it will take us back into the green zone:

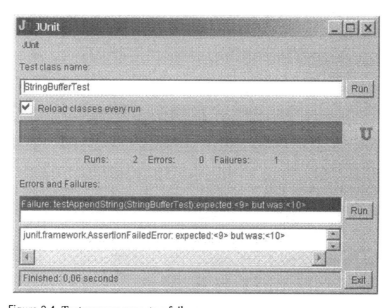

Figure 2.4 Test runner reports a failure.

```
public void testAppendString() {
  StringBuffer buffer = new StringBuffer();
  buffer.append("A string");
  assertEquals("A string", buffer.toString());
  assertEquals(10, buffer.length());
}
```

What is an error?   JUnit distinguishes between a failure and an error. An error occurs when an exception makes its way up to the test method while the test is running. The difference between "failure" and "error" is an important JUnit concept you should always keep in mind. For example, the following test case results in a NullPointerException and is registered by JUnit as an error:

```
public void testProvokeError() {
  StringBuffer buffer = null;
  buffer.append("A string");
}
```

Fixtures

Taking a closer look at the two test cases we have written so far, we can see a small code duplication:

```
public void testEmptyBuffer() {
  StringBuffer buffer = new StringBuffer();
  assertTrue(buffer.toString().equals(""));
  assertTrue(buffer.length() == 0);
}
public void testAppendString() {
  StringBuffer buffer = new StringBuffer();
  buffer.append("A string");
  assertEquals("A string", buffer.toString());
  assertEquals(9, buffer.length());
}
```

What is a test fixture?   The code was duplicated to generate our test object. This is typical for a set of tests referring to a specific component. Often, you will create not a single object but an entire mesh of objects, representing the starting point for all test cases of a test class. This "test basis" is also called a *fixture*.

setUp()   JUnit allows us to extract the code required to create a fixture into the setUp() method. This method is executed before the actual test code—and most important, once for each single test. This ensures that the changes effected on objects of the fixture by that one single test case cannot influence another test case. The integration of a fixture into our test class looks like this:

```
public class StringBufferTest extends TestCase {

    private StringBuffer buffer;
    protected void setUp() {
        buffer = new StringBuffer();
    }
    public void testEmptyBuffer() {
        assertEquals("", buffer.toString());
        assertEquals(0, buffer.length());
    }
    public void testAppendString() {
        buffer.append("A string");
        assertEquals("A string", buffer.toString());
        assertEquals(10, buffer.length());
    }
}
```

We can see that the local variable buffer blossomed into an instance variable, which can be accessed from within all tests. In addition, we have replaced all remaining assertTrue() calls by more meaningful assert-Equals(). This provides a clearer error message, which makes it easier for us to identify the cause of a failure.

tearDown()   As a counterpart to setUp(), JUnit also offers a way to release resources reserved in setUp—files, database links, and so on—in a tearDown() method after a completed test run. This tearing down occurs after the completion of each test, regardless of whether or not the test was successful.

Creating Test Suites

suite() So far we have used a hidden feature of our test runner: it takes the name of a class as parameter and tries to find a set of tests in this class. In order for that mechanism to work, the class is searched for a static suite() method, which returns an instance of TestCase or TestSuite, both of which implement the Test interface. If this method is missing, then the test runner builds a test suite from the set of all test cases with test methods beginning with test.

To bring the theory into practice we provide a first implementation of this famous suite() method:

```
public class StringBufferTest extends TestCase {
    ...
    public static Test suite(){
        return new TestSuite("StringBufferTest");
    }
}
```

This example is simple, so simple that it hardly does anything except generate an object of the TestSuite class. This suite does not contain any test yet, so the result of the test run is rather unspectacular: Runs: 0 Errors: 0 Failures: 0.

Now let's add our two test cases to the suite:

```
public StringBufferTest(String name) {
    super(name);
}
public static Test suite() {
    TestSuite suite = new TestSuite("StringBufferTest");
        suite.addTest(
            new StringBufferTest("testAppendString"));
        suite.addTest(new StringBufferTest("testEmptyBuffer"));
    return suite;
}
```

The addTest(...) method allows us to add tests to a suite. One single test case is created with the optional constructor of the test case class, which takes the name of the test method as parameter. This constructor is redundant in all other circumstances. This approach allows us to create test cases that do not observe the naming convention, but it is meaningful only in very rare cases. In addition, this approach is not type-save, which means that the statement of a nonexisting method name, due to a typing error for example, will become apparent as NoSuchMethodException only at runtime.

Although our previous example merely reproduces the default behavior (which means that we actually wrote superfluous code), implementing the suite() method can indeed be very useful in other cases. For example, it allows the execution of a subset of all test cases of a class or the composition of "normal" test suites into a higher-level suite. The nesting depth for suites can be arbitrary in that we can group single tests to a suite and then combine this suite with other suites or single tests to a new suite, ad infinitum. In this way, TestCase and TestSuite instances form a *composite* pattern [Gamm95].

AllTests　　　　One good example is the junit.samples.AllTests class we have already used. Its suite() method looks like this:

```
public static Test suite() {
    TestSuite suite = new TestSuite("All JUnit Tests");
    suite.addTest(VectorTest.suite());
    suite.addTest(new TestSuite(
        junit.samples.money.MoneyTest.class));
    suite.addTest(junit.tests.AllTests.suite());
    return suite;
}
```

This example uses a variant of the TestSuite constructor which requires a class object as parameter—MoneyTest.class in our example. A test suite created like this implements the known default behavior of test runners, which is to create a suite including all test cases of the specified class whose method names have the prefix *test*.

2.4 Summary

This chapter focuses on the reasons why unit test automation is necessary and how automated unit tests can be realized. While Section 2.2 formulated a few requirements to an automation framework, Section 2.3 showed how they can be implemented in JUnit:

- **Programming language equals test language.** JUnit is a pure Java framework.

- **Separation of application and test code.** Test cases are created in a separate class hierarchy, using the `junit.framework.TestCase`—base class.

- **Independence between test cases.** JUnit allows us to move the common features of tests to a `setUp()` method, which is executed separately for each test. This means that we do not have to worry about the test order.

- **Arbitrary grouping of tests into test suites.** The concept of a suite is available in the `junit.framework.TestSuite` class.

- **Test results are visible at a glance.** Assert methods serve for unique verification of the test results. Graphical test runners show successful test runs in green and failed test runs in red.

For these reasons, JUnit is ideally suited for use as an automation tool to automate developer-side component tests. Because it is freeware, we have used it as a basis for most of the code examples in this book.

In this chapter we discussed the technical aspects of the creation and execution of test cases in JUnit. The rest of this book will deal mainly with the creation of "the right" test cases. The word *right* relates to the creation time, quantity, size, structure, organization, and implementation. As in most aspects of our lives, we will see here too that there are no absolute rules and that we will have to give up looking for an optimal solution and instead settle for a sufficiently good solution.

Chapter 3

Basic Steps of the Test-First Approach

Remember our introduction? It explained that the approach discussed in this book is based mainly on the technique of writing a test **before** the actual program code to test this very code. Are we really serious about this? How should I test something that I don't know yet?

Let us go back to the programming problem of Chapter 1, Section 1.3 once again. We repeat the following requirements specification so you don't have to look back:

> We want to program a dictionary to translate a German text into a language of our choice, say English. This dictionary, in the form of a class, *Dictionary*, is initialized with a word file and allows us to query the translation of a German word. The program should allow several translation alternatives.

Let's assume that we were really serious about the test-first claim. What would that approach look like in this example?

3.1 Step by Step

"The development progresses in small steps, where testing and coding alternate. Such a 'micro-iteration' does not take more than 10 minutes." We will use this quotation from Chapter 1, Section 1.4 from now on as our guiding principle.

Requirements and test cases   When we begin to develop software, the requirements specification is our primary source of information. Accordingly, for the classes and objects at the outer border of a system, the majority of test cases will somehow be linked to those requirements. To be more precise, the more *testable* the requirements are, the easier it is to derive concrete and executable tests from them. Typically requirements documents are not as precise as we would like them to be and require some sort of interpretation. The following example is typical in that respect as we will see.

Let's begin with the first micro-iteration and create an empty test class:

```
public class DictionaryTest extends TestCase {
}
```

Empty test class   The name of the Dictionary class is already given so that we get the name of the test class, `DictionaryTest`, automatically. In many cases it will be sufficient to assign exactly one test class to one application class. This is a good starting point in any event. When starting the test runner with `DictionaryTest` as a command line parameter, we get the expected failure: No tests found in DictionaryTest. Now let's add the first test:

```
public void testCreation() {
    Dictionary dict = new Dictionary();
}
```

First design decisions   We have to make two decisions to this end: Which parameter is required by the constructor? How should we name the test? Considering that we do not currently have any clue for a parameter, our preliminary decision will be in favor of an empty constructor. The name of our test case—`testCreation`—is a typical name for a first test.

An attempt to run this test will fail from the outset, that is, the compilation fails. Compilation can be considered as our first testing cycle; successful compilation thus becomes an intermediate step on our way to a green bar.[1] So first the application code:

```
public class Dictionary {
}
```

---

1. Remember, a *green bar* is JUnit talk for having all tests run successfully.

As you can see, we see nothing. The default constructor does its job, but wonders will never cease! The test runs perfectly. We can now doubtlessly prove that we are capable of creating a `Dictionary` instance, but nothing else. We would at least like to make sure that a newly created dictionary is empty, so we expand the test

```
public void testCreation() {
    Dictionary dict = new Dictionary();
    assertTrue(dict.isEmpty());
}
```

Evolutionary design

Together with this expansion, we made our first design decision, namely that the interface of the Dictionary class provides the `isEmpty()` method. Such decisions have to be made constantly during the course of a test-first development. The sum of this large number of small progressions eventually leads to the overall system design, an approach we introduced as *evolutionary design* in Chapter 1, Section 1.2. With our tests we ensure that our design complies with the implementation; a design drawn on paper does not have this property. In addition, we can use the tests to revise our design decisions and do a refactoring.

Selecting a first test

Coming back to our example, you may wonder why we chose to test a newly created dictionary for being empty. Why not start by adding a couple of translations to the dictionary? The point is that we always try to test the most basic case first to have a stable point for further evolution. The most basic case we could think of here was an empty dictionary. Moreover, we were confident that we could fulfill this test case rather quickly:

```
public class Dictionary {
    public boolean isEmpty() {
        return false;
    }
}
```

As simple as possible!

The simplest implementation of a function is always to return a constant value, and simplicity is an important design goal. The corresponding rule from Chapter 1, Section 1.4 states, Write only as much production code as needed for the test.

Continuing with our example, we first select the return value that causes the test to fail, that of "false." Next we run the test to see if it really fails. This step is important for our confidence in the correctness of our test. And, now, we correct the implementation so that it will run successfully:

```
public class Dictionary {
    public boolean isEmpty() {
        return true;
    }
}
```

Faking the correct implementation   Although we have a vague inkling that the hardwired return of "true" will not be our final implementation, we obey our previous rule and are guided solely by the tests. We trust that some future test will force us to do the "correct" implementation. Keep that in mind: a premature "correct" implementation will lead to a situation where we would eventually write an insufficient number of tests, because we would naturally leave out all those tests already implemented by the application code. Writing only as much code as is forced by existing automated tests ensures that all code is being executed by those tests. This is a huge step forward on our travel to an adequate set of tests.

We want to take the first step towards a functioning dictionary in the next test:

```
public void testAddTranslation() {
    Dictionary dict = new Dictionary();
    dict.addTranslation("Buch", "book");
    assertFalse(dict.isEmpty());
}
```

This test looks a little meager since it does nothing but check whether or not a dictionary is no longer empty after adding a translation. Presumably, you expected bigger progress, for example, adding several translations and polling them. By the way, as the name suggests, assertFalse (...) is JUnit's counterpart to assertTrue(...) and checks that the passed predicate is evaluated to false.

Small steps   Remember that it is our objective to work in small steps to make sure we will never experience a sudden and unexpected test success or test failure. In practice, most developers take increasingly bigger steps, with the result of frequent surprises when they run their tests. That's where we will hopefully distinguish ourselves as test-first masters by making giant steps when moving in well known territory and making very tiny forward and sideward steps in unknown terrain and on slippery ground. However, this strategy requires that we know how to make the tiny steps in the first place.

You can now (and in the future) do the intermediate "empty" implementation leading to a failed test without any assistance. For this reason, let's make an attempt to meet the test requirements:

```java
public class Dictionary {

    private boolean empty = true;
    public boolean isEmpty() {
        return empty;
    }
    public void addTranslation(String german,
                               String translated) {
        empty = false;
    }
}
```

The implementation is simple and unexpected; after all, the given German word and its translation are not used at all. This points to a massive gap in our test, which we will try to close as follows:

```java
public void testAddTranslation() {
    Dictionary dict = new Dictionary();
    dict.addTranslation("Buch", "book");
    assertFalse(dict.isEmpty());
    String trans = dict.getTranslation("Buch");
    assertEquals("book", trans);
}
```

For the first time, this looks like a test that really does something useful, namely find and check the translation of a word. But if you had hoped to eventually see the final implementation code, you were mistaken. Adding the following method will perfectly satisfy the test requirements:

```
public class Dictionary {
  public String getTranslation(String german) {
    return "book";
  }
}
```

It looks like we are unable to get out of doing another test case. This test case should force us to give up on the unsatisfactory return of constants. How about this:

```
public void testAddTwoTranslations() {
  Dictionary dict = new Dictionary();
  dict.addTranslation("Buch", "book");
  dict.addTranslation("Auto", "car");
  assertFalse(dict.isEmpty());
  assertEquals("book", dict.getTranslation("Buch"));
  assertEquals("car", dict.getTranslation("Auto"));
}
```

Now look at the following. Even a malicious developer[2] wouldn't be able to come up with a *simple* implementation that won't move in the expected direction slowly but surely:

```
import java.util.Map;
import java.util.HashMap;
public class Dictionary {

  private Map translations = new HashMap();
  public void addTranslation(String german,
                             String translated) {
    translations.put(german, translated);
  }
  public String getTranslation(String german) {
    return (String) translations.get(german);
  }
  public boolean isEmpty() {
```

---

2. One reviewer suggested to look at this as a (programming) game where two players —the tester and the coder—try to outwit each other. I wonder if we programmers must have split personalities to develop successful code on our own?

```
        return translations.isEmpty();
    }
}
```

A Map serves us now to store translations; in turn, the variable "empty" landed in the waste bin. Once again, the tests ensured that we didn't forget the isEmpty() method while restructuring. The use of the hash map is definitely easier, compared to the solution drafted preliminarily in the introduction (see Chapter 1, Section 1.3). In case the introduction of a Translation class becomes necessary later on, the existing tests will protect the behavior achieved so far. But let's not speculate.

Refactoring tests

Now that we have the correct functionality built in, it is recommended to have a look at the test class to clean it up or do a *refactoring*. Several things leap to the eye:

- The names testAddTranslation and testAddTwoTranslations no longer reflect the entire contents of the test cases. The names testOneTranslation and testTwoTranslations look much better.

- The line that creates our Dictionary test object occurs several times. We turn this into a test fixture.

- The second and third test cases contain more than one assert. To facilitate future diagnostics, it is recommended to mark the individual assert calls by a descriptive comment as the first parameter. This variant is supported by all assert methods.

The freshly styled DictionaryTest class now looks like this:

```
public class DictionaryTest extends TestCase {
    private Dictionary dict;

    protected void setUp() {
        dict = new Dictionary();
    }
    public void testCreation() {
        assertTrue(dict.isEmpty());
    }
}
```

```
public void testOneTranslation() {
    dict.addTranslation("Buch", "book");
    assertFalse("dict not empty", dict.isEmpty());
    String trans = dict.getTranslation("Buch");
    assertEquals("translation Buch", "book", trans);
}

public void testTwoTranslations() {
    dict.addTranslation("Buch", "book");
    dict.addTranslation("Auto", "car");
    assertFalse("dict not empty", dict.isEmpty());
    assertEquals("translation Buch", "book",
                dict.getTranslation("Buch"));
    assertEquals("translation Auto", "car",
                dict.getTranslation("Auto"));
}
}
```

Comparing our set of tests with the specification reveals a yet unimplemented functionality: German words with more than one possible translation. First the test:

```
public void testTranslationWithTwoEntries() {
    dict.addTranslation("Buch", "book");
    dict.addTranslation("Buch", "volume");
    String trans = dict.getTranslation("Buch");
    assertEquals("book, volume", trans);
}
```

Bad design decisions   The choice to expect a comma-separated list of translations and not a collection object can be considered as bad since it speculates on a future textual user interface which is not yet defined. Don't get too involved in that discussion, though. Test-driven development allows us to make the wrong decisions since we can revise them later when the design weakness becomes obvious. At that time we will have the tests handy to show that changing a single aspect left the rest of our application untouched.

And here again, the simplest solution is the best only until a new requirement, and thus new tests, require a more complex design:

```
public class Dictionary {
    public void addTranslation(String german, String translated) {
        String before = this.getTranslation(german);
        String now;
        if (before == null) {
            now = translated;
        } else {
            now = before + ", " + translated;
        }
        translations.put(german, now);
    }
}
```

Reviewing the process   Let us review our test-driven development process as described so far in this chapter. At the beginning of each step, there was a test which was directly or indirectly motivated by the requirements specification. To be able to write this test, we had to make decisions about the *public interface* desired for our OUT (object under test). This public interface served both to "stimulate" the test object and to verify the correct behavior.

Once the compilation was successfully completed, we ran all tests created to this point, which resulted in a failure of the added or modified test, as expected. Next, we exercised some thought about the simplest way to realize the behavior specified in the test case. We used the "old" test cases as the constraint conditions; that is, the more test cases we had to satisfy, the more complex became our program design. At the end of each test-code cycle we reviewed the existing design, searching for refactoring opportunities to improve, which is to say, simplify it.

Test drives code—and vice versa!   This approach drove and controlled the development of our production code from the tests. Note, however, that there is also an opposite control mechanism: as soon as we find that a method has not been fully programmed, despite a green bar, there is a strong hint that there are still tests missing.

Public interface   So far, our tests have concentrated exclusively on the externally visible behavior of the OUT. In Java this theoretically includes all methods (and variables) with public, protected, or package scope visibility. In practice we restrict ourselves to use only what is intended to be used from the outside, that is from client code, which usually leaves out protected methods and members available for subclassing. This approach offers several benefits:

- The tests document the intended use of the tested class. This kind of documentation is always consistent, in contrast to prosaic documentation.

- Internal restructuring has no impact on the tests. For example, if we checked the structure of the hash map used, then a conversion to an independent class for each of the translations would be much more expensive.

This is why our guideline tells us to always use only the public interface in tests too. We will see later that we cannot always stick to this idealistic goal.

3.2 Dependencies

So far, in specifying our example program, we have ignored the part that deals with the dictionary file. Considering that the file format is not precisely specified, we must define one ourselves. Inspired by the numerous Java property files in other projects, we decide that each translation entry should be written to a separate line in the following form:[3]

```
<German word>=<translation>
```

Multiple entries are allowed. The first attempt at a test looks like this:

```
public void testSimpleFile() {
    dict = new Dictionary("C:\\temp\\simple.dic");
    assertTrue(! dict.isEmpty());
}
```

File dependency But now we find that we have made ourselves dependent on the content of an external file. We could delete this file at the beginning of the test case and create a new one with the desired content. However, this would also cause an undesirable dependency on a file path and platform-dependent

---

3. Any modern young programmer would choose XML and not be mistaken. We confess to being somewhat old-fashioned, and we wanted to forgo the introduction of yet another Java API here.

particularities. The solution is to permit any `java.io.InputStream` instance instead of using a file; this input stream can then be easily mapped to a file. This means that our test will become independent of files:

```
import java.io.*;
  ...

public void testTwoTranslationsFromStream() {
    String dictText = "Buch=book\n" + "Auto=car";
    InputStream in = new StringBufferInputStream(dictText);
    dict = new Dictionary(in);
    assertTrue(! dict.isEmpty());
}
```

At this point, we leave it up to our readers as a practical exercise to find the simplest way to the green bar.[4] Instead, we continue adding more assertions to the test:

```
public void testTwoTranslationsFromStream() {
    String dictText = "Buch=book\n" + "Auto=car";
    InputStream in = new StringBufferInputStream(dictText);
    dict = new Dictionary(in);
    assertFalse("dict not empty", dict.isEmpty());
    assertEquals("translation Buch", "book",
        dict.getTranslation("Buch"));
    assertEquals("translation Auto", "car",
        dict.getTranslation("Auto"));
}
```

Here lies a somewhat unpleasant thing: the `StringBufferInputStream` class enjoys the *deprecated* status since JDK 1.2. But for the time being we are short of a better idea and have to live with this little annoyance for now. Remembering the close relationship of our file format with Java property files leads to a simple implementation:

```
import java.util.*;
import java.io.*;
```

---

4.   Hint: The passed Reader instance can be totally ignored here.

```
public class Dictionary {

  ...

  public Dictionary(InputStream in) throws IOException {
     this.readTranslations(in);
  }

  private void readTranslations(InputStream in) throws
     IOException {
     Properties props = new Properties();
     props.load(in);
     Iterator i = props.keySet().iterator();
     while (i.hasNext()) {
        String german = (String) i.next();
        String trans = props.getProperty(german);
        this.addTranslation(german, trans);
     }
  }

}
```

Using "throws IOException" ensures that the test method must also throw an IOException. This is our way to entrust JUnit with exception handling to register an error just in case.

Departing from the existing tests, another one is built similarly:

```
public void testTranslationsWithTwoEntriesFromStream()
      throws IOException {
   String dictText = "Buch=book\n" + "Buch=volume";
   InputStream in = new StringBufferInputStream(dictText);
   dict = new Dictionary(in);
   String trans = dict.getTranslation("Buch");
   assertEquals("book, volume", trans);
}
```

At this point, it suddenly becomes obvious that the implementation by use of the Properties class led us to a dead end, because the load(Input-Stream) method overrides a property by the same name in the first entry, if there are duplicate entries; whereas, our specification states that all potential translations of a word should be read from the file. In addition, the behavior of the `Properties` class is undesirable in another aspect, namely the hash character (#).

The Single Responsibility Principle

We begin to realize that parsing the dictionary file really is a complex matter, so we eventually decide to move this functionality to a separate class, `DictionaryParser`. This decision is strongly backed up by an important object-oriented design heuristic: the *Single Responsibility Principle* [Martin02b]. This rule says that *a single class should have one and only one responsibility* in order to facilitate independent changes and to reduce coupling.

Refactoring before the test case

We have arrived at a point where we cannot or do not want to carry the current test to a successful end without doing some restructuring work first. This is the right point in time to take a step back. We preliminarily remove the *open test case* from the test suite[5] to be able to refactor with all tests running. A test case is called *open* when the behavior it specifies has not been (fully) implemented. In this example we want to move the parsing of `InputStream` objects to a class called `DictionaryParser`; the interface of this class allows the iteration over all translation entries of a stream. And while restructuring things, we replace `java.io.InputStream` by `java.io.Reader`; this class is better suited for reading text because it also takes care of the correct conversion between bytes and characters.

Extracting a class

To improve our readers' independent unit testing capabilities, we do not include a detailed description of all single refactoring and testing steps at this point, but limit ourselves instead to representing the result—test suites and implementation. First the test class:

```
import java.io.*;
    public class DictionaryParserTest extends TestCase {
    public DictionaryParserTest(String name) {...}
    private DictionaryParser parser;
    private DictionaryParser createParser(String dictText)
        throws IOException {
        Reader reader = new StringReader(dictText);
        return new DictionaryParser(reader);
    }
    private void assertNextTranslation(String german, String trans)
        throws Exception {
        assertTrue(parser.hasNextTranslation());
```

---

5. For example, by preceding the name of the test method with an underscore.

```
        parser.nextTranslation();
        assertEquals(german, parser.currentGermanWord());
        assertEquals(trans, parser.currentTranslation());
    }
    public void testEmptyReader() throws Exception {
        parser = this.createParser("");
        assertFalse(parser.hasNextTranslation());
    }
    public void testOneLine() throws Exception {
        String dictText = "Buch=book";
        parser = this.createParser(dictText);
        this.assertNextTranslation("Buch", "book");
        assertFalse(parser.hasNextTranslation());
    }
    public void testThreeLines() throws Exception {
        String dictText = "Buch=book\n" +
            "Auto=car\n" +
            "Buch=volume";
        parser = this.createParser(dictText);
        this.assertNextTranslation("Buch", "book");
        this.assertNextTranslation("Auto", "car");
        this.assertNextTranslation("Buch", "volume");
        assertFalse(parser.hasNextTranslation());
    }
}
```

Readability of test code   We can see that we also avoided code duplication in the test code and moved common functionality to private methods. In general, test classes are also part of the system, so that they should observe the same principles of simplicity and readability. A few more things got changed:

- We got rid of the deprecated class StringBufferInputStream and replaced it by StringWriter.

- We changed all throws-clauses so that they now throw a generic Exception instead of the more specific IOException. That way, no essential information gets lost and test case maintenance is simplified since we won't have to change the throws clause any more.

And now the pertaining implementation:

```java
import java.io.*;
public class DictionaryParser {
    private BufferedReader reader;
    private String nextLine;
    private String currentGermanWord;
    private String currentTranslation;
    public DictionaryParser(Reader unbufferedReader) throws
        IOException {
        reader = new BufferedReader(unbufferedReader);
        this.readNextLine();
    }
    public String currentTranslation() {
        return currentTranslation;
    }
    public String currentGermanWord() {
        return currentGermanWord;
    }
    public boolean hasNextTranslation() {
        return nextLine != null;
    }
    public void nextTranslation() throws IOException {
        int index = nextLine.indexOf('=');
        currentGermanWord = nextLine.substring(0, index);
        currentTranslation = nextLine.substring(index + 1);
        this.readNextLine();
    }
    private void readNextLine() throws IOException {
        nextLine = reader.readLine();
    }
}
```

The interface of the parser class is iterator-like. Each programmer will probably arrive at a different result as to how the best DictionaryParser interface should look. But this is not a major problem because the tests document the interface for other developers, and refactoring can be done in future changes if necessary. All that's left to do now is to integrate the parser into the dictionary:

```
public class Dictionary {
   ...

   private void readTranslations(Reader reader)
      throws IOException {
      DictionaryParser parser = new DictionaryParser(reader);
      while (parser.hasNextTranslation()) {
         parser.nextTranslation();
         String german = parser.currentGermanWord();
         String trans = parser.currentTranslation();
         this.addTranslation(german, trans);
      }
   }
}
```

Now we are ready to reactivate the test `testTranslationsWithTwo-EntriesFromStream()` and rename it in `testTranslationsWithTwoEntries-FromReader()`—and, well, it runs perfectly. We could now implement another constructor, `Dictionary(String filename)`, if desired. Yet another good exercise we leave for the ambitious reader to solve ;-)

Open tests   Taking a look back, what happened in the previous section? Our very normal approach—small tests and small implementation steps—has shown at some point that we had better move some functionality from the CUT (`Dictionary`) to another class (`DictionaryParser`). For this reason, we were not yet able to complete a full test, but had to deal first with the new object or new class, respectively. The open test had to migrate to a sort of "inactive test stack" for the time being, from where it was removed as soon as the implementation of the new class was completed, and was then "activated."

If you are afraid you may forget such open test cases, you may want to make some notes; this also applies to other code particularities we cannot deal with right away. Later, in Chapter 6, we will learn another possibility, specifically, the use of dummy implementations to avoid the temporary deactivation of test cases under implementation. And sometimes a dummy implementation evolves into a proper one over time.

Object dependencies   This approach is necessary whenever we need subordinate objects that do not yet exist during an implementation. Theoretically, the dependencies tree can have an arbitrary depth and an arbitrary width so that our "stack" can become arbitrarily confusing. However, in practice there are rarely more than two test cases in the "open, but deactivated" state. If you find that you are getting deeper into a large chain of dependencies, then it is normally due to the fact that the top test on the stack includes too big a chunk of functionality. If this happens, the best approach is to go back to the last 100% state and try to write a smaller test.

Top-down and bottom-up

It is interesting that one would have worked exactly the opposite way in a program designed in dry dock.[6] While we progressed in a *top-down* approach, that is, starting from the general functionality, it is much easier with a previously designed system to develop and test in a *bottom-up* approach, since a top-down approach requires the development of *stub* or *dummy* objects (see Chapter 6, Dummy and Mock Objects for Independence). Figure 3.1 shows a simple class diagram to highlight the difference:[7]

- **Top-down.** Programming and the class tests begin with class A; B and C are simulated by dummies. Next, B and C are dealt with, where the former needs another dummy for class D. In object-oriented systems, this normally means that we work our way from the outer (public) interface of a (sub) system towards the (private) inner life. Therefore, top-down is also an *outside-in* approach.

- **Bottom-up.** We begin with the nondependent classes and use them to compose the more complex, dependent objects. For example, the development order would be D - B - C - A.

If two (or more) classes depend on one another, then the bottom-up approach fails, i.e., all objects have to be developed en bloc; here again, the test-first development has an advantage.

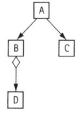

Figure 3.1 Top-down versus bottom-up approaches.

---

6. Also known as UML.

7. The direction of the arrows determines the navigability and thus the dependence.

Problems when
using complex
test fixtures

Both the top-down and the bottom-up approach can be problematic during testing as soon as the distance[8] between the class under test and the classes required for the test increases. The bigger the distance, the more difficult the creation of the required test fixture. This problem can be mitigated to some extent by using a centralized test object generation mechanism.[9] The cost for the creation and adaptation of these object meshes increases in line with the size of the application, and the dependencies between test cases and remote objects become more and more unclear. In addition, it becomes more difficult to allocate errors occurring in the tests to the CUT; they may be due to faulty behavior of one of the classes used. Chapter 6 will discuss in detail techniques to avoid such cases.

Grow or split?

There remains the question of the right point in time for separation of a new class during the development of another one. We would surely have been able to accommodate the functionality of the DictionaryParser in the Dictionary class. But then, a refactoring would probably have produced this or a similar class at some point in time, just later.

The time of relocation obeys two strategies: *Grow then split or split then grow* [Feathers00]. The right way is normally somewhere in the middle, since we first have to grow a little to understand the necessity of a new class. This may happen earlier or later, depending on the situation, but the important thing to remember is to eventually achieve a simple design.

Redundant tests

Splitting off a new object often leads to redundancy in test cases. Boundary and error cases that we already tackled in our tests for the higher-level object suddenly belong to the responsibilities of the new class, and thus a new test suite. For this reason, it is worth looking at existing tests to see whether or not we still need them. Our unit tests are aimed at verifying the functionality of a single unit, normally that of a single CUT. Any behavior pattern that this CUT delegates is not an integral part of that class.

What still has to be verified is that the delegation itself is correct. In our dictionary example, this would mean considering if the two test*From-Reader test cases are redundant. Both test goals (testing for two lines and testing for a duplicate entry) are also verified in DictionaryParserTest. For example, it would be meaningful to replace the two test cases by a single one that would then cover a more complex scenario. One argument against this approach is the documenting character of the test cases for the

---

8. In this context, "distance" means the number of objects in between.
9. Such a mechanism was introduced by the term *ObjectMother* [Schuh01].

users of the `Dictionary` class. There is no ideal method, but redundant tests are better than too few tests.

Dependent on external resources

Another case of dependence occurred within the scope of the previous implementation: files. Dependence of our code on files or other external resources makes testing more difficult, because we will suddenly have to stick to the rules of the game established by others. While the programming language and the local environment can be fully controlled, here we will have to deal with proprietary protocols, access restrictions, time dependencies, and other incalculable situations, making the success of a test indeterministic or at least its implementation more difficult. In the case of the dictionary file, the trick was to modify the interface so that its testability was improved. Of course, we cannot do without any file tests at all; this topic will be discussed in Chapter 6.

Testability as a design goal

Intuitively, many developers shrink back from changing their "correct" codes *only* to be able to test them better. Making a concession in the application code to facilitate testing is by no means damnable; it has a desirable effect: letting the tests drive the code forces us to design *testable* objects. "Testable" means in most cases *simpler.* "Simpler" means in most cases *less dependent.* As we know, reducing dependencies—both within a system and to the outside—is a central objective of good software design.

3.3 Organizing and Running Tests

Our mini-example has not placed major requirements on the test organization and test execution yet. The two test classes, `DictionaryTest` and `DictionaryParserTest`, can easily be restarted over and over again in the same test runner, and the execution time is negligible. However, as our project grows—and with it the number of test classes—this naive approach fails; we need to do some more thinking about test organization and test execution.

Organizing Tests

How many test classes?

The first question is, Over how many test classes should I distribute my tests? So far, we packed all tests of an application class into a separate test class. As a rule of thumb, *one test class per application class* is normally suitable as a starting point, but there are good reasons to deviate from it now and then:

- The goal of the test fixture we created in setUp() (see Chapter 2, Section 2.3) is to have an object configuration for all tests of that test class. If certain tests do not need this fixture, then they are extracted to a new test class. In our dictionary example, two groups of tests for the Dictionary class could well form during the further course of development: one needs a Reader as a fixture, while the other doesn't. The result would be two test classes for one application class, for example, DictionaryTest (as before) and DictionaryFromReaderTest.

- If the number of tests for a CUT becomes too big, then we should search for groups of tests with common properties and move them into a new test class. This is often a good point for refactoring towards an abstract test superclass, accommodating the common code of the two concrete test classes, as shown in Figure 3.2. A very large number of tests in a test class can also be an indication that the pertaining CUT should be split.

- If a trivial class does not require tests (e.g., DictionaryParserException discussed later in this section), then we would naturally also cut the test class.

- Tests referring to a configuration of classes or a subsystem and not to a single class deserve their own test classes.

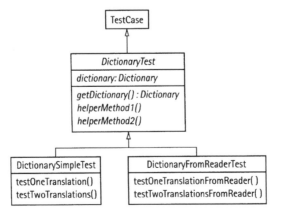

Figure 3.2 A small test class hierarchy.

Where to put the test classes? Another issue worth discussing is whether test classes belong to the same or a separate Java package and whether or not to separate test code from application code. Weighing up the benefits and drawbacks of the conceivable solutions does not lead to a clear judgement:

- **Test classes in the same package** allow access to method with *protected* or *package scope* visibility. This can improve the testability, but it also tends to create unstable tests (see also Chapter 8, Section 8.2).

  Another benefit is that the tests are near the tested classes. This means that lesser test classes will be "accidentally" overlooked when code is changed or moved. Also, it makes it harder to forget relevant test classes when renaming packages and classes.

  In contrast, the separation of application code from test code becomes more difficult, because when separating them one has to rely on a name convention. Test dummy classes can easily be taken as application classes by mistake.

- **Test classes in separate test packages** facilitate the separation of application code from test code. The downside is that non-public classes and methods can be accessed only over auxiliary tools or by the Java *reflection* mechanism. Whether or not the tests should be accommodated in a parallel hierarchy (e.g., tests.myproj.*) or whether each package should have its personal test package (e.g., myproj.pack1. tests) is simply a matter of taste.

- A third solution is to have *test code and application code* in **the same logical package but in different physical paths**. In this case, the test package looks like one and the same package from the Java perspective but can easily be separated for deployment purposes. Nowadays most IDEs support this distribution of sources among several base directories.

All three approaches have their specific benefits and drawbacks. The main thing is to use a common standard across the entire team.

All tests of one package Further advantages can be achieved by agreeing on how to address all tests of a package, a subsystem, or the entire project. To this end, AllTests classes represent a quasi-standard. Typically, such a class exists for each package where the test classes are located. This looks as follows in our example:

```
import junit.framework.*;
public class AllTests {
    public static void main(String[] args) {
        junit.awtui.TestRunner.run(AllTests.class);
    }

    public static Test suite() {
        TestSuite suite = new TestSuite("Test suite for chapter3.*");
        suite.addTestSuite(DictionaryTest.class);
        suite.addTestSuite(DictionaryParserTest.class);
        return suite;
    }
}
```

While the `suite()` method groups all test classes of the package, the `main()` implementation offers us a comfortable point to start the test suite without having to worry about parameters. Which one of the three test runners is used for this purpose is again a matter of taste. The important thing is that, when adding, deleting, and renaming test classes, we must not forget to adapt `AllTests` accordingly.

All tests of a project Depending on the system size and structure, at least one additional `AllTests` class exists, which groups all other `AllTests` suites into a test suite, for example:

```
package myproj.alltests;
import junit.framework.*;
class AllTests {
    public static void main(String[] args) {
        junit.awtui.TestRunner.run(AllTests.class);
    }

    public static Test suite() {
        TestSuite suite = new TestSuite("All tests of MyProject");
        suite.addTest(myproj.pack1.AllTests.suite());
        suite.addTest(myproj.pack2.AllTests.suite());
        suite.addTest(myproj.pack3.sub1.AllTests.suite());
```

```
        suite.addTest(myproj.pack3.sub2.AllTests.suite());
        return suite;
    }
}
```

The introduction of additional intermediate hierarchies for `AllTests` classes can simplify partial testing and updating of larger projects. Figure 3.3 shows a conceivable package and class structure for a fictitious project. Here, `myproj.pack3.alltests.AllTests` groups all tests from the subpackages of `myproj.pack3` together.

Generated test suites An alternative approach to the manual maintenance of test suites is to have all test classes of a package or even of an entire application generate and group automatically, by searching all subclasses of `junit.framework.TestCase`, for example. At first sight, this approach appears easier; the downside is that control over volume, organization, and distribution of all tests is easily lost.[10] One reviewer put it straight:

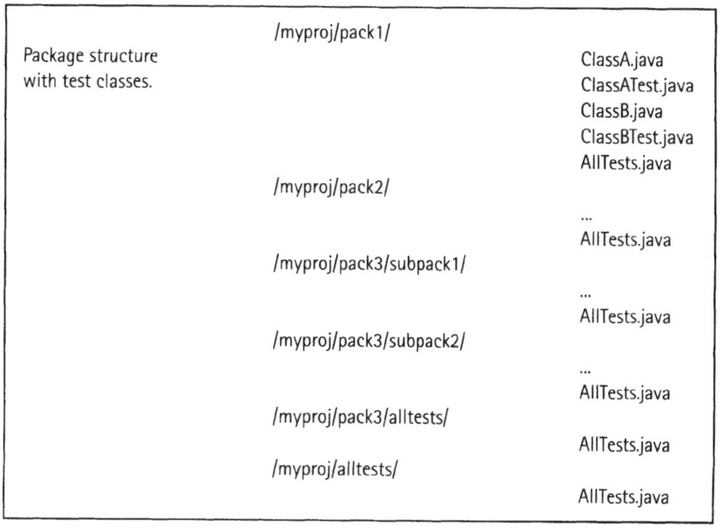

	/myproj/pack1/	ClassA.java
Package structure with test classes.		ClassATest.java
		ClassB.java
		ClassBTest.java
		AllTests.java
	/myproj/pack2/	
		...
		AllTests.java
	/myproj/pack3/subpack1/	
		...
		AllTests.java
	/myproj/pack3/subpack2/	
		...
		AllTests.java
	/myproj/pack3/alltests/	AllTests.java
	/myproj/alltests/	
		AllTests.java

Figure 3.3 Package structure with test classes.

---

10. Java code to automatically find all `TestCase` subclasses and create a `TestAll` suite is found in an article by Schneider [00].

Organizing groups of test suites requires some thought and is not a task well-suited to arbitrary automation. The reasons for grouping test suites (other than package-based grouping) is not likely to be something the compiler can figure out. For a very complicated project, suites might be organized to many different things.

I can add nothing to this and prefer the manual maintenance of test suites, myself.

Running Tests

There are numerous opportunities to run a test suite [Gassmann00]:

When to run
a test suite?

- Before and after refactoring of code.

- Before and after adding new functionality.

- Before and after integrating modified code into the overall system.

- Whenever you want to see a green bar to boost your mood.

In this respect, it is meaningful to select the number of executed tests so that as many test runs as possible are done, as long as this does not give a feeling that your work is hindered by unnecessary waiting. As long as a suite, including all tests of the system, runs in a few seconds, it won't hurt to start the full test set again whenever you make a local change. On the other hand, experience has shown that the runtime for all unit tests will be noticeable sooner or later. This is the reason we try to select a smaller execution granularity, depending on the individual case: subsystem suite, package suite, single test class, and sometimes even a single test case. The following is typical:

Which test
suite to run?

- Running a single test class during the development of a given class.

- Running all tests of a package before and after refactoring actions limited to that package.

At the latest, you should test upon completion of a task and before the integration of modified classes; however, all tests of the system should be run. If you have a feeling that the runtime of the tests hinder you in running the tests regularly, then you could try to reduce the runtime, perhaps by using the techniques described in Chapter 6.

3.4 | Summary

In this chapter, we discussed the typical approach taken in test-driven development and its numerous small micro-iterations, using the dictionary programming example from Chapter 1. More specifically, we demonstrated both the development of a single class and how this class can be separated into a parser and the actual dictionary.

The result of our test-first development clearly looks different from the previous solution designed in Chapter 1, Section 1.3. This means that the test-driven approach is not only a means to reduce program errors, but it also directs the system design towards as few internal and external dependencies as possible. The answer to the question How should I test something I don't know yet? is, therefore: I test it *because* I don't know it yet! But despite the *designing by testing* approach, a *rough* preliminary design is helpful to generate ideas if you are prepared to deviate from it when the implementation leads you somewhere else.

Finally, we focused on issues that come up when using JUnit for increasingly larger applications:

- If and how to separate test code from application code.

- How to organize individual test cases into suites and suites of suites.

- When to run which (sub) set of our tests.

Chapter 4

Test Ideas and Heuristics

So far in this book, we have written unit tests at exactly one point within the software development process: upon realizing a new requirement. However, there are more opportunities to write, modify, or edit tests:

- Once a task is completed, the application code is verified for refactoring possibilities and the test code is verified for quality and sufficient coverage.

- If an error occurs in subsequent development phases—during functional tests or after shipment—we need to write a unit test or expand an existing one to expose the error case **before** removing the error. This demonstrates that the developers really understood the cause of an error and prevents that same error from sneaking in later. Following this advice will often show that the bug we have just revealed was masking another one and that several unit tests and subsequent code changes are necessary to make the functional test that started it all work.

- Whenever we find inadequacies in test cases, for example, when trying to understand or modify existing code, testing is mandated.

- Testing is appropriate during or after a refactoring of program parts.

The developer in the tester's role   The greater experience one has in testing, the more tests will not be found necessary in later stages, but be written when adding new features. The difficulties in creating test cases do not result from a lack of experience, but from fundamental psychological reasons [Weinberg98]. While it is the objective of a tester to find as many defects as possible, developers like to see their software confirmed and may thus overlook errors in their own program that they would see at a glance in other people's code. Faulty programming concepts often lead to the same errors in a test. For this reason, we make efforts to give up the "developer ego" and instead assume the role of a "tester ego" when checking test cases for *sufficient coverage* (see also Chapter 8). Considering that we will never fully manage this, the cooperation of a second person can increase the quality of test cases considerably,[1] either within the scope of pair programming or in a subsequent review.

In the further course of this chapter, we will describe a few heuristics, ideas, and theoretical aspects to improve single unit tests and to find new test cases. As always we have to observe the most important rule: *Test code is treated like production code* and deserves the same attention with regard to readability and clarity. But we also have to observe another fact: *Less optimal tests are better than no tests.*

4.1   Reworking Single Tests

Looking at a single test case, a testXXX method, we can see that several points deserve our attention:

Naming conventions

- The **test name** should describe the functionality tested and perhaps the particular side conditions of that test. For example, a name like test-AddUser is surely easier to understand than test1, and testAddUser-WithoutPassword is better than testAddUserThrowException. The important thing is that it should be easy for *readers* of the test code to orient themselves and to identify the corresponding tests when changes are necessary. In particular, I do not recommend a naming convention that introduces consecutive numbers in any form. Numbering makes it more difficult to identify and maintain test cases.

- The **length of a test method** should be as short as possible. This can be achieved either by extracting method parts or by splitting the test. The

---

1. Sometimes we also have to deal with the requirement to fully separate the test group from the developer group from an organizational perspective to eliminate influences from the psychological phenomenon described here.

finer the granularity of a single test, the easier it will be to understand the purpose of a test and to modify it when necessary. Having more than a handful of assertions should make you consider splitting the test.

Testing complex scenarios and use cases often requires many individual steps. In such cases, we have to weigh carefully whether or not relocating parts of the test method to private methods could impair the readability of the test sequence.

- Test code contains **as little logic as possible**. Loops, branches, and case statements can be an indication that either the test is too complex or it tests more than a single unit. Auxiliary functions or auxiliary classes, to compare structured objects for instance, can represent exceptions to this rule and will require their own test cases.

When testing legacy software logically, complex testing code is often necessary. This should be an intermediate state, though, and be changed as soon as the major refactorings have taken place.

- **The expected results** should be stated **as previously determined constants** and not be calculated in the test. The next example compares two variants of the same test to better explain this rule:

```
public void testBalance1() {
    Account account = new account();
    account.deposit(10);
    account.withdraw(5);
    account.deposit(6);
    assertTrue(11, account.getBalance());
}
public void testBalance2() {
    Account account = new Account();
    account.deposit(10);
    account.withdraw(5);
    account.deposit(6);
    int balance = 10 - 5 + 6;
    assertTrue(balance, account.getBalance());
}
```

Following the example from testBalance2(), we can see that the test code implements almost all functionality of the application classes again. It is therefore meaningful to calculate the expected results in advance. An exception to this rule applies when the input data are already variable. In such a case, so-called *test oracles* (see Glossary) can help determine the correct result data to use in comparing the actual test results.[2] Note that oracles are used very seldomly in unit tests.

- **Test data and expected results** should be located close together. Consider this example:

```
public void testIsPasswordValid() {
    assertTrue(user.isPasswordValid("abcdef"));
    assertFalse(user.isPasswordValid("123456"));
}
```

A reader of this code can see whether or not this test is correct only by finding the place where the User object is created. In contrast, the following test is easy to understand:

```
public void testIsPasswordValid() {
    User user = new User("Name", "abcdef");
    assertTrue(user.isPasswordValid("abcdef"));
    assertFalse(user.isPasswordValid("123456"));
}
```

However, if we want to include the creation of User in the setup to avoid code duplication, then the use of constants offers a convenient middle course:

```
public void testIsPasswordValid() {
    assertTrue(user.isPasswordValid(CORRECT_PASSWORD));
    assertFalse(user.isPasswordValid(WRONG_PASSWORD));
}
```

The following rule applies in general: the bigger the distance between input and output data, the more difficult it will be to understand the test. For example, if we decide to relocate test data into a file, then the expected results should also be in this file. The next best solution would be to have a

---

2. Binder [99, p. 917] dedicates an entire chapter to oracles.

file with a similar name (e.g., `testData.input` and `testData.expected`) near the test itself.

To catch or
not to catch

- **Exceptions** that could potentially reach the test method and represent a test error should not be caught.[3] We therefore prefer:

```
public void testRetrieveUser() throws WrongPasswordException {
    assertNotNull(manager.retrieveUser("name", "password"));
}
```

instead of the following:

```
public void testRetrieveUser() {
    try {
        assertNotNull(manager.retrieveUser("name", "password"));
    } catch (WrongPasswordException e) {
        fail("Exception occurred: " + e.getMessage());
        e.printStackTrace();
    }
}
```

The `try-catch` code inflates the code without offering any real, informative gain when the `exception` or its `message` string are not specific enough. This negative example is still useful, because it demonstrates a JUnit command that we haven't covered yet: "`fail(String text)`." This command is also available in the `TestCase` class and always triggers a failure, which is meaningful, for example, when the correctness of a test case is determined by the program flow.

Usually we don't even declare the specific exception type(s) in the test method's `throws` clause but instead use the generic `Exception` or `Throwable`:

```
public void testRetrieveUser() throws Exception {
    assertNotNull(manager.retrieveUser("name", "password"));
}
```

The various possible exception types are of no interest to the invoking test method and the generic approach greatly reduces maintenance.

---

3. An excellent example of how greatly opinions can vary is demonstrated in Gassmann [00], where the opposite rule is stated.

Each team will develop their own basic vocabulary with test idioms and *guidelines* during the course of a project. Things that win through standardization include the use of the optional `string` parameter in `assert` calls or the naming of test fixture variables. One of the important aspects of guidelines is their consistent use. Far less important are the concrete contents of individual rules.

| 4.2 | **Black and White Boxes** |

Now that we have studied the anatomy of single test methods, we will focus our attention on the test suite as a whole. But first, it appears useful to know a little about test nomenclature.

Black-box and White-box tests

The literature [Binder99] distinguishes between *black-box tests* and *white-box tests:*

- Black-box tests—also called *specification-based* or *functional tests*— look at the behavior of a system or unit from the outside. Only behavior that is available and visible from the outside is used in the testing code. Black-box tests can be created before the implementation is available with only the unit's specification at hand. Most acceptance tests in XP are pure black-box tests.

- White-box tests are also called *implementation-based* or *structural* tests. They use knowledge about the current implementation of a function to determine *complementary,* critical test cases and execution paths.[4] A typical white-box test considers control flow or data flow of a program and derives the current input values for the test case from there.

The differentiation between black-box and white-box takes place on any level of focus. Seen from the outside, any testing of internal components is white-box testing. From a developer's point of view, however, the component itself can be tested with a black-box or a white-box mindset.

Adequate testing requires a combination of both approaches. All test cases we have developed so far were specification-based tests, because we

---

4. Knowledge about the implementation can also be used to identify superfluous black-box tests.

concentrated solely on the desired behavior of an object. However, unit tests cannot be uniquely assigned to either of the two categories. Although we will continue trying to limit ourselves to the use of "external" properties of an object in our test cases, the choice of tests we make will be influenced by what we know about the implementation.

4.3 | Testing the Typical Functionality

One common recommendation says, Write a test case for each public method. This rule has two catches. First, if we test the methods of an object in an isolated way only, we will not discover errors resulting from state changes of that object. The second catch results from the subliminal statement, One test for each public method is sufficient, since one test is often not enough. For this reason, we modify the preceding rule as follows: Test each *typical use* of an object. The difference is that a typical use normally consists of a sequence of messages.

For example, a typical use for our Dictionary object is adding new translations and polling existing translations. We have written test cases for both scenarios, but the isEmpty() method was used only within the scope of this "typical usage test." On the other hand, the rule should not lead to a situation where all individual tests are replaced by one complex and unclear test case. On the contrary, the important thing is to identify the smallest typical usage cases and to test them independently.

What is typical?   The typical usage is obviously nothing that can be fixed once and for all at the beginning of an application's life cycle. Right at the start we have nothing but the functional requirements to help us decide where to start. As for the outer boundary of a system, the use cases, user stories, or whatever we have as requirements specifications represent the primary source from which to derive the test cases. A good set of unambiguous and testable statements is an excellent starting point for developing an application test-driven from the outside in.

As for internal components, the developer figures out what tasks a unit is currently supposed to fulfill. As the component is used by more and more additional components, our initial guess of what is typical will often prove wrong. This insight will then be reflected in changes to the test cases.

One at a time

One reviewer made an important remark here that you should remember:

> We are only dealing with one usage situation at a time. We may add tests after we have written some code, but we do not add test cases in anticipation of future clients. . . . The primary quality benefit that we get from test-first comes from the small considered steps that we take and the design thoughts that we have when we are taking them.

Test ideas checklist

Over the course of time, other *test ideas* are added; these are often atypical but still legitimate usages for our code. Marick [00] recommends writing down these ideas and using them as a checklist for future editing of the tests, then discarding them. Editing in this context means to think about whether a test idea should manifest itself in a test, makes no sense at all, is not within the requirements, or the creation of its corresponding test would be too expensive. And again we are caught in the previous dilemma: should each idea fall to a separate test case or should we try to squeeze as many ideas into a single test case as we possibly can? Some of the benefits and drawbacks of the two approaches read like this:

- **One test per idea.** Simple tests facilitate debugging, are easier to read and to restructure, and generally can be created faster. The major drawback of simple tests is that they test only what we originally intended.

- **Many ideas per test.** Complex tests can test more than the test ideas we knowingly build into them; they find errors by pure luck. Building many ideas into one single test case requires more planning and is more error-prone. In addition, complex test scenarios resist subsequent modifications, because it will be very difficult for us to familiarize ourselves with them later on.

One potentially meaningful approach is to first implement all test ideas we find valuable in small, fine-grained, and well-documented test cases. We can then complete this scaffolding by adding a few more complex test cases; these are often scenarios directed at fulfilling a user goal and comprising the complete lifetime of objects. Finally, we have to be willing to discard and reconsider these more complex test scenarios when implementing changes and refactoring actions. The attempt to just slightly modify complex tests we don't really understand normally produces test cases of doubtful quality and little use.

4.4 | Threshold Values and Equivalence Classes

Testing along the margins

One important heuristic for effective testing is to increasingly test along the *boundaries of a permitted value range* because these are the areas where most errors occur. This plays an essential role in many situations, such as when selecting input parameters. For example, when testing the factorial function of our mathematics library, the numbers 0, 1, 2, and MAX-INTEGER are better input values than 5, 12, 69, and 101. The same heuristic suggests we also test a String input parameter with both an empty String and a very long character string.

However, the boundary rule does not apply only to input parameters. Boundary cases also exist with regard to the sizes of input files (e.g., length = 500MB), the number of a method's calls, the size of Collection objects, and many other factors. The more we think about this, the more points with potential problems in boundary areas we will identify. For example, although we tested DictionaryParser with an empty reader, we have not tested it with a large number of translation entries, which could lead to a buffer overflow or cause other problems. Let's try at this point to see how it works:

```
public void test10000Lines() throws IOException {
    StringBuffer buffer = new StringBuffer();
    for (int i = 0; i < 10000; i++){
        buffer.append("Wort"+i+"="word"+i+"\n");
    }
    parser = this.createParser(buffer.toString());
    for (int i = 0; i < 10000; i++){
        this.assertNextTranslation("Wort"+i, "word"+i);
    }
    assertFalse(parser.hasNextTranslation());
}
```

In addition, our tests have not yet paid any attention to the case where translation entries have empty strings. Empty strings do not represent a meaningful German word nor an English translation, so we postpone this issue to Chapter 4, Section 4.5, Error Cases and Exceptions.

Brian Marick offers a small catalog of test ideas at [URL:TestingCat], including more boundary cases interesting to test.

Threshold values normally depend on the implementation

Finding boundary cases can be very easy at times, as when the maximum admissible number of lines is stated in the specification. In most cases, however, we need to have a close look at the implementation to discover real boundary cases. Knowing only that an index type int is used to access a specific object will enable us to see MAXINTEGER as a threshold value.

Equivalence classes

Another commonly used example is the following sort function:

```
private final static int MIN_QUICKSORT = 15;
public List sort(List unsorted) {
   if (unsorted.size() < MIN_QUICKSORT) {
      return bubbleSort(unsorted);
   } else {
      return quickSort(unsorted);
   }
}
```

Analyzing the code is the only way for us to find that 15 is a threshold value which leads to two different code execution paths. Full code coverage requires that both paths be tested, necessitating two additional test cases, with 14 and 15 elements, respectively. When the space of all possible test cases is split in this manner, the space is said to be composed of two *equivalence classes.*

Equivalence classes are an old but still central concept in testing theory. Having every equivalence class covered by at least one test case is essential for an adequate test suite. Cem Kaner [93] defines equivalence class as follows:

> If you expect the same result[5] from two tests, you consider them equivalent. A group of tests forms an equivalence class, if you think that
>
> - They all test the same thing.
> - If one test catches a bug, the others probably will too.
> - If one test doesn't catch a bug, the others probably won't either.[6]

---

5. Here, "the same" obviously does not mean identical.
6. [Kaner93, p. 126].

The reasons why we consider these tests equivalent are normally found in the implementation details: the test cases of an equivalence class use the same input variables, manipulate the same output variables, and have a similar internal control flow. Equivalence classes in test cases often result from exceeding threshold conditions with regard to our input values. An object-oriented particularity in this context is *polymorphism,* which leads to a situation where the class membership of an object used can change the control flow, as we will see in Chapter 7. Thinking about test equivalence classes often leads to the discovery of new and yet unconsidered test cases. For example, equivalence classes for invalid input are being neglected by many programmers.

4.5   Error Cases and Exceptions

One aspect of our program has not been explicitly dealt with either in the tests or in the implementation: error cases. In general, we have to distinguish between two different categories of error cases:

Error categories
- The first error category includes errors we expect and would like to catch within the application. Correct handling of such cases has to be considered in our tests.

- The second error category includes errors we cannot foresee or those we can handle only with great effort. Such errors often point to programming errors and normally cause the application or a part of it to abort. In such a case, all that remains to be tested is to ensure that the application ends in a controlled way.

Checked exceptions and runtime exceptions

These two different error types can be represented in Java by *checked exceptions* or *runtime exceptions,* but this does not necessarily have to be the case. For example, expected faulty behavior is often marked by explicit return values, such as a result object that understands the isError() message or an implicit coding (e.g., -1 or null). On the other hand, it is absolutely common to transform runtime exceptions on one level into checked exceptions on another level, and vice versa.

Consistent handling of errors and exceptions is not trivial and requires frequent refactoring steps, especially in complex applications. A detailed discussion of this issue would go beyond the scope of this book; in fact, it could fill a book in itself.[7] Moreover, the test-first approach cannot solve this problem for us, but it forces us to think about consistency before implementing an error handling method of one type or another. The result of this consideration is more test cases with different test objectives:

- The occurrence of expected errors causes the correct error object to be returned or the correct exception to be thrown.

- The error object or the exception is correctly handled in the calling "client" object.

Let's try to transfer this finding to our example: So far, we have assumed that the Reader we passed to the DictionaryParser contains exclusively syntactically correct entries. But this assumption is more than naive, because the source we aspire to contains dictionary files written by humans. So we will first list a few errors that can potentially occur in the syntax:

1. A line is empty.

2. A line does not contain the "=" character.

3. The equal sign character (=) is preceded or followed by an empty string.

4. The word before or after the = character has blanks in its margins.

Note that this list does not include all conceivable error cases, but only a few typical ones. Our goal is to trace the most frequent problem cases rather than check for all potential errors. It is now a matter of finding the desired behavior of the parser. Cases 1 through 3 are obviously not suited for a meaningful parsing of the line, so we expect here the throwing of a DictionaryParserException. The following test results from error case 1:

Expected exception

```java
public void testEmptyLine() throws IOException,
    DictionaryParserException {
    String dictText = "Buch=book\n" +
        "\n" +
        "Auto=car";
    parser = this.createParser(dictText);
```

---

7. To our knowledge, this book has yet to be written. Do you feel like writing it?

```
this.assertNextTranslation("Buch", "book");
try {
    parser.nextTranslation();
    fail("DictionaryParserException expected");
} catch (DictionaryParserException expected) {}
this.assertNextTranslation("Auto", "car");
assertFalse(parser.hasNextTranslation());
}
```

Functioning after the error   Two things are unexpected in this test. First, we embedded an empty line between two correct lines. Especially when passing exceptions, it is meaningful to check our OUT for correct "continued functioning." The state of an object changes often before an error condition occurs, and the exception handler does not set it back afterwards. For this reason, the test ensures that everything continues functioning after the error.[8]

Test pattern for exception checking   The second thing is the pattern used to check an expected exception:

```
try {
    parser.nextTranslation();
    fail("DictionaryParserException expected");
} catch (DictionaryParserException expected) {}
```

I think that this check is simple and intuitive. As an alternative, JUnit offers a class, junit.extension.ExceptionTestCase, for the same purpose, but I find its use complicated, to say the least, because an (anonymous) subclass of ExceptionTestCase has to be created for each exception under test. In addition, the approach we selected expands easily in case we want to study the expected exception more closely, notably, with regard to its message string:

```
try {
    parser.nextTranslation();
    fail("DictionaryParserException expected");
} catch (DictionaryParserException expected) {
    assertEquals("message", expected.getMessage());
}
```

---

8. Keith Stobie [00] discusses this problem and similar ones during exception testing.

To induce the `testEmptyLine()` method to do faultless compiling, we have to create the `DictionaryParserException` class *and* add it to the throws clause of the `nextTranslation()` method. As a consequence, the majority of the methods in `DictionaryParserTest` cannot be recompiled until we give them `DictionaryParserException`. Whether we declare each single exception type or a simple `throws Exception` in the test methods is a matter of taste. Although the approach selected here documents the occurring exceptions much better, it also has a much higher adaptation cost.

The necessary change in the application code looks like this:

```
public class DictionaryParser {
   ...

   public void nextTranslation()
      throws IOException, DictionaryParserException {
      if ("".equals(nextLine)) {
         this.readNextLine();
         throw new DictionaryParserException();
      }
      int index = nextLine.indexOf('=');
      currentGermanWord = nextLine.substring(0, index);
      currentTranslation = nextLine.substring(index + 1);
      this.readNextLine();
   }
}
```

Accordingly, we can now define the test methods for cases 2 and 3:

```
public void testLineWithoutEquals() throws Exception {
   String dictText = "Buch=book\n" +
      "Auto car\n" +
      "Auto=car";
   parser = this.createParser(dictText);
   this.assertNextTranslation("Buch", "book");
   try {
      parser.nextTranslation();
      fail("DictionaryParserException expected");
   } catch (DictionaryParserException expected) {}
   this.assertNextTranslation("Auto", "car");
```

```
      assertFalse(parser.hasNextTranslation());
   }
   public void testLinesWithEmptyWords() throws Exception {
      String dictText = "Buch=book\n" +
         "Auto=\n" +
         "=car\n" +
         "Auto=car";
      parser = this.createParser(dictText);
      this.assertNextTranslation("Buch", "book");
      try {
         parser.nextTranslation();
         fail("DictionaryParserException expected");
      } catch (DictionaryParserException expected) {}
      try {
         parser.nextTranslation();
         fail("DictionaryParserException expected");
      } catch (DictionaryParserException expected) {}
      this.assertNextTranslation("Auto", "car");
      assertFalse(parser.hasNextTranslation());
   }
```

Once again, modification and refactoring of the nextTranslation()
method is left to the reader.

Case 4 differs from the first three cases in that the words are meaningful,
although they are enclosed in blanks. For this reason, we would like to
ignore the blank at the beginning or end of a word:

```
   public void testSpacesInWords() throws Exception {
      String dictText = "  Buch  =book\n" +
         "Auto=  car  \n" +
         " Buch=volume \n" +
         "Modultest=unit test  ";
      parser = this.createParser(dictText);
      this.assertNextTranslation("Buch", "book");
      this.assertNextTranslation("Auto", "car");
      this.assertNextTranslation("Buch", "volume");
      this.assertNextTranslation("Modultest", "unit test");
      assertFalse(parser.hasNextTranslation());
   }
```

How many error
cases should
be tested?

Again, we identified different cases, including one that should retain the blanks within a word. The questions we have to ask now—How many cases should be involved in the first attempt? How many should be added when reviewing the tests? and How many will eventually be added later when a problem occurs in practical operation?—can be answered based not least on experience and feedback. In the event that defects are found again and again in the shipped software, we have to invest more time in the test case creation. In contrast, if finding test cases devours 80% of available resources, we would do better to analyze the cost/benefit situation.

Correct
exception handling

So far, our tests have checked whether a faulty Reader leads to the correct exceptions. Our next step involves correct handling of these "exceptions" in the "client," the Dictionary class:

```
public void testInvalidTranslationsInReader() throws Exception {
    String dictText = "Buch=book\n"+
        "\n" +
        "Buch volume\n" +
        "Auto=car";
    Reader reader= new StringReader(dictText);
    dict = new Dictionary(reader);
    assertEquals("dict size", 2, dict.size());
    assertEquals("translation Buch", "book",
        dict.getTranslation("Buch"));
    assertEquals("translation Auto", "car",
        dict.getTranslation("Auto"));
}
```

Note that we had to deal with our actual test goal—check for correct handling of DictionaryParserException—by the back door. We created a Reader so that, based on our insider knowledge, it will throw the desired exceptions. This is a typical white-box test. Also, the correct handling—ignore faulty entries—was tested over a side effect, and we expanded the interface of the Dictionary class by the size() method for this purpose. This indirect approach is typical when a test includes several objects.

To prevent a sheer return of a constant from happening in the implementation of size(), we also add an assert statement verifying the size of the Dictionary object to all other tests, as in the next example:

```
public void testTwoTranslations() {
   dict.addTranslation("Buch", "book");
   dict.addTranslation("Auto", "car");
   assertFalse("dict not empty", dict.isEmpty());
   assertEquals("dict size", 2, dict.size());
   ...
}
```

And finally, a test that checks whether or not an IOException from the DictionaryParser also reaches the surface in the Dictionary constructor would definitely be useful:

```
public void testIOExceptionFromReader() {
   Reader reader = new StringReader("") {
      public int read(char cbuf[], int off,
         int len) throws IOException {
         throw new IOException();
      }
   };
   try {
      dict = new Dictionary(reader);
      fail("IOException expected");
   } catch (IOException expected) {}
}
```

One disturbing thing that makes the test hard to understand is that generating the IOException requires knowledge about implementation details of the StringWriter class. At times, it is even impossible to generate the desired exception in the conventional way. Fortunately, in Chapter 6, Section 6.7, we learn a technique to avoid exotic test tricks in most cases.

4.6 Object Interactions

Integration and interaction tests

One important feature of object-oriented programs is that the actual behavior of the system is determined by the interplay of many instances and not by single objects. However, classic unit tests are limited to checking the isolated behavior of a program unit, moving the test of the units' interplay to the so-called *integration tests*. Procedural integration tests focus on the syntactically correct use of the interfaces and verification of side effects. Today, these tasks are assumed by modern IDEs or data encapsulation, respectively. For this reason, McGregor and Sykes [McGregor01] suggest the new term *interaction test* to emphasize the shift of the test focus to the interplay of objects.

Types of
interaction tests
McGregor and Sykes distinguish between two main types of interaction tests:

- Testing *collection classes:* They use the term *collection class* for any class that stores references to other objects—normally as 1:n relationships— without "collaborating," or using their services. Such a test involves only the addition, creation and removal, or deletion of referenced instances. A small (incomplete) test suite for an imaginary collection that takes String objects could look like this:

```
public class MyCollectionTest extends TestCase {
    ...
    private MyCollection collection;
    protected void setUp() {
        collection = new MyCollection();
    }

    public void testAddString() {
        assertTrue(collection.isEmpty());
        assertEquals(0, collection.size());
        assertFalse(collection.containsString("string1"));
        collection.addString("string1");
        assertFalse(collection.isEmpty());
        assertEquals(1, collection.size());
        assertTrue(collection.containsString("string1"));
        collection.addString("string2");
        assertFalse(collection.isEmpty());
        assertEquals(2, collection.size());
        assertTrue(collection.containsString("string2"));
    }
```

```
public void testRemoveString() {
    collection.addString("string1");
    collection.addString("string2");
    collection.addString("string3");
    assertTrue(collection.containsString("string2"));
    collection.removeString("string2");
    assertFalse(collection.containsString("string2"));
    assertEquals(2, collection.size());
    collection.removeString("string3");
    collection.removeString("string1");
    assertTrue(collection.isEmpty());
    assertEquals(0, collection.size());
  }
}
```

Depending on the type of collection and the desired error behavior, various test cases have to be added. The important thing is that no messages have to be sent to the "collected" instances for testing.

- Testing *collaborating classes:* A class is called *collaborating* when it uses the services of other classes to meet its tasks, for example, when objects of the Dictionary class use an instance of DictionaryParser. The cooperation of objects can be either unidirectional or bidirectional; in other words, two objects can exchange messages in either direction.

There is no general approach to test collaborations. We have already seen several examples, including all test cases of the DictionaryTest class with fromReader in their names, and we will see more later on. The important thing here is that we want to test the direct exchange of messages between neighboring objects. The more mediator objects exist between our "collaborators," the more difficult it becomes to control the tests and the more often we will come up against the phenomenon of swallowed errors described in the next section. And we should limit ourselves to the public interface of the called object in our collaboration, or we will run the risk of designing very modification-sensitive tests.

Are interaction tests also unit tests?

Although interaction tests are no longer unit tests on a class level, they are still indispensable for the correct behavior of our larger units. Experiences gained with object-oriented systems in the testing community contradict the hope that the correct interplay of our objects can be ensured solely by acceptance tests on a system level. When the distance between the test interface and the tested class becomes too big, too many errors in the components no longer reach the surface; they will be "hidden," but can still come up again under slightly modified circumstances.

For this reason, as developer-testers we won't be able to avoid different types of interaction tests.[9] Indeed, several of our previous test efforts were oriented to the interplay of two objects. The fact that interaction tests are important parts of a test suite should not tempt us to test some objects only indirectly through other collaborating objects. On the other hand, testing a class in isolation is not sufficient to check the interplay of objects. We always have to keep an eye on the drawbacks inherent in inter-unit tests: increased cost of changes and refactorings.

4.7   Design by Contract

Design by contract (DBC) is a method originally proposed by Betrand Meyer [97] for the design of object-oriented and component-oriented systems. The main characteristic of DBC is that classes define their behavior and interplay by *contracts*. A contract in this context consists essentially of a *class invariant* and *pre-* and *post-conditions* for all methods of the class interface.

While *Eiffel*, the language preferred by Meyer, explicitly supports contracts, we have to find other ways in Java. There are both commercial Java expansions (e.g., JContract [URL:JContract] and JWAM-Contract [URL: JWAM]) and several free Java expansions (e.g., [URL:IContract]) available for DBC users.[10] One interesting alternative is the use of the contract parts for the construction or expansion of our unit tests:

Contracts provide ideas for unit tests
- The **pre-condition** of a method describes the limit of the defined system behavior. It tells us which input data is meaningful for the CUT, thus helping us in our decision of whether or not test X with input Y, Z

---

9. For this reason, there are also proposals to rename XP unit tests *mobility tests* or *build tests*.

10. The assert command available since JDK 1.4 is useful only to a very limited extent, because it does not support subtypes and invariants for DBC.

should still be written. Testing for compliance with the pre-condition itself is not meaningful.

- A **post-condition** can be converted directly into an additional `assert` call. However, the fact that not all CUT–internal matters required for verification are visible from the outside can be a problem. But post-conditions are actually not intended to serve this purpose.

- The **class invariant** can serve as an additional post-condition and be treated as such for unit-test purposes.

Let's use a part of the contract of `DictionaryParser` as an example:

- Pre-condition of the constructor: `in != null`

- Pre-condition of `nextTranslation()`: `hasNextTranslation() == true`

- Post-condition of `nextTranslation()`: `currentGermanWord != null && currentTranslation != null`

We can learn primarily from the pre-conditions which test we will not have to write: no test with `null` as `in` parameter and no test for `nextGermanWord()`, if we have not previously tested `hasNextTranslation()`. And the following lines could be produced from the post-condition:

```
parser.nextTranslation();
assertNotNull(parser.currentGermanWord());
assertNotNull(parser.currentTranslation());
```

We could insert the two `assert` lines in our test cases after each call of `nextTranslation()`. On the other hand, it would not make much sense because subsequent asserts would normally implicitly cover both conditions. This is typical because DBC conditions are not allowed to execute operations that change the state of an object and they are therefore often relatively weak in terms of their specificity.

Defensive programming
A design paradigm thought to be an antipole of DBC is *defensive programming*. This paradigm assumes that the pre-conditions of a function or method call are tested by the method itself and that a violation of the pre-condition leads to a defined error behavior. Fault-tolerant systems normally use this paradigm. The major drawbacks are higher development cost, increased runtime, and a potential veiling of programming errors.

Defensive programming is implicitly assumed in many specifications: developers are expected to respond to wrong input values by an understandable error message instead of an undefined behavior. In contrast to DBC, negative tests for pre-conditions are both meaningful and essential for adequate testing in this case (see Chapter 4, Section 4.5, Error Cases and Exceptions). The general rule here is that defensively developed classes require more isolated unit tests, whereas a contract-based design demands interaction tests [McGregor01, p. 224].

Compatibility of DBC and test-first developments

We can see that DBC contracts can serve as inspiration for our unit tests, provided that the contracts were formulated. Method-centered test cases can normally be translated directly into pre- and post-conditions, and vice versa. The big (unanswered) question is therefore, At what point in our test-first development cycle is it meaningful to *explicitly* specify the contracts? A DBC contract might play its most successful role as an unaware source of ideas during the test-first development, when the developer often has pre-conditions, post-conditions, and invariants in mind without explicitly formulating them. But the actual contracts represent the unit tests themselves.

Explicit contracts are advantageous in any event when they already exist—for example, during subsequent creation of unit tests for existing software (see also Chapter 15, Section 15.1)—and when it is a matter of defining and documenting interfaces for external development teams. If we also use an appropriate DBC expansion, we can reduce the number of unit tests to be written by those that test the contract verified elsewhere.

4.8 More Ideas to Find Test Cases

Those who think they still don't have sufficient material to find test cases are referred to the huge amount of test literature; see the references in Bibliography and List of References, Further Reading. A few additional tips and ideas follow from various sources:

- Compile a *test catalog with typical error cases* and use it for inspiration. A good starting point might be the catalog at [URL:TestingCat].

- Test *all* of your *different result categories* ("distinct results") of a function call. The above explanations about error cases and exceptions are based on this principle.

- Sometimes it is meaningful to *randomly generate test data* and to find the desired result based on a test oracle, instead of using only test cases with exactly defined input and output data. This is normally the case when certain errors cannot be caused in a deterministic way. A typical example is the creation of correct random input strings for a parser to discover potential ambiguities in the underlying grammar [Metsker01].

Such tests remove the causal relationship between failure and previous changes to the code so that these tests should be separated from "normal" unit tests.

What if time is short? Developers who take their role as testers seriously will hardly encounter the problem of not testing enough, but rather when to stop. Chapter 8 discusses this issue in detail. The following heuristics may be helpful to decide on the minimal set of tests when deadlines are looming or when you have to trade off your testing effort:

- Test at least the explicit functional requirements.

- Add a unit test whenever a bug slipped through to functional testing or production.

- Test wherever you have already found many bugs. Statistical studies have shown that bugs normally come in clusters; they are not equally distributed over the entire application.

4.9 Refactoring Code and Tests

Let's recapitulate the definition of refactoring:

> Refactoring is the process of changing a software system in such a way that it does not alter the external behavior of the code yet improves its internal structure.[11]

At first sight, this definition suggests that nothing will change in the tests either in the course of refactoring. This holds true for all those tests that view the behavior of the *component under refactoring (CUR)* from the

---

11. [Fowler99, p. xvi].

outside, for example, all acceptance tests. In contrast, unit tests are normally a mixture of specification-based and implementation-dependent tests. For this reason, changes in the course of refactoring cannot be avoided. We can identify the following basic types and their impact on unit tests:

The impact of refactoring on unit tests

- **Renaming** methods, classes, or packages forces the renaming of test cases and move test classes.

- **Removing parameters** results in the corresponding adaptation of the test cases. Sometimes test cases can become superfluous, such as when they differ from another test case only by a parameter that was removed.

- **Adding parameters** requires not only a correction of the corresponding method calls, but often also expansion of the test fixture by the new parameter object.

- **Extracting a class** causes the tests to be moved—when these tests concentrated on the behavior—which is now implemented by the new class. In addition, interaction tests between the original and the added class are necessary. After the extraction, it is also important to look at the new class as an independent CUT to identify missing test cases.

  A special case of extracting a class is the **extraction of a subclass**. This often leads to a parallel hierarchy of test classes (see Chapter 7, Section 7.1).

- As a countermove, the **inlining of a class** means that tests have to be moved in opposite direction. This can cause some tests to lose their right to exist, especially the tests dealing with the interaction of both classes.

- **Moving a public method** into another class has consequences similar to the extraction of a class, that is, either moving the test cases that concentrate on this method or duplicating the test cases, if the method remains in the old class and delegates the call to the new class.

- **Modifying the implementation** of a single method has no impact on black-box tests, but implementation-dependent test cases have to be reconsidered. For example, if we were to modify the implementation of the sort() method from Section 4.4 as follows:

```
private final static int MIN_QUICKSORT = 10;
public List sort(List unsorted) {
    if (unsorted.size() < MIN_QUICKSORT) {
        return bubbleSort(unsorted);
    } else {
        return quickSort(unsorted);
    }
}
```

Then the correct test cases would no longer be equipped with 14 and 15, but with 9 and 10 elements.[12]

Refactoring approach
A common approach in refactoring is to first identify the test cases which should still be valid after refactoring. Next, you restructure in small steps and evaluate after each step whether some test is now superfluous or should be moved or expanded. The next action would always be the start of the remaining tests to validate your assumptions. If you think a refactoring task is complete, you once more swap your developer hat for your tester cap and reconsider all existing test cases with regard to adequacy and redundancy.

Throw away existing tests
Marick [00] emphasizes not trying to desperately keep all existing tests when doing system modifications. The more complex the tested scenario, the more difficult it will be to adapt it subsequently to the new situation. Such complicated tests should sometimes be thrown away and replaced by new ones for reasons of cost.

Adaptation cost
The cost arising to adapt our test suites to the constantly changing program can be considerable, but it is seldom a waste of effort. One positive effect is that the developers are constantly confronted with their previous assumptions and get opportunities to improve things. After all, learning is a never ending process.

On the other hand, if we find that maintaining our test suites takes much more time than the actual modifications to the system, then this is a sign that we are writing the wrong tests. Here "wrong" means that we may be testing things that change too often, so that automated tests, such as testing private methods and attributes of a class, are of no use.

---

12. A few people suggested making the constant MIN_QUICKSORT public and using it to build the appropriate test data in the test case. This would indeed save us the labor of changing the test when changing the value, but it would (a) reveal an implementation detail and (b) require more complex test logic.

| 4.10 | **Summary** |

This chapter concentrated on clues and theoretical basics to explain how you can improve and expand your existing test cases and how you find missing ones. Focusing on individual tests, improvements in test method naming, length, and simplicity were suggested. Test cases should concentrate on the typical usage of the CUT, on threshold values, and on equivalence classes. Error cases are equally important to test and the interaction of several objects must not be neglected. Moreover, the ideas in design by contract can give valuable hints for certain kinds of tests. Last but not least, one should never forget to adapt the test suite during and after refactoring; this can induce considerable but worthwhile effort.

Model-based test case creation I intentionally did not discuss the algorithmic and formal implementation of various software models in test cases—an aspect frequently discussed in the test literature. My reason was twofold: First, there are very few up-front models available in the course of test-first development. Second, the methods suggested there usually generate an overwhelming number of different test cases. This has a deterrent effect on "normal" software developers, and it also omits the meaningful balancing between testing costs and benefits.[13] In addition, although formal test case generation methods theoretically achieve a larger code coverage, their drawback is that they can hinder intuitive testing. Effective testing derives from intuition; restrictive rules hinder the intuition. Nevertheless, those who reach the limits of the test ideas described here, or those who are simply curious, will hopefully find more help in Bibliography and List of References, Further Reading.

---

13. [URL:TestingAgile] is all about finding the balance between no testing and complete testing given the needs of different kinds of software.

Chapter 5

The Inner Life of a Test Framework

As mere users of a test framework, we should not bother about its internal structure, unless we are programmers and, as such, interested in the inner parts of each piece of software we can get a hold of. In addition, unit testing is such an individual activity that we may sometimes not get around expansions and adaptations of the framework. JUnit does not cover every functionality anyone may need during testing; it is an open core that can be expanded and completed in different places. And if we find that JUnit limits our own test needs too much, then it may still serve us as an example for the benefits and drawbacks of certain design decisions in the development of our own test support tools.

5.1 Statics

JUnit as a "pattern tutorial"
So far, we have introduced three classes: TestRunner (in three different variants), TestCase, and TestSuite. But JUnit has much more in store. The inner structure of JUnit—mainly the package junit.framework—is a small tutorial in itself for the use of a large number of *design patterns* [Gamma95]. Kent Beck and Erich Gamma [Beck99] describe the patterns used and their motivation.[1] The article and the accompanying study of the JUnit sources is recommended to everyone and is an absolute must for all who want to understand and expand JUnit, even though JUnit has been further developed in the interim.

---

1. This article is included in the JUnit documentation as cookstour.htm.

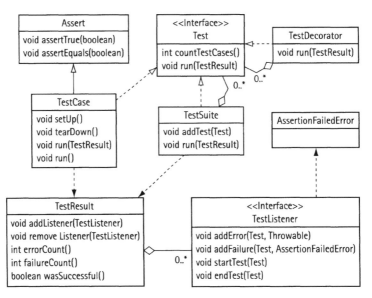

Figure 5.1 JUnit class diagram.

Figure 5.1 shows a small section from the inner life of JUnit Version 3.8. Except for `TestDecorator`, this class diagram shows a section from the `junit.framework` package. What is new for us are the "extension hooks" for project-specific and functional expansions of the JUnit framework:

- `TestResult` is the container of all results from a test run. All classes implementing the test interface—`TestCase`, `TestSuite`, and `TestDecorator`—become an instance of the class `TestResult` in its run() method.

- A `TestListener` can be registered with a `TestResult` by using `addListener()` to obtain information about start, end, failure, and error events in a test. This possibility is used by all of the three `TestRunner` classes to get notification about the current state of a test run.

The class `TestDecorator` serves as a superclass for a large number of expansions of the test framework. As the name implies, it implements the *decorator* pattern described by Gamma et al. [95], allowing the use of several concurrent expansions. Practical examples are included in the `junit.extensions` package.

Most JUnit expansions are developed as subclasses of `TestCase`. If we use `TestDecorator` instead, then we have the benefit that several expansions can be used concurrently. The drawback is that the application becomes more complex, because a decorator instance has to be added explicitly to a test or test suite.

■ AssertionFailedError is an exception thrown when an assert call fails, is caught by TestCase instances, and finally passed on to a TestResult for registration.

■ Assert is a superclass of TestCase and accommodates all variants of the assert method, all of which are also static. In this way, other classes, like test decorators, can also use the assert functionality. The extent of the assert variants available and their implementations is the focus of constant discussion in the JUnit discussion group [URL:YahooJUnit]. Project-specific expansions normally include a new assert method in one form or another to compare certain collection classes or other data structures.

Knowing how JUnit is built inside is very useful, especially when you decide to start peeking behind the TestCase scene to enjoy some well written source text of the framework.

5.2 The Life Cycle of a Test Suite

The dynamic side of a program is hard to grasp by the sole study of class diagrams. Consider the following AllTests class:

```
public class AllTests {

    public static void main(String[] args) {
        junit.awtui.TestRunner.run(AllTests.class);
    }

    public static Test suite() {
        TestSuite suite = new TestSuite("All tests of MyProject");
        suite.addTest(pack1.AllTests.suite());
        suite.addTestSuite(pack2.ExampleTest.class);
        return suite;
    }
}
```

Look what happens when we call this class from the command line:

1. The `AllTests` class itself is used as an argument to start the AWT test runner.

2. The test runner calls the static `suite()` method of the `AllTests` class. The latter, in turn, builds a complex test suite in tree structure by adding other test suites—in this case `pack1.AllTests` and `pack2.ExampleTest`—to its own. The difference between `addTest(Test)` and `addTestSuite(Class)` is that `addTestSuite(Class)` asks the class passed on—a subclass of `TestCase`—for its test methods, using Java's reflection mechanics, and uses them to build a suite.

   At the ends of this building chain, there are individual test cases. Each test case is represented by an instance of the class `TestCase` or a subclass. For example,

   ```
   public class ExampleTest extends TestCase {
       public void testFoo() {...}
       public void testBar() {...}
       public void testFooBar() {...}
   }
   ```

   becomes an instance of `TestSuite`, with three instances of the `ExampleTest` class, which differ only in the name of the called test method. This name is stored internally as the name of the test case and can be retrieved by `getName()`.

3. Clicking the *Run* button first generates a `TestResult` instance and then starts the `run(TestResult)` method of the top test suite. This test suite, in turn, calls the `run(TestResult)` method of all involved tests sequentially.

   In the "leaves" of this call tree—the `TestCase` instances—`run(TestResult)` first causes the execution of `setUp()` and then the `runTest(TestResult)` method, followed by `tearDown()`. Unless `runTest()` was explicitly overloaded, it will now start the actual test method; it learned the name of this method from the constructor's String parameter. Figure 5.2 shows a simplified process from the beginning to the execution of a test case.[2]

---

2. As usual, reality is a little more complicated, and the details are best taken from the JUnit source code itself.

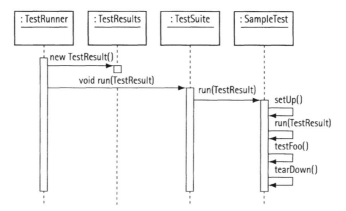

Figure 5.2 Sequence diagram for the start of a test case.

We can learn two things from the previous process description: First, it makes a difference whether we build the test fixture—normally identical to the instance variables of the test class—in the constructor or in the setUp()method, because a test setup should occur only during the execution of a test. Second, the tests are executed sequentially, but not in a defined order, so that we cannot rely on it.

Repeated test execution   What will happen when we click the *Run* button a second time depends on the status of the *Reload* checkbox. If the Reload option is deselected, then another run(TestResult) is sent to the top test suite. In contrast, if Reload is selected, all classes are reloaded,[3] the test tree is created again, and finally the suite is started. We need to know that the instances of the test cases have to be such that they *could* be restarted repeatedly.

5.3	## Project-Specific Expansions

Project-specific requirements   Many projects have particularities that also have an impact on testing. In the simplest case, an additional or modified assert variant is needed, for example, to compare files. In difficult cases, the test results should be logged in XML. And then, there is this project that has to run the same test with hundred different records.

---

3. Dynamic reloading may cause problems (see JUnit FAQs in Appendix A, Section A.1).

Go ahead, expand JUnit with your own test functionality.[4] Or better yet, have a look around for expansions readily available (see also Appendix A, Section A.2, JUnit Expansions), and don't hesitate to hit your keyboard in case the wheel hasn't been invented yet. Oh, and finally, don't forget to make your expansion available to other JUnit users at some point in time. We will see a few small and a few larger expansions in the further course of this book.

Warning   Note that building a test framework should not turn into an end in itself, but rather facilitate and support our test effort. Any framework handicraft beyond this scope is useless for the progress of the project and amounts to nothing more than killing after work hours.

5.4 | Summary

This chapter served to shed some light into the hidden interior of JUnit. It was not our goal to examine every detail of this open test framework, but instead to give the interested developer some useful hints for his or her entry into source text reading. In addition, a certain basic knowledge of the static structure and the dynamics of the most important objects is useful for those who want to evaluate the usability of test frameworks for specific test projects and scenarios. In fact, project-specific expansions of JUnit are often required, whereas complex expansions and reorganizations of the framework are involved in a project only in rare cases.

---

4. But think it over 10 times before you change the JUnit source code itself. Each new version will entail changes and here we are, caught up in a time-consuming and unnecessary maintenance spiral.

Chapter 6

Dummy and Mock Objects for Independence

In an averagely complex application, an object can hardly do without the cooperation of many other objects of the same or another class. So how can we test an object that depends on so many others? The most pragmatic and (probably) intuitive way out of this dilemma is the *bottom-up approach:* we begin our development and testing with the classes that build themselves on system-owned classes. Then we use these tested components to build independent classes.

This approach is called *bottom-up* because we start from the very bottom, with the most concrete objects, working our way up to the more abstract components. We saw in Chapter 3, Section 3.2 that working *top-down* (or *outside-in*) is easier in the test-first approach. In that section, we also identified problems caused by the dependence of various classes upon each other and external sources. This chapter shows how to avoid these dependencies or subsequently eliminate them in many cases.

6.1 | Little Dummies

Locality and independence

One important unit-testing rule comes up over and over again: a single test case should be as *local* as possible; that is, it should test only the object we are currently dealing with and not all the others it requires for its job or with whom it cooperates and to which it delegates tasks. One way to come a step closer to the goal of maximum independence of a test is through the use of *dummy objects*. This means that we replace part of our objects by others that are only pretending. A simple example will explain this idea.

We want to program a Euro calculator that converts and returns a given amount of currency into Euros;[1] an instance of class ExchangeRateProvider shall be used for retrieving the actual exchange rates. Naturally, we first do the tests:

```
public class EuroCalculatorTest extends TestCase {

    public void testEUR2EUR() {
        double result = new EuroCalculator().valueInEuro(1.0, "EUR");
        assertEquals(1.0, result, 0.00001);
    }

    public void testUSD2EUR() {
        double result = new EuroCalculator().valueInEuro(1.0, "USD");
        assertEquals(1.1324, result, 0.00001);
    }

}
```

We use the class ExchangeRateProvider as a readily available component; it provides the rate of exchange for all common currencies over a network connection:

```
public class ExchangeRateProvider {
    public double getRateFromTo(String fromCurrency, String to) {
        double retrievedRate = ... // Access to server over network
        return retrievedRate;
    }
}
```

Problems   Although implementing the EuroCalculator class is easy, our tests still have a few problems. First, the testUSD2EUR() test case will probably function only for a short time, namely as long as the exchange rate between Dollar and Euro does not change. Second, accessing the exchange rate server is a very insecure matter, because we access it over a network. The server may have long response times or even be unavailable for an unknown time due to overload. This dependence upon an external service

---

1. To simplify things, we use the primitive type double to represent monetary amounts, but this primitive type is rarely used in the real world due to its rounding problem.

can mean that our test may go wrong, even though our program does not
have any error.

First dummy   One way to solve this problem is the use of a fake exchange rate server to
which we can give the expected exchange rate right away:

```java
public class DummyProvider extends ExchangeRateProvider {

    private double dummyRate;
    public DummyProvider(double dummyRate) {
        this.dummyRate = dummyRate;
    }
    public double getRateFromTo(String from, String to) {
        return dummyRate;
    }
}
```

Now we have to find a way to smuggle our dummy into EuroCalculator.
One option is to expand the signature of the valueInEuro() method by a
parameter of the ExchangeRateProvider type. This is one possible design
decision which requires that all clients of EuroCalculator have an instance
of ExchangeRateProvider available; if necessary, this decision can be
changed later on (see Chapter 6, Section 6.8). Anyway, we seize this opportunity to drag the expected accuracy to a constant, ACCURACY. The modified
test looks like the following:

```java
public class EuroCalculatorTest extends TestCase {
    private final static double ACCURACY = 0.00001;

    public void testEUR2EUR() {
        ExchangeRateProvider provider = new DummyProvider(1.0);
        double result = new EuroCalculator().
            valueInEuro(2.0, "EUR", provider);
        assertEquals(2.0, result, ACCURACY);
    }

    public void testUSD2EUR() {
        ExchangeRateProvider provider = new DummyProvider(1.1324);
        double result = new EuroCalculator().
            valueInEuro(1.5, "USD", provider);
```

```
        assertEquals(1.6986, result, ACCURACY);
    }
}
```

And here we are: our test runs fast and stable and it is independent of fluctuating exchange rates. But we have to be aware of the fact that we are testing only the EuroCalculator class and not the exchange rate server. We assume that the exchange rate server was (hopefully) tested by the provider of the component. If we are the provider, then we also test the server, but in another test suite.

6.2 | Weltering in Technical Terms

Before we deal with more challenging falsifications, we will have a look at the terms used. There are many terms used for what we are calling a dummy object, including *stub, mock,* and *shunt.* Unfortunately, these terms are used inconsistently in the literature and, we have to assume, randomly. We will be using the different flavors as follows.

Stub A *stub* is part of a software that has been implemented rudimentarily and will later be replaced by the correct implementation. A stub object serves as placeholder for a functionality we have planned but not yet implemented.

Dummy In contrast, a *dummy* (or *testing stub*) can replace the real implementation for test purposes. Whether or not we will use the real object or a dummy object will be determined by the internal or external configuration.

Mock A *mock* differs from a *dummy* by additional functionality. If necessary, a mock object allows us to set the reactions desired by the object and to verify the correct behavior of its "client." Chapter 6, Section 6.5 discusses mock objects in detail.

6.3 | Big Dummies

Its simplicity makes the Euro calculator example attractive. It does nothing but replace a complex function from the real world by hardwired values, which are exactly tuned to the tests. Let's look now at a more complex problem:

In most applications, we need a way to log a large variety of events in a central place during the program runtime. To be able to implement this *logging functionality* consistently over the program, we define a standardized interface:

```
public interface Logging {
    int DEFAULT_LOGLEVEL = 2;
    void log(int logLevel, String message);
    void log(int logLevel, String message, String module);
    void log(String message);
}
```

This interface allows us to log a message and state a log level, the parameter logLevel, to distinguish between error messages and debug messages. In addition, we need a way to work without an explicit log level, to have instead a standard value, DEFAULT_LOGLEVEL.

A first implementation of the Logging interface should be the class LogServer, which is created by stating a file name and used to write all log entries to this file. As usual, we start with a test:

```
public class LogServerTest extends TestCase {

    public void testSimpleLogging() {
        Logging logServer = new LogServer("log.test");
        logServer.log(0, "line One");
        logServer.log(1, "line Two");
        logServer.log("line Three");
        // assertTrue(??) Oops, and now?
    }

}
```

How to test file access? While the first four lines were easy game for us, we are now in a dilemma. How do we get inside the log.test file to check whether or not the log server really does its job properly? One way to check this would be to expand our log server by a function, getLoggingFile(). However, this would mean that we commit ourselves to file logging and disclose an implementation detail merely for test purposes. In addition, opening and reading a file could cause problems that make controlled and repeated test runs more difficult:

- How do I find a path that is readable and writable for test purposes?

- How can I ensure that the access rights on this path are correct?

- How can I ensure that the file doesn't already exist or wasn't deleted before the test?

All of these are problems we have to consider for productive operation, but should be of no meaning for the current state of development.

PrintWriter instead of a file

This is where our knowledge of the Java IO classes comes in handy. How about simply passing an instance of the java.io.PrintWriter type within the constructor to our LogServer, instead of using a file name. This offers a way to output our log message by use of println() and it is useful not only for files but for any type of OutputStream. Therefore, we will modify our test as follows:

```java
public void testSimpleLogging() {
    PrintWriter writer = new PrintWriter(
                            new FileOutputStream("log.test"));
    Logging logServer = new LogServer(writer);
    logServer. log(0, "line One");
    logServer.log(1, "line Two");
    logServer.log("line Three");
    // assertTrue(??) Oops, and now?
}
```

Unfortunately, we are still facing the problem that we first have to get a hold of the file to be able to do the necessary checks. On the upside, knowing that our log server should do nothing but use the println(...) method to output a combination of log level and log message leads to another intuitive idea. Why not implement our own subclass of PrintWriter, as in the previous Euro calculator example? The instances of the PrintWriter subclass record everything they get from println(), and everything would be available for later checks. This idea produces the following dummy class:

```java
import java.io.PrintWriter;
```

```
import java.util.*;
public class DummyPrintWriter extends PrintWriter {
    private List logs = new ArrayList();

    public DummyPrintWriter() {
        super((OutputStream) null);
    }

    public void println(String logString)
{
        logs.addElement(logString);
    }

    public String getLogString(int pos) {
        return (String) logs.get(pos);
    }
}
```

With the help of this DummyPrintWriter class, we can now formulate our
test much more simply and clearly:

```
public void testSimpleLogging(){
    DummyPrintWriter writer = new DummyPrintWriter();
    Logging logServer = new LogServer(writer);
    logServer.log(0, "first line");
    logServer.log(1, "second line");
    logServer.log("third line");
    assertEquals("0: first line", writer.getLogString(0));
    assertEquals("1: second line", writer.getLogString(1));
    assertEquals("2: third line", writer.getLogString(2));
}
```

Lack of aesthetics   Looks like we made it, or did we? Taking a closer look, we can see that
our test still contains a few ugly things. To make DummyPrintWriter a useful
subclass of PrintWriter, we had to use a few tricks. On the one hand, our
constructor does a *cast* on the null object; this is ugly but necessary to
allow the Java compiler to statically determine the correct super constructor. On the other hand, we dangerously assumed that our log server would
exclusively call the println(...) method of the PrintWriter instance. Why

not simply turn this implicit assumption into an explicit one by introducing an interface? Well said; now let's do it:

```java
public interface Logger {
    void logLine(String logString);
}
```

Of course, this also changes the constructor of our log server and thus the test:

```java
public void testSimpleLogging() {
    DummyLogger logger  = new DummyLogger();
    Logging logServer = new LogServer(logger);
    logServer.log(0, "first line");
    logServer.log(1, "second line");
    logServer.log("third line");
    assertEquals("0: first line", logger.getLogString(0));
    assertEquals("1: second line", logger.getLogString(1));
    assertEquals("2: third line", logger.getLogString(2));
}
```

And our DummyPrintWriter turns into a DummyLogger:

```java
import java.util.*;
public class DummyLogger implements Logger {
    private List logs = new ArrayList();

    public void logLine(String logString) {
        logs.add(logString);
    }

    public String getLogString(int pos) {
        return (String) logs.get(pos);
    }
}
```

The actual implementation of LogServer appears trivial, compared to our efforts in making everything "testable":

```
public class LogServer implements Logging {
   private Logger logger;
   public LogServer(Logger logger) {
      this.logger = logger;
   }

   public void log(int logLevel, String message) {
      String logString = logLevel + ": " + message;
      logger.logLine(logString);
   }
   public void log(String message) {
      this.log(DEFAULT_LOGLEVEL, message);
   }
}
```

**Is it worth
the effort?**

Now, was this really worth all the effort? Don't we see at a glance that the class does exactly what it is supposed to do? Before answering this question, it is worthwhile to have a look at what we achieved with the introduction of our dummies and what we didn't achieve. By introducing the Logger interface, we obtained a log server with an implementation independent of system-specific IO classes. This interface also allows us to implement different loggers that our server can use without modifying them.

**The Dependency
Inversion Principle**

In this effort, we have observed important heuristics in object-oriented design, namely the so-called *Dependency Inversion Principle* [Martin96b, Meade00]), which states:

- High-level modules should not depend upon low-level modules. Both should depend upon *abstractions* (interfaces). In our example, this means that the log server should not depend on the file logger.

- Abstractions should, in turn, not depend upon details. Instead, details should depend upon abstractions.

Figure 6.1 shows this simple principle based on a dependence diagram of the HighLevelClass class upon an abstract interface, AbstractServer. The two implementations, ConcreteServer1 and ConcreteServer2, in turn depend only on this interface.

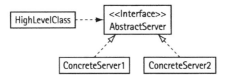

Figure 6.1 Schematic view of the Dependency Inversion Principle.

Design improvement   Another achievement is that we can now test the *correct interaction of the log server with its logger* in a very simple way. By following the one objective, namely to make our log server testable, we won a second objective for free: a modified design. It is a design that reduces dependencies and increases expandability. However, we (still) do not have a log server that really writes to a file. But that should be no trouble at all for us, considering what we have learned so far. First the test:

```java
import java.io.*;
public class FileLoggerTest extends TestCase {
    private final String TEMPFILE = "C:\\temp\\test.txt";

    public void testLogLine() throws IOException {
        FileLogger logger = new FileLogger(TEMPFILE);
        logger.logLine("Line 1");
        logger.logLine("Line 2");
        logger.close();
        BufferedReader reader = new BufferedReader(
                            new FileReader(TEMPFILE));
        assertEquals("Line 1", reader.readLine());
        assertEquals("Line 2", reader.readLine());
        assertNull("end of file reached", reader.readLine());
        reader.close();
    }
}
```

This test still contains one little ugly thing, namely the dependence upon an absolute file path. But we will discuss this later (see Chapter 6, Section 6.11). And now there is no magic about the implementation of the FileLogger class:

```
import java.io.*;
public class FileLogger implements Logger {
   private PrintWriter writer;
   public FileLogger(String filename) throws IOException {
      writer = new PrintWriter(new FileOutputStream(filename));
   }
   public void close() {
      writer.close();
   }
   public void logLine(String logMessage) {
      writer.println(logMessage);
   }
}
```

Objective partly achieved Although the dependencies of our tests upon the file system are not fully eliminated yet, we reduced them to a single one, namely the one that verifies the cooperation with files.

6.4 Extending Our Mansion

Was *this* worth all the effort? Let's look at a few extensions of our small framework and think about the impact they may have on our tests.

Additional parameter **Extension 1:** We extend our Logging interface by a log method with an additional module parameter. This parameter specifies which module of the application is currently logging.

Impact: One additional test method and some minor refactoring in the LogServerTest, along the following lines:

```
public class LogServerTest extends TestCase {
   private LogServer logServer;
   private DummyLogger logger;
   protected void setUp() {
      logger = new DummyLogger();
      logServer = new LogServer(logger);
   }
```

```
public void testLoggingWithModule() {
    logServer.log(0, "first line", "test");
    assertEquals("test(0): first line",
                    logger.getLogString(0));
}

public void testSimpleLogging() {
    logServer.log(0, "first line");
    logServer.log(1, "second line");
    logServer.log("third line");
    assertEquals("(0): first line", logger.getLogString(0));
    assertEquals("(1): second line", logger.getLogString(1));
    assertEquals("(2): third line", logger.getLogString(2));
}
}
```

The tests for the actual loggers remain untouched.

Several loggers per server   **Extension 2:** We allow a log server to accommodate several loggers, to which it will distribute all log messages.

Impact: A few tests here to check for adding and removing of the loggers, and a few tests there to check whether or not each logger receives all messages. Even this bigger functional extension leaves the tests for the actual loggers untouched.

Keeping errors at bay   Separating LogServer from Logger and introducing a dummy implementation brought us the additional advantage that, if a *test failure* occurs, we will be able to precisely locate the problem in the source code. This is possible because we know for a fact that a test failure would be due solely to our log server and not to an error when accessing the file system.

| 6.5 | **Endoscopic Testing** |

Testing from inside   In the XP world, dummy objects are normally called *mock objects*. To our knowledge, this term was initially used in the commendable article by Mackinnon [00] about *endo-testing*—a pun on endoscopic surgery. We too are talking about "testing from inside" by smuggling in a test medium, namely the dummy object. In fact, the dummy logger enabled us to check for correct behavior of the log server without having to delve too deeply.

Mock objects that deserve to be called by that name take us a step further than the dummy objects studied so far. Mock objects fetch the majority of the actual test code. Let's rebuild our dummy logger into a mock logger:

```java
import java.util.*;
public class MockLogger implements Logger {

    private List expectedLogs = new ArrayList();
    private List actualLogs = new ArrayList();
    public void addExpectedLine(String logString) {
        expectedLogs.add(logString);
    }
    public void logLine(String logString) {
        actualLogs.add(logString);
}

    public void verify() {
        if (actualLogs.size() != expectedLogs.size()) {
            Assert.fail("Expected " + expectedLogs.size() +
                    " log entries but encountered " +
                    actualLogs.size());
        }
        for (int i = 0; i < expectedLogs.size(); i++) {
            String expectedLine = (String) expectedLogs.get(i);
            String actualLine = (String) actualLogs.get(i);
            Assert.assertEquals(expectedLine, actualLine);
        }
    }
}
```

The two methods, addExpectedLine() and verify(), are typical for a mock object. While the first one serves to set the *expected behavior* of our "client" (the log server), the second one does the actual checking for correct behavior *at the end of the test*. Naturally, our test class has to adapt to this new situation:

```
public class LogServerTest extends TestCase {
    private LogServer logServer;
    private MockLogger logger;
    protected void setUp() {
        logger = new MockLogger();
        logServer = new LogServer(logger);
    }

    public void testLoggingWithModule() {
        logger.addExpectedLine("test(0): first line");
        logServer.log(0, "first line", "test");
        logger.verify();
    }

    public void testSimpleLogging() {
        logger.addExpectedLine("(0): first line");
        logger.addExpectedLine("(1): second line");
        logger.addExpectedLine("(2): third line");
        logServer.log(0, "first line");
        logServer.log(1, "second line");
        logServer.log("third line");
        logger.verify();
    }
}
```

So far, we have not moved much code, so a few changes to our mock logger won't hurt:

```
import java.util.*;
public class MockLogger implements Logger {
    private List expectedLogs = new ArrayList();
    private List actualLogs = new ArrayList();
    public void addExpectedLine(String logString) {
        expectedLogs.add(logString);
    }

    public void logLine(String logLine) {
        Assert.assertNotNull(logLine);
        if (actualLogs.size() >= expectedLogs.size()) {
            Assert.fail("Too many log entries");
```

```
        }
        int index = actualLogs.size();
        String expectedLine = (String) expectedLogs.get(index );
        Assert.assertEquals(expectedLine, logLine);
        actualLogs.addElement(logLine);
    }

    public void verify() {
        if (actualLogs.size() < expectedLogs.size()) {
            Assert.fail("Expected " + expectedLogs.size() +
                        " log entries but encountered " +
                        actualLogs.size());
        }
    }
}
```

What we gained here appears to be subtle: one part of the verification code was moved from the verify() method to the logLine() method. This has the benefit that the feedback of a faulty log entry will occur immediately and not at the end of the test. We can see this easily, for example, by changing the line

```
logServer.log(0, "first line");
```

to

```
logServer.log(0, "first line wrong");
```

and then let the debugger track down exactly when the TestFailure exception will be thrown. In complex test cases, this exact localization of an error could shorten the debugging time noticeably. Another one of our changes was the following additional line:

```
Assert.assertNotNull(logLine);
```

Testing this important pre-condition with our "old" DummyLogger would have entailed adding it separately for each single log line.

We can see that the progress achieved with mock objects versus simple dummy objects consists mainly in avoiding duplicate code. This benefit increases in line with the increasing number of mock objects we build, because the code we need to compare the expected with the actual behavior is very similar from one mock object to another so that it can be moved to separate classes.

Patterns for test case creation using mock objects

Another benefit is that mock objects enhance the communication capability of our code. Using them in the way suggested by Mackinnon et al. [00], we obtain a standardized *pattern* that simplifies the actual test code, thus making it more readable. Just as with the other patterns, this pattern improves communication between all who know the pattern. Our slightly modified version of the pattern for unit testing suggested in *Endo-Testing* [Mackinnon00] consists of the following steps that describe what a single unit test looks like:

1. Create instances of mock objects.

2. Set state in the mock objects.

3. Set expectations in the mock objects.

4. Invoke the code under test with mock objects as parameters.

5. If applicable, use direct tests to verify state changes in the objects under test.

6. Use verify() to verify consistency in the mock objects.

Mock objects for state tests?

Mackinnon [00] does not list step 5; he thinks that even simple state changes are best verified through mock objects for consistency reasons. However, our experience has shown that direct polling of sheer state changes is often much simpler than building corresponding mock objects, which would be used only in this place. Once again, there is no rigid rule; whether or not the use of mock objects can improve our code remains to be seen from case to case.

The direct state test is often the simplest way, at least initially. Once the internal objects become more complex and we find code duplication in our tests, then we can gradually introduce corresponding interfaces and mock implementations. The iterative approach is the method of choice for testing, too.

6.6	**Mock Objects from the Assembly Line**

The fact that mock objects are a standard technique of the test-first approach has led to the emergence of some very interesting software products, which simplify or avoid mock object creation. A look at these freely available libraries and tools is recommended to all who use mock objects more than sporadically.

Mock Library

Expectation classes Mackinnon [00] mentions a mock object library, which is now freely available [URL:MockObjects]. It can relieve us from a lot of implementation effort. The basic principle consists in the use of so-called *expectation classes*. These expectation classes encapsulate the expected behavior, the actual behavior, and a balance between the two aspects in verify().

To better explain this idea, we will implement the above MockLogger class by using the library:

```
import com.mockobjects.*;
public class MockLogger2 extends MockObject implements Logger {

   private ExpectationCounter closeCalls =
      new ExpectationCounter("MockLogger.close");
   private ExpectationList logLines =
      new ExpectationList("MockLogger.logLine");
   public void addExpectedLine(String logString) {
      logLines.addExpected(logString);
   }

   public void close() {
      closeCalls.inc();
   }
   public void logLine(String logLine) {
      junit.framework.Assert.assertNotNull(logLine);
      logLines.addActual(logLine);
   }
```

```
public void setCloseExpected() {
   closeCalls.setExpected(1);
}
}
```

The resulting implementation, `MockLogger2`, has shrunk by almost half, compared to `MockLogger`, and it is better readable, once you get used to working with expectation objects. If you derive your own mock class from `com.mockobjects.MockObject`, you can normally do without implementing the `verify()` method, because all expectation objects declared in instance variables will be verified automatically.

In addition to a basic set of expectation classes, the library offers ready-made mock classes, including classes to test servlets and JDBC invocations (see also Chapter 9, Section 9.4).

Mock Generators

The idea to generate mock classes based on the interfaces they implement suggests itself. I am aware of two approaches are known to the author for this purpose:

- MockMaker [URL:MockMaker] is a tool to create source code for mock objects, building on the described expectation classes. Given an interface, it writes the source code for a mock object class that implements the interface and allows instances of that class to have expectations set regarding how many times a method is called and what parameters each method is called with, and to pre-set return values for methods.

- Similar to MockMaker, MockCreator [URL:MockCreator] offers an environment for automatic creation of mock objects. The tool is currently available as a command line version, as an Eclipse plug-in, and for VisualAge for Java.

Mock Objects the Easy Way

From JDK 1.3 up   Driven by the tiresome effort involved in mock class implementation, the *EasyMocks*-Library [URL:EasyMock] pursues a new idea. EasyMock is a class library that provides an easy way to use mock objects for given interfaces. This means that we don't have to write interfaces and mock implementations for all kinds of uses. Instead a mock implementation of a given Java interface can be created and controlled at runtime.

To see how this works, we use an example that implements part of the LogServerTest class:

```
import org.easymock.*;
public class LogServerTestUsingEasyMock extends TestCase {
    private LogServer logServer;
    private MockControl control;
    private Logger logger;
    public LogServerTestUsingEasyMock(String name) {...}

    protected void setUp() {
        control = EasyMock.strictMockControlFor(Logger.class);
        logger = (Logger) control.getMock();
        logServer = new LogServer(logger);
    }

    public void testSimpleLogging() {
        logger.logLine("(0): first line");
        logger.logLine("(1): second line");
        logger.logLine("(2): third line");
        control.activate();
        logServer.log(0, "first line");
        logServer.log(1, "second line");
        logServer.log("third line");
        control.verify();
    }
}
```

java.lang. reflect.Proxy   First, we need an additional MockControl object that rids us from having to create and eventually verify a Logger instance; we will achieve all of this with EasyMock.strictMockControlFor(Class aClass). This detour is necessary because the underlying Java proxy mechanism does not allow us to extend the "simulated" interface.

The actual test is a kind of capture and replay mechanism. First, we record the desired behavior—the three lines logger.logLine(...). Next, we activate the mock functionality, run the code under test, and use the final verify() call to verify whether or not the recorded behavior was actually executed. We opted for the "strict" variant of the MockControl object so that the invocation order is included in the verification part.

In addition to what the preceding example demonstrated, *EasyMocks* allow the specification of return values and exception throwing. This saves us from having to implement a dedicated mock class. However, we won this shortcut at the cost of poorer readability of the test code. On the upside, EasyMocks are more stable towards changes to the interface of a class.

It is interesting to ask whether consequent refactoring of the mock code created in this way would eventually take us back to standard mock classes. We are curious to see whether this approach will become firmly established in the test-first community.

6.7 Testing Threshold Values and Exceptions

We argued in Chapter 4, Section 4.4, that test cases should concentrate particularly on the boundary areas of inputs and outputs. Provided that we know these threshold values, we can run our tests easily when they are passed to the testing method as parameters.

Taking one example, let's assume that our class TextFormatter is ready to be tested. This class is supposed to reformat a passed text line by line. Our boundary condition is that lines with a maximum of 32 characters should be processed; longer lines will be truncated. On these grounds, our test based on threshold values is as follows:

```
public void testLongLines() {
    TextFormatter formatter = new TextFormatter();
    String line32 = "  abcdefg   hijklmn opqrs tuvwxy";
    String line33 = "  abcdefg   hijklmn opqrs tuvwxyz";
    assertEquals("abcdefg hijklmn opqrs tuvwxy",
        formatter.formatLine(line32));
    assertEquals("abcdefg hijklmn opqrs tuvwxy",
        formatter.formatLine(line33));
}
```

So far, so good. In the course of development the text formatter's responsibility changes. It should not format single lines, but instead complete files and then write the result to a file. This means that its public interface is no longer line-based, but file-based. So we are facing a problem similar to the one we had to solve with the LogServer (see Section 6.3). Except this time we have to create an input file with corresponding content, in addition to the output file, **before** the test. If we use a pair of mock classes, one MockLineReader and one MockLineWriter, implementing the LineReader and LineWriter interface, respectively, then writing the test based on the presented mock pattern is easy:

```
public void testLongLines() {
    MockLineReader reader = new MockLineReader();
    String line32 = "  abcdefg   hijklmn opqrs tuvwxy";
    String line33 = "  abcdefg   hijklmn opqrs tuvwxyz";
    reader.addLineToBeRead(line32);
    reader.addLineToBeRead(line33);
    MockLineWriter writer = new MockLineWriter();
    writer.addExpectedLine("abcdefg hijklmn opqrs tuvwxy");
    writer.addExpectedLine("abcdefg hijklmn opqrs tuvwxy");
    TextFormatter formatter = new TextFormatter();
    formatter.format(reader, writer);
    writer.verify();
}
```

Uncontrollable threshold values

While creating appropriate test files would still be conceivable in this fabricated case, there are other cases where boundary conditions can hardly be handled other than by using dummy or mock objects. For example, think of accessing a server that has a maximum of x seconds to send a reply before the client throws a TimeOutException. How do I get a remote server to wait exactly $x-1$ or $x+1$ seconds with its reply to ensure that I can verify the correct response of my client in these boundary cases? A MockServer class where I can configure both the desired response and the delay time makes this test child's play.

Uncontrollable exceptions

Exceptions are similar to boundary cases. Using the example from Section 6.1, we can modify the interface of our getRateFromTo() method as follows:

```
public double getRateFromTo(String from, String to)
   throws ServerNotAvailableException;
```

It may take some persuasion to get our financial information provider to remove the exchange rate server from the network for a few milliseconds whenever we need to do some testing. But with a minor change to the class DummyProvider, we can spare ourselves from such negotiations:

```
public class DummyProvider extends ExchangeRateProvider {
   private double dummyRate;
   private boolean serverAvailable = true;
   public DummyProvider(double dummyRate) {
      this.dummyRate = dummyRate;
   }

   public double getRateFromTo(String from, String to)
      throws ServerNotAvailableException {
      if (!serverAvailable) {
         throw new ServerNotAvailableException("Test");
      }
      return dummyRate;
   }
   public void setServerAvailable(boolean isAvailable) {
      serverAvailable = isAvailable;
   }
}
```

We would like our EuroCalculator to use an exchange rate of 1.0 whenever the exchange rate server is not available (we don't want to discuss here whether or not this specification is meaningful ;-). The test for this might look something like this:

```
public void testServerNotAvailable() {
   //Rate of DummyProvider doesn't matter;
      it will thrown an exception
   DummyProvider provider = new DummyProvider(1.1324);
   provider.setServerAvailable(false);
   double result = new EuroCalculator().valueInEuro(1.5, "USD",
      provider);
```

```
        assertEquals(1.5, result, ACCURACY);
}
```

Should every
possible exception
be tested?

In this way, we can use mock objects to test for correct behavior in exceptional situations and boundary cases that would otherwise be ignored. But here, too, the following applies: we should beware of bombarding each object with all kinds of exceptions just because we can. For example, if we want to test all places in our program where a NullPointer-Exception could occur, then we would be busy doing only this. Careful balancing between cost and benefit is particularly important in such cases.

6.8 How Does the Test Get to the Mock?

In all our previous examples, we had little trouble foisting the dummy or mock object on the test object. While the interface of the valueInEuro() method passed ExchangeRateProvider in our Euro calculator example, LogServer was passed to Logger within the constructor in our logger example. The choice between the two options depends on different points:

- If we add the helper object as parameter to the corresponding method, as in EuroCalculator, we can reuse the OUT with different helper instances. In turn, we have to consider carefully where to take the correct helper instance from, without stealing it, for each method call.

- If the helper object is passed in the constructor of the test object, as in our LogServer, then we will never have to think again which instance we will need when. This is meaningful mainly when the helper is needed in several methods of the object, and if it remains unchanged for the object's entire lifetime.

Subsequent
modification

Either option lets us simply replace a helper or server object with dummy or mock objects. However, most existing programs were written without testing requirements in mind; that is, objects used internally are hardwired. The required helper objects are often created and maintained in instance variables during the initialization of an object. It is relatively easy to make such objects testable by offering additional methods to replace these helpers. Our EuroCalculator would then look like this:

```
public class EuroCalculator {

   private ExchangeRateProvider provider =
      new ExchangeRateProvider();
   public void setProvider(ExchangeRateProvider newProvider) {
      provider = newProvider;
   }

   double valueInEuro(double amount, String currency) {...}
}
```

Accordingly, our test class has to explicitly replace the correct provider with a dummy provider in the test methods:

```
public void testUSD2EUR() {
   ExchangeRateProvider dummyProvider = new DummyProvider(1.1324);
   EuroCalculator calculator = new EuroCalculator();
   calculator.setProvider(dummyProvider);
   double result = calculator.valueInEuro(1.5, "USD");
   assertEquals(1.6986, result, ACCURACY);
}
```

We can see that the test is now longer and harder to read. In addition, there is a risk of forgetting to replace another component with its mock counterpart in more complex test scenarios. This can lead to subtle failures or errors in the test that will be hard to discover. However, we now have the benefit that the application code does not have to know anything about the replacement of a provider object.

Testing by use of dummies is even more difficult if a new server object is created in each place it is used, for example, to avoid synchronization problems. Our (simplified) valueInEuro() method would then look like the following:

```
public double valueInEuro(double amount, String currency) {
   ExchangeRateProvider provider = new ExchangeRateProvider();
   double exchangeRate = provider.getRateFromTo(currency, "EUR");
   return amount * exchangeRate;
}
```

In this case, our constructor invocation new ExchangeRateProvider() is nothing but an implicit constant, playing the same ugly role when the software is maintained and tested. If we change the constants, we need to search for all places they occur throughout the code—a first step towards the "maintenance trap."

Being determined to properly test such a method, we have to do major restructuring work: the ExchangeRateProvider has to be structured so that it can be replaced. If we do not want to pass the provider as an additional parameter, there is only one last trick left: instead of the instance itself, we pass a *factory* object. When testing, we can replace the factory object by a *mock factory*. To this end, we need an interface with two implementations:

Last resort: Factory

```java
public interface ProviderFactory {
    public ExchangeRateProvider createProvider();
}

public class RealProviderFactory implements ProviderFactory {
    public ExchangeRateProvider createProvider() {
        return new ExchangeRateProvider();
    }
}

public class MockProviderFactory implements ProviderFactory {
    private double rate;
    public MockProviderFactory(double rate) {
        this.rate = rate;
    }
    public ExchangeRateProvider createProvider() {
        return new DummyProvider(rate);
    }
}
```

Now we can either pass the appropriate factory object in the EuroCalculator class with the constructor or replace it by using a setter method. The following would be a typical case:

```java
public void testUSD2EUR() {
    ProviderFactory factory = new MockProviderFactory(1.1324);
    EuroCalculator calculator = new EuroCalculator(factory);
    double result = calculator.valueInEuro(1.5, "USD");
    assertEquals(1.6986, result, ACCURACY);
}
```

Drawbacks of the
"factory solution" However, the testability here is at the cost of simplicity and readability. The additional detour is harder to understand than a straight constructor invocation. To our advantage, though, we win independence of the Euro-Calculator from a specific ExchangeRateProvider.

| 6.9 | ## Evil Singletons |

A special case of the, How do I get the dummy into the object? problem are *singletons*. The popularity of *design patterns* [Gamma95] in today's programming community has led to a situation where simple patterns are commonly used without previously weighing their drawbacks. A singleton represents the simplest of all commonly used patterns. It is supposed to ensure that only one instance of a specific class is created and that this instance is easily accessible by all objects within the system. This approach appears practical for objects used across a system, such as resource management systems, database systems, pre-settings, and generally all global objects that the developer would like to have freely available everywhere and always.

Singleton ==
global variable But caution is needed here, because singletons used without much thought given are nothing more than global variables in object-oriented systems, along with all their drawbacks, like sensitivity to side effects and weakened encapsulation [Rainsberger01]. Also, if singletons are heavily used in application servers, we are often confronted with unexpected problems caused by the use of threads and application-specific class loaders. But enough of this! We do not want to discuss the issue "Singletons are evil,"[2] but instead to study a test-specific problem: Considering that there is exactly one instance of each singleton class at a program's runtime and that there is only read access to that instance, the question is how can we replace this instance by a mock instance, if necessary.

The following solution appears feasible (this time, our singleton class abstracts from all meaningful activities):

```
public class Singleton {

    protected static Singleton instance = null;
    public static Singleton getInstance() {
```

---

2. This issue is discussed at [URL:CoSingle] and [URL:WikiSAE] in detail.

```
        if (instance == null) {
            instance = new Singleton();
        }
        return instance;
    }
}
```

Our mock singleton as subclass can now offer an initialization possibility for test purposes:

```
public class MockSingleton extends Singleton {
    public static void initMockSingleton() {
        instance = new MockSingleton();
    }
}
```

In our tests, we have to ensure that the initMockSingleton() method is executed at the beginning of the test or in the setup:

```
public class MockSingletonTest extends TestCase {
    public void testInitialization() {
        MockSingleton.initMockSingleton();
        assertTrue(Singleton.getInstance()
                   instanceof MockSingleton);
    }
}
```

This is a feasible method for us, if we really don't want to part with our singleton, but it has several drawbacks:

- We always have to ensure that each test puts all required singletons into the correct test state at the beginning, and then replaces them with the original. If we forget this—say, for a newly added singleton—we may have to face painful debugging sessions.

- Sometimes, each test requires an individually configured instance of our mock singleton. This could lead to a situation where initialization code piles up in the singleton or MockSingleton class.

Both problems can be solved by providing a *setter method* for the singleton. Naturally, the singleton would then no longer be a real singleton; it would have mutated into a dangerous species: a globally accessible state container, subject to all kinds of side effects.

Singleton alternatives

There is a way out of this singleton crisis, because another concept hides behind most singletons, but escape is not free: we need objects that remain the same within a specific context and exist only once. This context can be our *system,* our *user,* or perhaps our *session.* So why not use a *system object,* a user object, or a session object that will give us access to the objects we would otherwise have turned into singletons? We could then either pass this system object to all objects that need it when we create them, or—being ready for a compromise—turn them into singletons. This way, we will be sitting on only one single singleton in the end, but we will have to watch it closely.

This discussion shows again that the wish for local testability challenges common programming patterns, drawing our attention to design problems that we might otherwise have simply overlooked or ignored. Creating software based on the *test-first approach* lets us avoid most of the difficulties in advance. On the other hand, trying to equip an existing application with a dense mesh of developer tests in arrears will take us to a point where the implementation of these tests will demand extensive program restructuring actions. We hardly dare say it again: careful balancing between cost and benefit is mandatory to avoid many months of restructuring effort.

6.10 | Lightweight and Heavyweight Mocks

So far, we have seen two approaches to build a dummy object:

1. The first approach derives the dummy object as subclass from the real implementation, for example, `DummyRateProvider`.

2. In the second approach, both the real class and the mock class implement the same interface.

Although the first variant is the simpler of the two, because we do not have to implement a separate interface, it has certain risks. For example, it can easily happen that we forget to adapt the mock class when changing the signature of the real class. This means that the OUT would invoke the new method, and the test would create an unexpected failure that is normally hard to trace.

In contrast, the second variant causes additional programming work, because it first needs to extract the interface and then implement all methods in the mock class. Accordingly, any change to the signature would entail a change in (at least) three different places: in the interface itself, in the real implementation, and in all mock classes. Nevertheless, we normally prefer the second variant, because the interface also assumes a documenting function, and it reduces complexity, as in our transition from DummyPrintWriter to DummyLogger (see Section 6.3). In addition, the cost for synchronization between the interface and the implementation can be minimized by an appropriately equipped development environment or use of EasyMocks (see Section 6.5).

The UML diagram in Figure 6.2 shows the full structure of our small pattern for the introduction of mock objects. The idea behind it is that the class AbstractMock throws a NotImplementedException for all methods declared in the interface. This allows specific mock classes to extend AbstractMock and override only the methods they are interested in. Moreover, common features of specific mock objects can be moved up to AbstractMock to avoid code duplication in the tests.

Consider the following example to better understand this approach; our logging framework should be extended so that single loggers can be replaced in the course of active operation. First of all, we need to insert the method:

```
public void setLogger(Logger newLogger) {...}
```

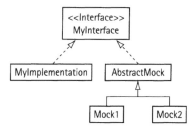

Figure 6.2 Schematic view of the mock objects hierarchy.

into the LogServer class. Next, we have to extend our logger interface by the method:

```
public void close();
```

to ensure that a logger to be replaced gets a chance to free resources it no longer needs before it retires. Before the implementation, we write two tests for this new functionality:

```
public void testSetLogger() {
   MockLogger newLogger = new MockLogger();
   logServer.setLogger(newLogger);
   newLogger.addExpectedLine("(1): Test");
   logServer.log(1, "Test");
   newLogger.verify();
}
public void testCloseOnSetLogger() {
   logger.setCloseExpected();
   logServer.setLogger(new MockLogger());
   logger.verify();
}
```

In the second test, we have a close() message sent to a logger before it is replaced. Subsequent extensions are now necessary in the MockLogger class:

```
public class MockLogger implements Logger {
   ...
   private boolean closeExpected = false;
   private boolean closeInvoked = false;
   public void close() {
      closeInvoked = true;
   }
   public void setCloseExpected() {
      closeExpected = true;
   }

   public void verify() {
```

```
        if (closeExpected) {
          Assert.assertTrue(
            "close() should have been called", closeInvoked);
        }
        if (actualLogs.size() < expectedLogs.size()) {
          Assert.fail("Expected " + expectedLogs.size() +
                    " log entries but encountered " +
                    actualLogs.size());
        }
      }
    }
  }
```

The most conspicuous change was in the verify() method; we extended it by an additional verification. We can easily imagine that verify() will develop into a reservoir for all kinds of possible and impossible validation functions as we continue extending the logger functionality. Out of all these validation functions, we will probably need only one or two in each test. Although we could avoid this excessive wealth by introducing an abstract mock logger and various subclasses (e.g., TestCloseMockLogger and Test-LinesMockLogger), we would have to deal with a constantly increasing number of mock classes over the long run. And we would probably use each of these classes only once.

Tricks to limit the number of classes Java offers two little tricks to prevent this excessive reproduction of classes:

1. If a specific mock implementation is needed for only one single test, we can create it as an *anonymous class* directly in the test method.

2. If a specific mock implementation is needed within only one test class, we can create it as an *internal class* of the test class.

Trick 1 is suitable mainly to simulate methods that return fixed values in the test. To achieve complex validation functions in anonymous classes, we would have to perform light to medium contortions, because Java imposes some restrictions on these lightweight classes. Our Euro calculator can serve as a typical example to illustrate this technique. Its tests could do without the DummyProvider class, but each single test would become more cumbersome:

```
public void testUSD2EUR() {
   ExchangeRateProvider provider = new ExchangeRateProvider() {
      public double getRateFromTo(String from, String to) {
         return 1.1324;
      }
   };
   double result = new EuroCalculator().valueInEuro(1.5,
      "USD", provider);
   assertEquals(1.6986, result, ACCURACY);
}
```

Trick 2 does nothing but reduce the visibility of the mock class. We leave it up to the interested reader to transfer this principle to a TestLine-MockLogger. Whether we should implement a mock class as an internal or "normal" class in a specific case depends not least on how this Java feature is supported by the development environment we use.

Finally, we should mention that there is a possibility to use the test class itself as a mock object by letting the test class implement the corresponding interface. This is a slightly modified form of the internal class approach, but without the option to inherit from an existing abstract class. This approach has been described as the *self-shunt* test pattern [Feathers00].

Evolution of a mock object   And which one of these numerous possibilities is recommended in practice? The best option is surely to stick to the XP rule, "We generally do the simplest thing that could possibly work!"[3] In our EuroCalculator example, we would begin with an anonymous class and then switch to an internal class that overrides the getRateFromTo() method in the second test. As soon as we need this class externally, or as soon as we find that a loss in manageability of the internal class neutralizes the small benefit of reduced visibility, we extract the internal class and make it a fully fledged member of our Java company.

Notice that the development of our MockLogger was similar. In the first approach, we had a DummyPrintWriter as direct subclass of PrintWriter. But then we found out that a dedicated interface (Logger) communicates the true purpose of the object much better and makes the code easier to read, although at the cost of programming a new interface and two new classes. In a subsequent step, we found that we can simplify our test by

---

3. [Jeffries00, p. 74].

moving the actual validation from the test class to the dummy class, which promoted our DummyLogger to a MockLogger.

Finally, extending the logging framework led to an extension of the Logger interface and, during the test, to the wish to have different MockLogger classes. This is the hour of birth of our AbstractMockLogger:

```java
public class AbstractMockLogger implements Logger {
    public static class NotImplemented extends RuntimeException {
    }
    public void close() {
        throw new NotImplemented();
    }
    public void logLine(String logMessage) {
        throw new NotImplemented();
    }
}
```

We can now turn this logger into a specific mock logger object in an anonymous, internal, or real class. Once again, the iterative approach and development of our test framework replace the rigorous observance of rigid rules.

6.11 File Dummies

We wrote a test for the FileLogger class in Section 6.3. The ugly thing about this test was that we had to state the name of a test file as constant. The consequence was that we became dependent not only upon the file system used, but also upon things like *security* settings and available disk space. Although the class java.io.File since JDK 1.2 offers us a mechanism to create temporary files regardless of a constant file path, the dependence upon the file system's availability and its access privileges still prevails in this method.

Generic mock files

Why not use our newly gained knowledge about dummy and mock classes to program our own MockFile class? Easier said than done, because the JDK developers built a few obstacles to make things a little more difficult for us. The biggest obstacle is the fact that the class java.io.File does not hold what its name promises. It is not an abstraction of all the things we would like to do with files, but merely an abstraction of a file name and its access path within a specific file system.

The actual file functionality is hidden in the classes java.io.FileInputStream and java.io.FileOutputStream. Is it worth our while to create mock classes for these two streams by overriding several read and write methods?

In most cases, it is not worthwhile, because the functionality of streams which write their data into buffers and read data from buffers are already available in the form of various other stream classes (e.g., ByteArrayInputStream and ByteArrayOutputStream). These can then take the place of file streams for testing purposes.

To better understand this, we will use our FileLogger example again (see Section 6.3). First, we turn FileLogger into a StreamLogger, which offers us two constructors:

```java
import java.io.*;
public class StreamLogger implements Logger {
   private PrintWriter writer;
   public StreamLogger(OutputStream out) throws IOException {
      writer = new PrintWriter(out);
   }
   public StreamLogger(String filename) throws IOException {
      this(new FileOutputStream(filename));
   }

   public void close() {
      writer.close();
   }
   public void logLine(String logMessage) {
      writer.println(logMessage);
   }
}
```

Now we can pass an arbitrary InputStream within the constructor, allowing us to test independently of any file access:

```java
public void testLogLine() throws IOException {
   ByteArrayOutputStream out = new ByteArrayOutputStream();
   StreamLogger logger = new StreamLogger(out);
```

```
      logger.logLine("Line 1");
      logger.logLine("Line 2");
      logger.close();
      ByteArrayInputStream in =
         new ByteArrayInputStream(out.toByteArray());
      BufferedReader reader =
         new BufferedReader(new InputStreamReader(in));
      assertEquals("Line 1", reader.readLine());
      assertEquals("Line 2", reader.readLine());
      assertNull("end of file reached", reader.readLine());
      reader.close();
   }
```

All this messing about with different Stream and Writer classes can now be nicely put inside a reusable mock class:

```
import java.io.*;
import java.util.*;
public class MockTextOutputStream extends OutputStream {
   private ByteArrayOutputStream outputStream;
   private List expectedLines = new ArrayList();
   private boolean streamClosed = false;
   public MockTextOutputStream() {
      outputStream = new ByteArrayOutputStream();
   }
   public void addExpectedLine(String line) {
      expectedLines.add(line);
   }
   public void close() throws IOException {
      streamClosed = true;
      outputStream.close();
   }
   public void flush() throws IOException {
      outputStream.flush();
   }
   private InputStreamReader getReader() {
      InputStream input =
    new ByteArrayInputStream(outputStream.toByteArray());
```

```
        return new InputStreamReader(input);
    }
    public void verify() throws IOException {
        if (!streamClosed) {
            Assert.fail("Stream was not closed");
        }
        BufferedReader reader =
            new BufferedReader(this.getReader());
        Iterator i = expectedLines.iterator();
        while(i.hasNext()) {
            String expectedLine = (String) i.next();
            String actualLine = reader.readLine();
            Assert.assertEquals(expectedLine, actualLine);
        }
        Assert.assertNull("EOF expected", reader.readLine());
    }
    public void write(byte[] b) throws IOException {
        outputStream.write(b);
    }
    public void write(int b) throws IOException {
        outputStream.write(b);
    }
}
```

We can use this MockTextOutputStream whenever it is a matter of validating an OutputStream. Normally, we will have to adapt this mock class to the local requirements. Our unmodified test, using MockTextOutputStream, now looks like this:

```
public void testLogLine() throws IOException {
    MockTextOutputStream mockStream =
        new MockTextOutputStream();
    mockStream.addExpectedLine("Line 1");
    mockStream.addExpectedLine("Line 2");
    StreamLogger logger = new StreamLogger(mockStream);
    logger.logLine("Line 1");
    logger.logLine("Line 2");
    logger.close();
    mockStream.verify();
}
```

Note that the actual test code has become shorter. The more tests of this kind we have, the more rewarding our investment in the mock stream.

We can see in this example that the testLogLine() method is very similar to the last version of the testSimpleLogging() method in LogServerTest (see Section 6.5). The reason is that StreamLogger does nothing but move incoming log lines into a PrintWriter. Whether or not this sheer delegation requires its own test at all may be viewed differently, but we are in favor of creating that test. Even when we currently see that the code of our logLine() method does exactly what it should do, the situation could be totally different after the next refactoring.

Testing a simple delegation

Following the MockTextOutputStream example, we recommend at this point to implement a MockTextInputStream class as a practical exercise, or better yet a coffee break....

| 6.12 | **More Typical Mock Objects** |

Other fields of application

The use of mock objects is convenient in various places in our code. The mock streams described in the previous section are just as typical as the examples we will see later in the realm of databases (see Chapter 9) and Web applications (see Chapter 12). Here are a few additional ideas:

- We can use *MockListeners* to check for correct sending of *events* to appropriate *listener objects.* Depending on the complexity of event instances, we could describe the expected sequence of events by using String objects corresponding to the toString() representations of these events.

- If we want to verify the exact *order of messages received,* then it would be meaningful, here again, to convert the messages into strings inside the mock object. Note that this approach may require frequent adaptations as you rename methods.

- Validating a message or event sequence across several clients (and thus mock objects) can be done by furnishing all mock objects concerned with a *message registrator.* This registrator will then play the actual mock's role and compare the expected with the actual message sequence.

This type of testing is very sensitive to minor modifications of our CUT's implementation, therefore we recommend it exclusively for cases where the exact sequence is part of the specification. This is often the case with frameworks, where abstract framework superclasses guarantee the invocation sequence of abstract methods.[4]

6.13	## External Components

Using dummy objects for testing works wonderfully as long as our helper or server objects allow the simple creation of dummies. Working exclusively with our own code, we can produce this type of testability, at worst, by major refactoring actions. If we proceed entirely by the *test-first approach*, then testability will just turn out that way, without making a major effort.

Testability of external classes   The situation is different for our interfaces to the Java library or third-party components. The external APIs we use are encapsulated by means of interfaces or abstract classes and can be replaced by mock objects in our tests only if we are extremely lucky. One good example for this is the class java.io.OutputStream; remember how easy it was for us to replace it by our MockTextOutputStream. In contrast, when working with third-party libraries or dealing with parts of the Java library left over from JDK 1.0, the situation normally looks like this:[5]

```
import thirdparty.*;
public class MyClient {

    public void doSomething(String arg) {
        TheirRequest request = new TheirRequest(arg);
        TheirResponse response = request.send();
        String answer = response.getAnswer();
        // do something with answer...
    }

}
```

---

4. This corresponds to the *Template Method* design pattern [Gamma95].

5. This example was adapted from the discussion at [URL:WikiUTATP].

In this example, the Their* classes are the interfaces provided by the third-party vendor; MyClient is our own class. Based on what we have learned so far, we now plan the following approach: We build a class, Mock-Request, derived from TheirRequest. The latter will then return an instance of MockResponse upon send(), where MockResponse is derived from Their-Response. Of course, we have previously defined the latter's response to getAnswer(). If we manage to realize this plan, we will also have managed to tame this external interface. However, such an attempt often fails due to one or several of the following reasons:

- TheirRequest and/or TheirResponse are *final* and no subclasses can be derived from them.

- The classes themselves are not *final,* but the methods send() and/or getAnswer() are.

- The existing constructors of TheirResponse are not usable for a mock subclass, because they need parameter objects, which cannot be created outside the library, or we need new parameters to create them and so on.

- The library classes do things that we wanted to avoid with our mock approach, such as accessing a network.

Complaining about the shortcomings of unknown developers won't help either. Nope, we have to solve our test problem ourselves. With the source code on hand, we could modify the corresponding classes so they will no longer conflict with our testing efforts. However, this could represent a millstone around our necks with regard to future versions of that external library.

Introducing an adapter

Isn't there another way? There is. Let's simply build another layer around that external interface. First, we define an interface that defines the functionality of the external library for our special needs. This approach is described as the *adapter* pattern in *Design Patterns* [Gamma95]. In our current example, things would look like this:

```
public interface AnswerFactory {
    String getAnswer(String arg);
}
```

From now on, our own client uses only this "factory" to create an answer object:

```
import thirdparty.*;
public class MyClient {
   private AnswerFactory factory;
   public MyClient(AnswerFactory factory) {
      this.factory = factory;
   }
   public void doSomething(String arg) {
      String answer = factory.getAnswer(arg);
      // do something with answer...
   }
}
```

What's missing now are only the two implementations of Answer-Factory:

```
public class MockAnswerFactory implements AnswerFactory {
   private String answer;
   public MockAnswerFactory(String presetAnswer) {
      answer = presetAnswer;
   }
   public String getAnswer(String arg) {
      return answer;
   }
}
```

```
import thirdparty.*;
public class AnswerFactoryAdaptor implements AnswerFactory {
   public String getAnswer(String arg) {
      TheirRequest request = new TheirRequest(arg);
      TheirResponse response = request.send();
      return response.getAnswer();
   }
}
```

And here we are, exactly where we wanted to be: we now have a mock object we can use to test our MyClient class. But wait, there is now a gap in the whole thing: the class AnswerFactoryAdaptor is left untested. If we were able to test it, we could have saved ourselves a lot of trouble. For this reason, the methods of this "forwarding class" should remain as simple as possible. If we need more logic in this class, in addition to the sheer translation of method calls, then another separation into *adapter* and *delegator* is recommended.

We won independence

By the way, we won something else in addition to testability: our client is now independent of the external interface. Just in case we decide to use another library later on, we would *only* have to replace the Adaptor class.

Tests for external libraries

It is normally not our job to test the functionality of an external library; this should have been done elsewhere. Still, it appears meaningful to add a handful of tests covering our special use of a library to ensure that we understand the interface and that a new version of that library would function properly. But that's another story.

6.14 The Pros and Cons

The use of dummy and mock objects is not uncontested, both in the software tester community and in the XP world. We tried to collect the most important arguments from both camps. We begin with the benefits of dummy objects:

Benefits of dummy objects

- We can test with a finer granularity and higher accuracy. This shows that we can always trace a *test failure* back to an error in the test object or the test itself. This means that we won't have to dig deep into program layers that are currently of no interest.

- A dummy allows us to concentrate on the object under test and to create the initial state required for the test more easily. In contrast, building a complex initial state with the right (perhaps persistent) objects can represent a major problem.

- Dummy objects belonging to the test ensure reusability of our test. Real server objects may change their states due to a test and have to be reset after the test. This means additional effort in the best case; it might even be totally impossible.

- The use of real server objects in the test represents a kind of *micro integration test*. However, *integration tests* overlap heavily with function tests, and they are part of *developer tests* only in rare cases. Experience has also shown that tests integrating objects from many different layers can become too slow for a reasonably fast and continuous *feedback*.

- Dummy objects allow us to test the behavior of the test object along the margins of admissible value ranges. They also allow us to simulate error cases and exceptions in a very dedicated manner. Creating certain marginal conditions and error cases across several abstraction and access layers is very difficult and in some cases even impossible.

- In addition, dummy objects allow us to use a top-down approach in software development. Due to dependencies among objects, we would otherwise have to develop from layer to layer, in a bottom-up approach. This also means that, when using mock objects, we no longer have to define the complete infrastructure of our system upfront. Instead, we can build and expand it iteratively and incrementally.

- Dummy objects also help us test when a service provider we depend on is not yet implemented but has published its API.

- Testing with dummy objects improves the structure of the resulting program, because it prefers small objects and makes sure that the *Dependency Inversion Principle* and the *Law of Demeter* (see Glossary) are observed.

Mock objects are special dummy species, offering additional benefits:

Benefits of mocks

- Conventional tests rely on the validation of return values and state changes of the test objects visible from the outside. Mock objects allow us to validate whether or not the test object's access to its helper and server objects is correct. This means that we actually test from the inside.

- Mock objects serve as containers, collecting duplicated test functionality. They facilitate *refactoring* of test code and represent a pattern that improves the communication ability of our code.

Drawbacks

All points listed above relate to either increase of independence (of tests and code) or improvement of communication. All these benefits are confronted with drawbacks:

- Dummy classes can contain errors. However, this problem is relative because the probability that errors in the dummy class and errors in the test class will cancel each other out is small. Errors in the dummy class are normally discovered right away.

- Mock-based testing does not find errors resulting from the interplay of several components. We simply cover this error category by function tests. If we still find that such errors cause a frequent problem, then we should think about additional local integration tests in the critical places in the system. Ideally, they should integrate only two adjacent layers.

- Changes to the interface of the real implementation require changes to the dummy object. However, experience has shown that this additional effort accounts only for a small part of the total effort involved in updating all tests. The IDE also often helps find the signatures to be modified or extended.

- Using dummies for testing is something developers have to learn. However, both their experience and the reusable dummy and mock objects library increase over time.

- "Testing from the inside" means that we need to know what happens or should happen in the class. If the implementation changes, for example, because we found a better way to work with a server object, we also have to change the test code (including mock objects) frequently, even though the test object's behavior to the outside remained unchanged. For this reason, mock objects are used to test relatively stable implementations.

Costs of dummy programming

Robert Binder estimates the effort involved in creating *stubs* as being very high [Binder99, p. 662]. In particular, the large number of stub objects needed to supply each single test with the required responses is a big obstacle in the general use of this technique, according to Binder. Our experience does not confirm this theory; we normally manage with one single and easily configurable mock object per test. This discrepancy in experiences results partly from differences between development by the *test-first* or *test-after approach*, where the latter is based on the classic testing theory. Moreover, conventional stubs often simulate the real behavior of a system, requiring a much higher implementation effort, compared to slim mock objects.

Brian Marick [00, p. 110] identified two major problems in the use of stubs: (1) We implement each *misconception* we have about the real object in the dummy object. (2) Errors we would otherwise have found through indirect invocation in the helper object slip through. Reason (2) warns us against the assumption that, when using the mock technique, interaction tests like the ones described in Chapter 4, Section 4.6, can be totally omitted; at best, their number reduces.

Heuristics for the Use of Mocks

Careful balancing between the large number of benefits and drawbacks takes a lot of experience and the courage to experiment. We use dummy and mock objects in the following situations:

- We cannot do without them when the tests run too slowly, when the "right" class does not exist yet, or when certain boundary and error cases cannot be tested any other way.

- They improve the readability and maintainability of our test code, by removing duplicate code, for instance.

Whenever we can write the test as easily and clearly with the same or less redundancy without dummy objects, then we will do without them. The more we get used to them, the more often we will find good reasons to use them.

Temporary dummy One reviewer pointed out that it's common to start using a stub class for unimplemented functionality that evolves into the real class later on. This kind of temporary dummy is found most often during the development of model code.

However, we have to be careful to ensure that our mock objects do not get too complex. Signs of excessive complexity include:

- They duplicate program logic from the "right" classes.

- They call other mock or dummy objects directly.

- We want to write test cases for mock objects ourselves.

In these cases, it makes sense to take a step back and ask ourselves whether we can simplify our mocks (e.g., by distributing them over several mock classes), whether we need them at all, whether a simple dummy class would do the trick, or whether the mock problem actually turns our attention to a design problem.

6.15 Summary

A *dummy* object is an object that replaces another object for the duration of a test. It implements the same interface as the "real" object, but replaces complex calculations with constant returns, throws exceptions when ordered to do so, and does some additional parameter validation or other things needed only in the test. *Mock* objects are special dummy objects that additionally handle the specification of the expected behavior and the validation of the actual behavior.

The main argument in favor of using dummies is independence in the tests and related design improvements. There are many more benefits and drawbacks such that mock objects should not be used reflexively but solely by carefully weighing the positive and negative implications against each other. Typical applications include access to files or other external resources and integration of external components. Dummy objects and mocks will also play an important role later on in Chapter 9, Persistent Objects, and Chapter 12, Web Applications.

Chapter 7

Inheritance and Polymorphism

Java is an object-oriented language, as we know. In addition to object identity and data encapsulation, *inheritance* and *polymorphism* are other important concepts of the object-oriented paradigm.[1] These two concepts have not played a major role in the previous chapters of this book, except in the implementation of our test cases. As useful and convenient as inheritance and polymorphism may be for software development, the problems they can cause during testing can be equally big. But all complaints are useless: we have to deal with the positive and negative effects.

7.1 | Inheritance

Well-Shaped Inheritance Hierarchies

Inheritance as a reuse mechanism

Many inexperienced developers consider inheritance between classes mainly as a practical means to simplify their implementation: once they know a class that possesses the capabilities they need for a new class, they often extend this class. After all, the key word is *extends*. Then they add a method here, override another one there, and—voilà—the new marvel is ready.

---

1. Some languages (e.g., the prototype-based *Self*) do without classes and class-based inheritance.

Using the inheritance mechanism in this way has a harmful effect, mainly since we take both the desired and the undesired properties of the superclass. And because Java links a subtype relationship to the extends relationship, like most other statically typed languages, the door is wide open for unintended use of the new, derived class. Inheritance is commonly used as a reuse mechanism and is one of the main reasons for poor maintainability of larger object-oriented systems.[2]

Substitution principle

The problems with this kind of inheritance can be avoided by observing the *Liskov Substitution Principle (LSP)* [Liskov93, Martin96a] for the creation of subtypes when we build inheritance hierarchies. This principle states that an object of a subtype—and thus also an instance of a subclass —must be able to substitute the object of the supertype at any given time. Not following that rule will lead to nasty problems when using polymorphic operations (see Section 7.2).

At first sight, the LSP appears intuitive, but it has its pitfalls once we let ourselves become inspired by the specialization relationships found in the real world while building class hierarchies. This problem shows in the commonly used example of the relationship between a rectangle and a square. A programmer with basic knowledge of mathematics knows that a square is a rectangle with two equal sides. This programmer would probably write the following code:

```java
public class Rectangle {
    private int x;
    private int y;
    public Rectangle(int x, int y) {...}
    public int getX() {...}
    public int getY() {...}
}

public class Square extends Rectangle {
    public Square(int x) {
        super(x, x);
    }
}
```

---

2. The situation gets worse when multiple inheritance is used.

So far, so good. The trouble begins when the programmer adds the method stretchX(int factor) to the Rectangle class. The decisive post-condition of this method is that x will be extended by factor, while y remains unchanged. The subclass Square can never meet this property, because its sides always have to keep the same length. For this reason, an instance of Square can no longer substitute an instance of Rectangle in all occurrences, thereby violating the substitution principle.

Well-shaped hierarchies   In this specific example, there are several solutions, which will not be discussed here.[3] What we should take home from this example is the fact that *well-shaped inheritance hierarchies*—those fulfilling the substitution principle—do not necessarily correspond to natural generalization and specialization hierarchies. Instead, they should be determined by our program's specific requirements.

Rules for well-shaped inheritance hierarchies   In the general case, observation of the following two rules ensures a well-shaped hierarchy:

1. A subclass can leave the **post-conditions** of a public method unchanged or **strengthen** them by introducing additional conditions. This applies equally to the class invariant, because we can consider it as an implicit post-condition for all public methods.

2. A subclass can leave the **pre-conditions** of a public method unchanged or **weaken** them by removing or softening some conditions. At first sight, this appears unintuitive, but it is an immediate consequence of the substitution principle.

These two rules correspond to those of the design by contract approach (see Chapter 4, Section 4.7), which shows its strong side especially in testing inheritance hierarchies for well-shapedness. However, most difficulties arise from nonexplicit conditions.

In the further course of this chapter, we assume that we are dealing with well-shaped hierarchies, at least with regard to those features that are part of our test suite; otherwise, the reuse of test cases would hardly make sense. Depending on the individual case, violating the substitution principle may be justified, provided that we understand the consequences, which is to say, a more difficult testability.

---

3. For example, inverting the extends relationship, extracting a common superclass, or introducing *value semantics*.

Reusing Superclass Tests

A pleasant and intuitive assumption appears to turn testing of class hierarchies into an easy task. When a subclass obeys the rules of the substitution principle, namely, it is a real subtype of the superclass, then (a) unchanged methods should not have to be tested, and (b) overridden methods should allow adequate testing in the test suite of the superclass.

Test axioms   Unfortunately, both assumptions are wrong. This evolves from Weyuker's [88] three *test axioms*, which establish limits on the transferability of code coverage for test suites applied to modular—and thus including object-oriented—systems:[4]

- The **antiextensionality axiom** states that a test suite that covers one implementation of a specification does not necessarily cover a different implementation of the same specification. A responsibility may be implemented in many ways.

- The **antidecomposition axiom** states that the coverage achieved for a module under test is not necessarily achieved for a module that it calls. A test suite that covers a class or a method does not necessarily cover the server objects of this class or method.

- The **anticomposition axiom** states that test suites that are individually adequate for segments within a module are not necessarily adequate for the module as a whole.

Effects of test axioms   All of this has a few implications on our strategy for testing of class hierarchies. First, we also have to test unchanged methods of a subclass, if this class directly or indirectly invokes overridden methods. Second, the test suite of the superclass is often insufficient to test overridden methods of the subclass. The reason is that another implementation requires both new implementation-based and extended specification-based tests, if pre- or post-conditions have changed. The good news is that we can reuse at least part of the test suite of the superclass to test the subclass.

Let's use an example to put theory into action. Our example deals with a very simple hierarchy, involving two classes, as shown in Figure 7.1. The attributes in this example are not publicly accessible; they represent getter

---

4. Taken from Binder [99, p. 505]. One can argue whether or not the term *axiom* is correct for these mainly empirical rules.

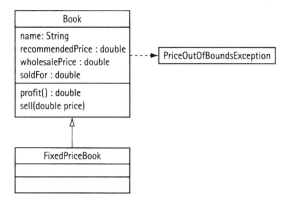

Figure 7.1 A simple inheritance hierarchy.

and setter methods. The diagram does not show that PriceOutOfBound-Exception can be thrown by the sell(double price) method. This method has the additional condition that it must not be invoked again after one successful attempt. Also, there is a pre-condition for Book.profit() stating that it may be invoked only after a successful sale. This pre-condition no longer exists for FixedPriceBook.profit(), because the amount of the (potential) profit is already known before a sale occurs. Let's first look at the test class for Book:

```
public class BookTest extends TestCase {
    private Book book;
    private final String NAME = "A Test Book";
    private final double WHOLESALE = 10.0;
    private final double RECOMMENDED = 12.0;
    protected void setUp() {
        book = new Book(NAME, WHOLESALE, RECOMMENDED);
    }
    public void testCreation() {
        assertEquals(NAME, book.getName());
        assertEquals(WHOLESALE, book.getWholesalePrice(), 0.00);
        assertEquals(RECOMMENDED, book.getRecommendedPrice(), 0.00);
        book = new Book("Another Book", 20.0, 23.0);
        assertEquals("Another Book", book.getName());
        assertEquals(20.0, book.getWholesalePrice(), 0.00);
        assertEquals(23.0, book.getRecommendedPrice(), 0.00);
```

```
        }
        public void testSellAtRecommendedPrice() throws Exception {
            book.sell(RECOMMENDED);
            assertEquals(RECOMMENDED, book.getSoldFor(), 0.00);
            assertEquals(2.0, book.profit(), 0.00);
            book = new Book("Another Book", 20.0, 23.0);
            book.sell(23.0);
            assertEquals(23.0, book.getSoldFor(), 0.00);
            assertEquals(3.0, book.profit(), 0.00);
        }
        public void testSellAtWholesalePrice() throws Exception {
            book.sell(WHOLESALE);
            assertEquals(WHOLESALE, book.getSoldFor(), 0.00);
            assertEquals(0.0, book.profit(), 0.001);
        }
        public void testSellBelowWholesalePrice() {
            try {
                book.sell(WHOLESALE - 0.01);
                fail("PriceOutOfBoundsException expected");
            } catch (PriceOutOfBoundsException expected) {}
        }
        public void testSellAboveRecommendedPrice() {
            try {
                book.sell(RECOMMENDED + 0.01);
                fail("PriceOutOfBoundsException expected");
            } catch (PriceOutOfBoundsException expected) {}
        }
    }
```

The last two test cases show that the allowed price margin is limited to range between Wholesale Price and Recommended Price.

Parallel test class hierarchy

Considering that the subclass FixedPriceBook should have exactly the same public interface as Book, we also want to use the existing test suite of the Book class. The easiest way to achieve this, from the technical perspective, is a test class hierarchy that maps the structure of our application classes. Next, we substitute the constructor invocations in the tests by invoking an overridable *factory* method and encapsulating the access to our OUT in a getter and a setter. Now the reusability of existing test cases is child's play:

```
public class BookTest extends TestCase {
    ...

    protected Book createBook(String name,
            double wholesale, double recommended) {
        return new Book(name, wholesale, recommended);
    }

    protected Book getOUT() {
        return book;
    }

    protected void setOUT(Book newBook) {
        book = newBook;
    }

    protected void setUp() {
        this.setOUT(this.createBook(NAME,
            WHOLESALE, RECOMMENDED));
    }

    public void testCreation() {
        assertEquals(NAME, this.getOUT().getName());
        assertEquals(WHOLESALE,
                this.getOUT().getWholesalePrice(), 0.00);
        assertEquals(RECOMMENDED,
                this.getOUT().getRecommendedPrice(), 0.00);
        this.setOUT(this.createBook("Another Book", 20.0, 23.0));
        assertEquals("Another Book", this.getOUT().getName());
        ...
    }

    ...

}

public class FixedPriceBookTest extends BookTest {
    ...
    protected Book createBook(String name,
            double wholesale, double recommended) {
        return new FixedPriceBook(name, wholesale, recommended);
    }
}
```

Completing and
adapting existing
test cases

And really, our FixedPriceBookTest suite runs perfectly, provided no method in FixedPriceBook got overridden. But that was exactly the purpose of this exercise: A Fixed Price book should (a) be sold only at the recommended price, and (b) allow the invocation of the profit() method even when there was no previous sale. Therefore, we have to check the inherited test cases for usefulness and add new test cases:

1. testCreation(), testSellAtRecommendedPrice(), and testSellAbove-RecommendedPrice() still appear to be meeting our specification and remain unchanged.

2. testSellAtWholesalePrice() no longer corresponds to our intensified condition, and must be overridden:

```java
public class FixedPriceBookTest extends BookTest {
    ...
    public void testSellAtWholesalePrice() {
        try {
            this.getOUT().sell(WHOLESALE);
            fail("PriceOutOfBoundsException expected");
        } catch (PriceOutOfBoundsException expected) {}
    }
}
```

3. Although testSellBelowWholesalePrice() is not wrong, it actually refers to a boundary case of the superclass. But it doesn't hurt either.

4. We need an additional test case to be able to do some testing directly below the recommended price:

```java
public void testSellBelowRecommendenPrice()
    try {
        this.getOUT().sell(RECOMMENDED - 0.01);
        fail("PriceOutOfBoundsException expected");
    } catch (PriceOutOfBoundsException expected) {}
}
```

5. And finally, we need a test case to check for correct functioning of profit() without previous sale:

```java
public void testProfitBeforeSale() {
    assertEquals(2.0, this.getOUT().profit(), 0.00);
}
```

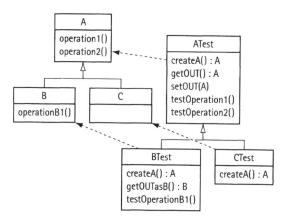

Figure 7.2 A parallel test hierarchy.

The methods sell() and profit() in the class FixedPriceBook from Book have to be overridden to ensure that the modified test suite will end with a green bar. If we had decided not to let some of the tests from Book-Test loose on instances of FixedPriceBook, then we would have had two options to choose from: either override the test method with an empty body, or extract all Book-specific test cases into a separate test class.

Parameterizing the factory method In the general case, it can happen that creating an instance of the subclass demands other parameters than those needed in the instantiation of the superclass. In that case, the OUT factory method (i.e., createBook(...) in this example) needs additional parameters, and not all of them can be used in all test subclasses.

If new functionality is added to the subclass, and thus new specific tests are added to the test class, then it is recommended to use a getOUT() variant, which already takes care of the necessary typecast. Figure 7.2 shows a class diagram of the parallel test hierarchy in general form.

Test Class Hierarchies by Refactoring

In the last example, we added the tests for our class hierarchy in arrears. In this case, the top-down approach is easiest, because it allows us to evaluate from class to class which tests of the superclass are still meaningful and which are not.

The situation is slightly different in test-first programming. The decision whether or not to derive a class as a subclass from another class is taken in the course of refactoring. This means that we already have an independent test suite for the subclass. Here, too, we encounter the typical phenomenon described in Chapter 4, Section 4.9: First, there is a small refactoring step based on existing test cases. Next, we think about modifications and extensions that may be required for our unit tests.

In our Book example, there would probably have been an `isFixedPrice` attribute of the class `Book` to distinguish regular books from fixed price books, before introducing our class hierarchy. The test suite would have distinguished between tests where this attribute is set and those where it is not set. At some point in time, the introduction of our subclass would have caused the setter for that attribute to disappear. And upon this modification at the latest, we would have built our parallel test hierarchy. Subsequently, those test cases that concentrate on differences in behavior through `isFixedPrice` would have been decomposed and eventually moved into the test subclass.

Delayed test refactoring Refactoring of tests often lags behind restructuring of the application code by one step. This is the opposite of the approach used to add functionality, where our test cases are always a step ahead of the application classes.

Testing Interfaces

Interfaces are Java's way to deal with the problem of multiple inheritance. As we know, each class can implement an arbitrary set of interfaces, and it additionally inherits all implemented interfaces of its direct and indirect superclasses.

Relationship between superclasses and interfaces From the tester's perspective, "`MyClass implements MyInterface`" is very similar to "`MyClass extends MySuperclass`." The first difference is that an interface does not come with an implementation, thus we can derive only specification-based test cases from it. Second, the parallel test hierarchy described above fails as soon as `MyClass` implements more than one interface, or additionally extends `MySuperclass`, because Java does not support multiple inheritance in an implementation for classes.

We still have the idea in mind that a test suite `MyInterfaceTest` for `MyInterface` should be executed for all implemented objects. When trying to realize this idea in Java, a few thoughts prove useful:

- Test classes can also be *abstract*.

- Abstract classes can be made instantiable by using *static internal* classes.

- JUnit allows us to implement a separate `suite()` method for each test class.

Consider the situation shown in Figure 7.3. We have two interfaces and two classes; one class implements both interfaces and the other one implements one of the two interfaces. Based on this structure, we would also like to have test classes (Figure 7.4). The `implements` relationship between the classes and interfaces should be replaced by a *uses* relationship of some kind between the corresponding test classes.

We now have to answer the question of what the implementation of the abstract interface test classes and the `suite()` methods might look like. The schematic suggestion below follows along the lines of our initial idea:

```
public class InterfaceATest extends TestCase {
    private InterfaceA out; // object under test
    protected abstract InterfaceA createInterfaceA();
    protected void setUp() {
        out = this.createInterfaceA();
```

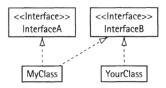

Figure 7.3 Interfaces.

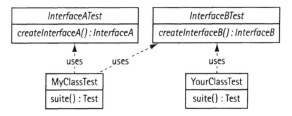

Figure 7.4 Interface test classes.

```
      }
      public void testXXXX() {...}
   }

   public class InterfaceBTest extends TestCase {
      private InterfaceB out; // object under test
      protected abstract InterfaceB createInterfaceB();
      protected void setUp() {
         out = this.createInterfaceB();
      }
      public void testYYYY() {...}
   }

   public class MyClassTest extends TestCase {

      public static class MyClassInterfaceATest extends InterfaceATest {
         protected InterfaceA createInterfaceA() {
            return new MyClass();
         }
      }
      public static class MyClassInterfaceBTest extends InterfaceBTest {
         ... // accordingly
      }

      public static Test suite() {
         TestSuite suite = new TestSuite(MyClassTest.class);
         suite.addTestSuite(MyClassInterfaceATest.class);
         suite.addTestSuite(MyClassInterfaceBTest.class);
         return suite;
      }
   }
```

Note that suite() initially creates the standard test suite—new TestSuite (MyClassTest.class)—and then the interface test suites are appended. Considering that InterfaceATest and InterfaceBTest (can) include exclusively specification-based test cases, we need additional implementation-based test cases in MyClassTest for the implemented interfaces.

Usage criteria   The technique introduced here for reusing abstract test classes by means of internal classes means reaching deeply into Java's bag of tricks, and it is hard to understand. For this reason, we will not use this technique mechanically for each interface to be implemented. Instead, we will use it only when there is actually a nontrivial specification-based test suite. There are often very few semantic requirements to the implementing class, apart from the requirement to make the interface public. In this case, the interface tests would be better off in the test suite of that class.

Testing Abstract Classes

The root and some of the classes in the center of a class hierarchy are normally abstract; that is, no instances can be created from them. Some design heuristics even require that only the leaves of an inheritance tree may be specific.[5]

From the test implementation perspective, abstract classes do not cause us major problems. We only have to ensure that the corresponding classes of the parallel test hierarchy are really abstract and that they are not admitted as independent test suites.[6]

Direct testing of abstract classes McGregor and Sykes [McGregor01] discuss whether or not exclusive testing of abstract classes in specific derivations is sufficient. Alternatively, they study a way to create a specific subclass exclusively for testing purposes. However, they arrived at the result that the complexity of an abstract class is rarely great enough to justify this effort. Instead, they recommend additional code *inspections.*

Our personal experiences support this recommendation, with one exception. If *no* specific subclass of our abstract class exists, then a specific derivation is *mandatory* to be able to test in the first place. We generally encounter this case only in a framework development situation.

<table>
<tr><td>7.2</td><td>**Polymorphism**</td></tr>
</table>

Dynamic polymorphism *Polymorphism* means *the quality or state of being able to assume different forms.* In the object-oriented context, polymorphism means the multitude of forms that object references (e.g., a variable or parameter) can take. We are interested in *dynamic polymorphism,* or the ability of an object reference to be bound to many different kinds of objects. It is "dynamic"

---

5. A different discussion of this issue is found in Riel [96].

6. This can indeed be a problem with aggregate suites created automatically.

precisely when the object's class cannot be determined at compile time, but only at runtime. The only thing that is determined is a type the object has to obey.

By invoking an operation on such a reference, we cannot previously determine the concrete method (implementation) that will eventually be executed, since method execution depends on both the operation invoked and the class of the invocation receiver. For example, if we have the variable myBook of type Book (see Section 7.1), then an instance of either the Book class or the FixedPriceBook class can hide behind it.

Difference between
type and class

In this context, it is important to distinguish between the terms *type* and *class*. To ensure correct compilation of an operation call, such as myBook.sell(10.0), only the type of the objects is decisive. In Java, an object can embody many different types. A type is defined by its class and all of its superclasses, and additionally by all interfaces implemented by its class or one of its superclasses.[7] This means that instances of the class FixedPriceBook can assume the following forms: Object, Book, or Fixed-PriceBook. When an operation is invoked on a polymorphic object reference, then the signature of the operation—including its name and number, type, and the order of its parameters—determines the method that will actually be executed.

Developer's
perspective

A running object-oriented program can be regarded as a world where client objects invoke operations on other objects. Those other objects provide some kind of service for the client; let's therefore call them server objects for the rest of this chapter. From the developer's perspective, polymorphic server objects facilitate the programming work, because they reduce the size and the complexity of the client code on the one hand, and the maintenance effort when adding or removing new server classes on the other hand.

Tester's
perspective

From the tester's perspective, polymorphism represents the counterpart of inheritance. While we reused test suites of the superclass and special interface test classes in our previous example to ensure that all implementations of a type would obey the specification, we are now testing the interplay, or *interaction*, between the service classes under test and their clients.

Problems with
polymorphism

Polymorphic operations represent a kind of case statement, rendering the control flow of the client code under test more complicated. The com-

---

7. Depending on the programming language, types are identified in a totally different way. For example, Smalltalk defines the type solely by the implemented methods.

plexity of the logic is hidden behind syntactic simplicity. In addition, server code can be modified regardless of its clients, as long as it continues to formally meet the interface specification. Therefore, the optimistic assumption that it is sufficient to adequately test all server classes and the interaction of our client with one single server is wrong once again. The following things can go wrong:

- Our reference object could be bound to a wrong server object.

- The wrong method of the server is invoked. This is often caused by signatures that differ only in the type of their parameters.

- The client code does not consider the full spectrum of a method's return values. This also includes correct handling of all possible exceptions.

- Certain server classes violate the rules of the substitution principle, causing the client code to stumble.

- The pre- or post-condition of a polymorphic method was changed, but the server was not adapted accordingly.

Let's use the Book example again to better explain these issues. Our two "servers"—Book and FixedPriceBook—were adequately tested. Now we proceed to programming the first client, an automated seller called Mr. BookSeller, with an interface that looks like this:

```java
public class BookSeller {
    public void setBookToSell(Book book);
    public Book getBookToSell();
    public String sellFor(double price);
}
```

Probably the only big surprise here is that sell() should return a string telling us whether or not the sales transaction was successful. And we can build the following test suite swiftly; it is pretty neat, but not complete yet:

```java
public class BookSellerTest extends TestCase {
    private BookSeller seller;
    private Book book;
```

```
protected void setUp() {
   seller = new BookSeller();
   book = new Book("test book", 10.0, 12.0);
   seller.setBookToSell(book);
}

public void testNormalSell() {
   assertEquals(book, seller.getBookToSell());
   String answer = seller.sellFor(11.0);
   assertEquals("OK", answer);
   assertEquals(11.0, book.getSoldFor(), 0.0);
}

public void testSellAboveRecommendedPrice() {
   String answer = seller.sellFor(12.01);
   assertEquals("Price too high", answer);
   assertEquals(0.0, book.getSoldFor(), 0.0);
}

public void testSellBelowWholesalePrice() {
   String answer = seller.sellFor(0.99);
   assertEquals("Price too low", answer);
   assertEquals(0.0, book.getSoldFor(), 0.0);
}
}
```

What's mainly missing in this test class are cases for repeated sales attempts after a success or failure, yet another practical exercise for our readers. However, the problem lies somewhere else. The following **correct** client code shows where we have a flaw:

```
BookSeller seller = new BookSeller();
Book book = new FixedPriceBook("Pygmalion", 10.0, 12.0);
seller.setBookToSell(book);
String answer = seller.sellFor(11.0);
System.out.println(answer);
System.out.println(book.getSoldFor());
```

This code generates the output:

```
OK
0.0
```

Despite the "OK" there was no sale. We can see the reason if we take a closer look at the implementation of BookSeller.sellFor():

```
public String sellFor(double price) {
    if (price < bookToSell.getWholesalePrice()) {
        return "Price too low";
    }
    if (price > bookToSell.getRecommendedPrice()) {
        return "Price too high";
    }
    try {
        bookToSell.sell(price);
    } catch (PriceOutOfBoundsException impossible) {}
    return "OK";
}
```

Selling a fixed price book at a price not equivalent to its fixed price makes it throw a PriceOutOfBoundsException. The developer of the class BookSeller was not expecting that to happen. Calling the exception variable impossible shows that he started from the wrong assumption. Such a misconception can happen easily when fixed price books are introduced *after* the implementation of the BookSeller class.

And the moral of this story?
Never trust a single class!

Guidelines for testing polymorphic interactions

Or, rephrased as a guideline: For polymorphic operations, design your interaction tests so that *all possible implementations* of the addressed type are tested. And because this may mean a very high effort, here is another (weaker) rule: When creating test cases, consider the possibility that a reference might be polymorphically bound; edit the interaction tests of all your clients when you modify the server class.

At least two additional test cases are needed in our current example:

```
public void testNormalSellFPB() {
    Book fpBook = new FixedPriceBook("FPB", 10.0, 12.0);
    seller.setBookToSell(fpBook);
    assertEquals(fpBook, seller.getBookToSell());
    String answer = seller.sellFor(12.0);
    assertEquals("OK", answer);
    assertEquals(12.0, fpBook.getSoldFor(), 0.0);
}

public void testSellFPBBelowRecommendedPrice() {
    Book fpBook = new FixedPriceBook("FPB", 10.0, 12.0);
    seller.setBookToSell(fpBook);
    String answer = seller.sellFor(11.99);
    assertEquals("Price too low", answer);
    assertEquals(0.0, fpBook.getSoldFor(), 0.0);
}
```

In the general case, the effort for adequate testing of polymorphic interactions can be much higher. This is the price we have to pay for the flexibility and apparent simplicity of our multifaceted object meshes. There's no such thing as a free lunch!

7.3 Summary

Inheritance hierarchies, interfaces, and polymorphism are different variants of the same object-oriented idea: objects can present themselves from different angles as they take one type or another. For the user of objects, only the type and not the concrete implementation plays a role.

From the developer's perspective, this idea results in a number of benefits, while the tester has to struggle with the traps of complexity hidden behind the cloak of simplicity.

This chapter discussed both the theoretical foundations for a better understanding of the problems involved in inheritance and polymorphism and techniques to solve some of these problems. These techniques include reuse of the superclass tests and testing of interfaces.

Chapter 8

How Much Is Enough?

The previous chapters dealt mainly with what should be tested, how, and why. If we were to turn all our testing ideas into automated test cases, then the test effort to implementation effort ratio would be at least 10 to 1, if not higher. One important question is therefore, When will we have sufficiently tested?

Let's be honest, only very few of us are addicted to testing. Most development teams suffer rather from the opposite phenomenon. There are too few tests for us to always deliver or restructure with a clear conscience. The other important question is therefore, When have we tested too little?

Factors influencing the test optimization

There are numerous factors that play a role in determining the optimal testing effort. The most important ones follow:

- *Complete testing* with the declared intention to verify the correctness of a program *is impossible to achieve for all nontrivial programs.* The objective of our testing efforts; therefore, can only be to find as many faults as possible at a manageable effort level.

- There is an *acceptable error level* for each system. How high this level is depends on the type of system: the software to control a radiological unit should certainly not contain as many errors as a Web application for sock subscriptions.[1] The acceptable error level is normally specified by the customer in metrics like *mean time between failure* or the like. The actual error level achieved by an implementation is usually hard to predict without running the application productively for some time.

---

1. There is no such thing? Check it out at [URL:Soxabo].

- The *effort* required to achieve a specific error level *grows in a nonlinear way with regard to the benefit.* For this reason, we can achieve an average error level at a relatively small testing effort. But the effort will be much higher for only half as many bugs in the program.

- Not all faults are created equal—some are cosmetic, some are catastrophic. If possible, testing should concentrate on finding the severe bugs.

- The correct number of *unit tests* has *positive effects on the development velocity,* as soon as the project term exceeds a certain duration.

- Test-first development requires at least a sufficient number of tests so that all developers will have *enough confidence in their own work.* When a developer is forced to fall below his or her personal minimum quality standard, due to time pressure for instance, then identification with the result of their work and their motivation and productivity will suffer.

- Unit tests are *not only a quality-assurance technique.* Above all, they steer the development of our evolutionary design.

- Unit tests are *not the only tests* we use, so they don't have to fully guarantee the desired error level. The acceptance tests specified by the customer are another responsible element. A life-critical system demands additional test steps and quality-assurance measures.

- Too few tests hold another danger: we get lulled into a false sense of security.

For these reasons, we have to weigh two aspects against each other: the economic side (How much does which error level cost me?) and the technical side (How many tests will bring me maximum velocity, flexible design, and happy developers?).

8.1 The XP Rule

Extreme Programming has a simple answer to our question about the required test quantity:

"Test everything that could possibly break."[2]

Unfortunately, this sentence may initially sound like a prediction from the oracle of Delphi. If I knew everything that could possibly break, then I would naturally test it or take care not to get it wrong in the first place.

Interpretation
The actual core of this statement is something else: each developer and each team makes different mistakes. Looking at one's own mistakes over time, you will find that they are often similar.[3] This also applies to a team, if there is a team. And then hopefully we are always learning, with the result that we will make different mistakes over the long run, sometimes fewer than before, but still mistakes. Therefore, the optimum test quantity includes only all of those tests that find or prevent our *actual errors.*

Iterative adaptation to the test level
In practice, this means that each team has to find its own optimal test level and, above all, iteratively feel its way towards the correct volume. Note that this volume can change over time.

If we discover that many faults are found only after the release, we have either too few or the wrong tests. We then have to look at the bugs closely, write unit tests for them, and add test cases for recurring error types to the test suite in advance.

In contrast, there will be times when we feel that a big testing effort slows us down inappropriately, without apparent benefit from refactoring or fitting new requirements. In such a situation, we will naturally try to identify unnecessary tests for errors that never occur.

8.2 Clear Answers to Clear Questions

Well, isn't that typical! you will probably say. The author gives fishy, commonplace answers to the most important questions. I'd like to know what I should test and what I shouldn't! To contain your temper a little, I will try to give you a few "concrete" answers in the following sections.

---

2. Jeffries[00, Ch. 34] dedicates an entire chapter to this sentence.
3. This phenomenon is described in the literature [Weinberg98].

Tests per Class

Should each class have its own test class?

Yes. Each nontrivial class should have *at least one* test class. Trivial classes are, for example, exception classes that do nothing but implement standard constructors and pass parameters to super. The differentiating answer is, Does that class have its *own* logic?

Getters and Setters

Should I test simple getters and setters of attributes?

Ron Jeffries says no, because we can see at a glance that they are correct. I don't accept that as a sufficient argument because we cannot be sure that extensions and refactorings will have an impact on the code which we *currently* know to be correct. However, most of the time these trivial methods don't require dedicated tests since they are already used—and thereby tested—in other test cases. If this is not the case, then a dedicated setter-getter test method will at least do no harm.

Non-Public Object Properties

A brief definition of terms appears to be useful at this point. We use the term *public* for everything that can be accessed from outside of our unit under test. When testing a single class, then *protected* and *package-scope* methods are also regarded as public. In contrast, when testing a subsystem where all classes are within one package, then only methods and constants with the access specification *public* are public.

This leads us to two related, but different questions:

Should we test non-public methods?[4]

The supporters argue that even private methods can be very complex so that something in them can go wrong. However, the drawbacks in testing private methods predominate. They make refactoring more difficult

---

4. This question is one of the most fiercely discussed issues in the field of unit tests under XP (see [URL:WikiUTNPMF]).

and increase the maintenance effort, because they are strongly implementation-dependent tests, and we have to use a few tricks to be able to invoke them at all (as we next discuss).

When using the test-first approach, wishing to test private methods is mainly a *code smell* matter. Either the method in question is actually part of the public interface (for which there is no client code yet) and if so, we should simply replace private with public and everything will be alright. Or, a new helper object is waiting to be born and in that event the method would be public.

However, everything will look different during subsequent testing. Unfortunately, there is rarely an alternative to grasping the nettle: before we can start cleaning up inherited unknown code, we need workable tests as a safety net (see also Chapter 15, Section 15.1, Unit Testing for Existing Software. In such a case, we can only hope that these tests will prove to be a mere transitional stage.

Should we allow tests to access internal things?

By "internal things," we mean non-public methods and attributes. The benefit is that it would allow us to test many post-conditions with much less effort, compared to the situation where we have to rely on the public interface. The drawback is again the high implementation dependence of such test cases.

Ron Jeffries answers this question pragmatically: "those who believe that an important test can be realized only by accessing implementation details should do this. If the implementation proves to be too erratic, we will notice it very quickly. On the other hand, if the implementation remains stable, then the non-public feature may be an unrecognized public feature looking for its client."[5]

Once we have decided to break the object's private sphere, we will have to clarify how to technically access private methods and attributes. The following options are available: we can change the access restriction for testing purposes, or we can use reflection (from JDK 1.2 up) or mock objects to mitigate the problem and possibly avoid it.

---

5. One question closely related to this issue is whether data encapsulation is generally overvalued, such that all methods would better be public. Some argue that the Smalltalk world copes wonderfully with the fact that "private" represents merely a guideline and is not forced by the language. You can read the discussion and get involved at [URL:WikiMSBP].

What is the bottom line? Try to avoid testing private methods and accessing internal properties of a class within your tests. If you change your mind after careful consideration, then this won't mean the end of the world in most cases.

Complex Interaction Tests

We explained in Chapter 4, Section 4.6, why interaction tests between *two* objects are sometimes necessary to create an adequate test suite. However, if we do unit testing without dummy or mock objects, we will soon get to a point where we have to create a complex object mesh to be able to create a test fixture, and where the distance between the OUT and the basic objects of the fixture becomes large. Such tests are difficult to read and maintain, and they also violate the rules requiring maximum independence and minimum granularity for our tests.

The benefit of such *micro integration tests* is that they can uncover "random" errors by indirect use of numerous other objects. The successful tester lives on such planned chances. So when should we avoid this type of complex test? The following comments can give us useful indications:

Contraindications for integration tests

1. The test runs are very long, because they access databases or other external resources.

2. We can no longer adapt our tests after changes to the code or when new requirements emerge, because there are excessive cross-dependencies.

3. The tests often raise false alarm, because things in the remote object have changed, while these things are not relevant for the actual test case.

4. The tests overlap functionally with the acceptance tests.

5. The tests use real data—production data dumps provided by the customer—which are too complex for us developers to remember all the details.

6. Understanding the test scenarios requires extensive customer-specific knowledge that the average developer does not typically have.

Points 1 through 3 occur mostly when the code under test was not at all or only partly developed by the test-first approach, because test-first code is generally less dependent than *design-first code*. If we have a feeling that we cannot test our CUT in isolation or without a complex fixture, then this clearly indicates that there is a design problem that will have to be solved sooner or later.

Points 4 through 6 indicate that we have exceeded our developer competence and entered the realm of acceptance tests. This may be necessary when customers do not supply their own acceptance tests. But in these cases, too, we should draw an organizational separation between the "real" unit tests and the *developer's own acceptance tests*, by using separate packages, for example.

Testing the Tests

No tests for the sake of tests

One frequently asked question is whether or not we should write tests for the tests themselves. The simple answer is no, because test cases do not contain logic that has to be verified. If they do contain logic (e.g., in the form of branches) then that test case has to be simplified (see also Chapter 4, Section 4.1). According to our experience a trivial error in the test code, for instance, a wrong assertEquals(...), will be discovered during the first test run in most cases. From this perspective, the application code is sort of a test for the test code.

One exception to the rule, No tests for the sake of tests, is testing helper classes with their own logics (e.g., reusable dummy objects). They actually need their own test suite.

8.3 | Test Coverage

Test coverage

One frequent keyword in the testing literature is *test coverage*. The term describes the answer to the question, How much of X will be covered by my tests? (where X stands for different coverage types). At least two types of coverage can be differentiated: *specification-based coverage* and *code-based coverage*.

Specification–Based Coverage

This coverage type refers to the completeness of taking account of our software specification in the test cases. The background can be, for example, requirement tables, use-case models, and state transition diagrams. This type of coverage is normally determined by manual inspections.

Requirements coverage   That our test suite covers the functional requirements is undoubtedly one of the most important aspects of adequate testing. A pragmatic approach to reach this goal is to have the customer (or the analysts as customer representatives) write testable requirements, those which can be translated unambiguously into unit tests. Then these test cases can be reviewed by the customer to check for accuracy and sufficiency. A more XP-like approach would be to ensure that all acceptance tests can be found as unit tests for system boundary classes and to make sure that whenever an acceptance test fails a unit test will also fail.

Code–Based Coverage

Code-based coverage can refer to the *control flow* or the *data flow* of a program or even to both. A large number of coverage metrics have been proposed, including the following commonly used (control flow) metrics:

- **Line Coverage.** This code coverage measure tells you the percentage of your program lines that were "touched" in the test run. This is the weakest measure, because even 100% coverage permits many errors.

- **Branch Coverage.** This code coverage measure tells you how many of the branches in the control flow were visited during the test. This measure is somewhat stronger, but again, even 100% coverage does not guarantee that there are no errors.

- **Path Coverage.** This coverage measure shows you the percentage of all possible paths—branching combinations—that are getting tested. However, despite 100% coverage, which is not realistic for commercial systems, there could still be hidden errors.

How helpful are
coverage tools?

The commercial coverage tools currently available for Java[6] support only line coverage. Academic tools try to determine stronger metrics. However, the determination of all possible branches in the control flow of polymorphic messages is difficult or even impossible when dynamic class loading is permitted, which conflicts with the above coverage goal. Nonetheless, such a coverage model can be useful even if we cannot know when 100% coverage is obtained, as long as we can determine that progress with regard to the model being made.

If it were our only goal to increase the value of a specific coverage measure (e.g., to achieve 100% line coverage), then we would fall victim to the phenomenon normally observed when the quality of human work is evaluated on the basis of derived numbers: "People tend to optimize the metric rather than the goal. Tools should complement not replace programmer judgement."[7]

Meaningful use of
coverage metrics

Therefore, it appears to be meaningful indeed to use an appropriate tool now and then to determine the (change of) percentage coverage and, above all, to identify code pieces not executed within the tests. In contrast, it would be a doubtful goal if we were to achieve a specific value at all costs to then happily lean back. The results of our effort in determining the coverage can show us flaws in our tests. In this respect, we have to distinguish between the following categories of uncovered code:

- Code not being tested, but which should be tested. This discovery is the greatest benefit for us.

- Dead code that should be removed. This is also very useful.

- Code generated automatically, which is not invoked in our application.

- Code that can be reached only against a very high testing effort. This often concerns error handling code, because Java's concept of *checked exceptions* provokes (at least the interim) insertion of empty try-catch blocks. These uncovered lines occur less frequently in programs developed by the test-first approach.[8]

---

6. For example JProbe with its coverage module [URL:JProbe].
7. Kent Beck in a Yahoo! discussion of the "code coverage" issue.
8. Ron Jeffries even gives an inductive proof that test-first development can always achieve 100% line coverage ([URL:YahooXP], Message 26626).

In a paper entitled, How To Misuse Code Coverage [URL:TestingCoverage], Brian Marick states more reasons why code coverage can never be the goal, but merely a nice addition to a tester's common sense. In summary, Marick writes in the Yahoo! discussion previously cited:

> Coverage can't tell you that you're missing code, because coverage tools work on the code you have. How much assurance should you expect from a tool that is oblivious to so many bugs?

Mutation testing

Mutation testing is an interesting addition to conventional coverage analysis and was originally proposed by DeMillo [78]. This testing type is based on targeted changes to the application code and on subsequent verification of whether or not the original test suite can detect such a change as an error. In contrast to conventional coverage metrics, this method can be used to identify code parts that are executed within the suite but have implications not verified in the tests. One representative of this type of tools is Jester [URL:Jester], which uses JUnit to run mutation tests.

8.4 | Summary

Complete testing is impossible. A question that must be answered is when to stop testing and where to concentrate available resources. There is no right or wrong answer. Each project and each team has to find the answer to this question themselves, or worse yet, the right answer can change from day to day. Still, there are a few guidelines and arguments that help speed up a team's learning process. This chapter discussed the most important guidelines, the XP mantra, Test everything that could possibly break, being one of them. Requirements also play a fundamental role in striving for an adequate test suite. Finally, the chapter described the role code-coverage metrics and tools can play in controlling and steering our own testing efforts.

Part II

Advanced Topics

Chapter 9

Persistent Objects

Most programs have a common problem: they want to save part of their state, (i.e., part of their objects), in certain moments to make sure they survive the end of the program run. This process is called *persisting*. In another moment, and frequently in another program run, *persistent objects* should eventually be taken back from their exile to operative use.

There are many options to make data and objects "durable" in Java. Typical variants include:

Persistence
mechanisms

- Saving the object attributes to a file(e.g., in XML format).

- Serialization of an object graph in a stream.

- Saving the objects to a relational database (RDBMS)—with or without the use of a *mapping tool.*[1]

- Using an object-oriented database (OODBMS).

RDBMSs are
most common

A full discussion of the benefits and drawbacks of available persistence mechanisms goes beyond the scope of this book. These issues are covered in the literature [Barry96], which discusses in detail why and how an OODBMS can make our programming life easier. After all, we developers would like persistence to become a seamless part of object-oriented principles. In contrast, more than 10 years after the appearance of the first commercial object-oriented databases, most companies still favor their

---

1. A mapping tool maps objects to relational tables. One of the most popular tools of this kind is TopLink [URL:TopLink].

relational counterparts for software development, for good or bad reasons. In this chapter, we concentrate on the RDBMS variant and on *Java database connectivity (JDBC)* as a standardized programming interface to databases. The following problems occur when testing relational objects:

Problems when testing persistent objects

- Accessing an external persistence medium takes much longer than accessing "normal" objects. This increases the runtime of a test suite (even with a small number of tests) beyond the limit we are willing to accept without grumbling. As a consequence, we take bigger steps in the test-driven development to cut down on test starts.

- The consistency conditions of the data schema often require the existence of a very large number of supporting objects in order to be able to create our OUT in the database at all. The creation of these helper objects not only costs additional runtime, further slowing down the test suite, it can also turn into a maintenance nightmare, especially with complex schemas. For example, a new constraint in one place can mean that some of our tests fail during setup, or an additional relation in another place can mean that we have to create additional records to be able to get hold of a consistent instance of our CUT.

- Before it actually starts, each test case has to ensure that both the number and state of all considered objects comply exactly with expectations. This means that no previous test case may leave garbage and that no other program (of another developer) interferes with the test.

- Developers often have to use non-local databases for test purposes. This means that the underlying network generates additional runtime delays and increases the probability that problems unrelated to the test case itself cause it to fail.

Persistent testing can be a real drag

Other persistence mechanisms can cause the same or similar troubles. These problems contribute to a situation where many developers who had initially been happy to work with the test-first approach throw in the towel when trying to integrate the persistence mechanism. This chapter explains how a combination of certain design principles and techniques can help to make unit testing for and with persistent objects less painful.

9.1 | Abstract Persistence Interface

Example:
CRM system

Consider a small application to maintain customer relationships, a tiny *customer relationship management (CRM)* system. The persistent object model of this example system has stabilized in the course of the first few iterations to the structure shown in Figure 9.1. In the center is the customer (Customer), who is assigned to *exactly one* category (CustomerCategory), and who can be contacted an arbitrary number of times (CustomerContact).

A naive testing approach handles persistent objects like all other objects and uses a database like an internal resource. Opting for this approach often means that we will have a persistence interface that is either static or implemented as a singleton. The following static database class is conceivable for the objects represented in Figure 9.1:

```
public class CRMDatabase {
    public static void initialize(String dbURL)
        throws CRMException {...}
    public static void shutdown() throws CRMException {...}
    public static CustomerCategory createCategory(String name)
        throws CRMException {...}
    public static void deleteCategory(CustomerCategory category)
        throws CRMException {...}
    public static Set allCategories() throws CRMException {...}
    public static Customer createCustomer(String name,
        CustomerCategory category) throws CRMException {...}
```

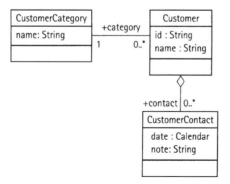

Figure 9.1 Object model of the CRM application.

```
        public static void writeCustomer(Customer customer)
           throws CRMException {...}
        public static void deleteCustomer(Customer customer)
           throws CRMException {...}
        public static Customer getCustomer(String id)
           throws CRMException {...}
        public Set allCustomers(CustomerCategory category)
           throws CRMException {...}
    }
```

There are methods for initializing and stopping the database and for creating, writing, deleting, and retrieving categories and customers. Cus-tomerContact instances depend on customer objects and are stored, written, and deleted through these objects.

Naive test implementation   One of the important tasks of this CRM system is to create regular *reports.* For example, a daily report (DailyReport) determines the number of customer contacts with specific customer categories. The following piece of code was taken from the pertaining test class:

```
public class DailyReportTest extends TestCase {
    private DailyReport report;
    private Calendar reportDate;
    private CustomerCategory catFortune100,catSmallCompany;
    private final String DB_URL = "jdbc:odbc:CRM";
    private List customersToDelete = new ArrayList();
    protected void setUp() throws Exception {
        reportDate = Calendar.getInstance();
        report = new DailyReport(reportDate);
        CRMDatabase.initialize(DB_URL);
        catFortune100 =
            CRMDatabase.createCategory("Fortune 100");
        catSmallCompany =
            CRMDatabase.createCategory("small company");
    }
    protected void tearDown() throws Exception {
        Iterator i = customersToDelete.iterator();
        while (i.hasNext()) {
            Customer each = (Customer) i.next();
```

```
            CRMDatabase.deleteCustomer(each);
        }
        CRMDatabase.deleteCategory(catFortune100);
        CRMDatabase.deleteCategory(catSmallCompany);
        CRMDatabase.shutdown();
    }
    public void testAllContacts() throws Exception {
        Customer customer1 = CRMDatabase.createCustomer(
            "Customer 1", catFortune100);
        customersToDelete.add(customer1);
        Customer customer2 = ...
        Customer customer3 = ...
        Calendar dayBefore = (Calendar) reportDate.clone();
        dayBefore.add(Calendar.DATE, -1);
        customer1.addContact(dayBefore, "note 1");
        customer1.addContact(reportDate, "note 2");
        CRMDatabase.writeCustomer(customer1);
        customer2.addContact(reportDate, "note 3");
        CRMDatabase.writeCustomer(customer2);
        customer3.addContact(dayBefore, "note 4");
        CRMDatabase.writeCustomer(customer2);
        List contacts =
            report.allContactsForCategory(catFortune100);
        assertEquals(1, contacts.size());
        // ...
    }
}
```

The following problems emerge:

- Although the DailyReport class should be fully independent from our database, the unit tests for this class require extensive code to initialize the database and create objects in the database itself. This code is errorprone and causes long runtime.

- The complete deletion of all previously created persistent objects from tearDown() requires active cooperation in the test code by using customersToDelete.add(...) within the test method. If we forget this just once, our database will eventually be in an undesirable state.

- In addition, we make ourselves conditional upon the availability of the database. A failure in the connection or excessive database-specific resources (e.g., sessions) would be enough to cause all subsequent tests to "say goodbye" with strange exceptions and error messages.

Abstraction of the persistence interface

Again, the *Dependency Inversion Principle* (see Chapter 6, Section 6.3) offers a way out of this tricky test situation. In the above code example, the `DailyReport` class depends directly upon the database interface. This violates the rule stating that high-level modules should not depend on lower-level modules. We break this dependence by encapsulating persistence in an abstract interface:

```
public interface CRMPersistence {
    void shutdown() throws CRMException;
    CustomerCategory createCategory(String name)
        throws CRMException;
    void deleteCategory(CustomerCategory category)
        throws CRMException;
    Set allCategories() throws CRMException;
    Customer createCustomer(String name,
        CustomerCategory category) throws CRMException;
    void writeCustomer(Customer customer) throws CRMException;
    void deleteCustomer(Customer customer) throws CRMException;
    Customer getCustomer(String id) throws CRMException;
    Set allCustomers(CustomerCategory category)
        throws CRMException;
}
```

All currently static methods of the CRMDatabase class are now found in CRMPersistence, with one exception, `initialize(String url)` is an implementation detail so that it has no business in the abstract interface.

9.2 Persistent Dummy

Separating the persistence interface from the database connection puts us in a position to supply several implementations of that interface. One of them is a *dummy implementation;* we can use it in the tests for higher layers instead of a real database. The most important part of the dummy for our sample test looks like this:

```java
public class DummyCRMPersistence implements CRMPersistence {
    private int id = 0;
    private Set customers = new HashSet();
    private Set categories = new HashSet();

    public CustomerCategory createCategory(String name)
        throws CRMException {
        CustomerCategory category = new CustomerCategory(name);
        categories.add(category);
        return category;
    }

    public Set allCategories() throws CRMException {
        return categories;
    }

    public Customer createCustomer(String name,
        CustomerCategory category) throws CRMException {
        Customer customer = new Customer(name, category);
        customers.add(customer);
        return customer;
    }

    public Set allCustomers(CustomerCategory category)
        throws CRMException {
        return customers;
    }
    ...
}
```

As simple as possible
All methods not shown here can remain empty for this test case. Note that the method allCustomers(...) returns all created customers and does not filter by category, in contrast to what the functionality actually requires. This complies with our principle to design dummy objects as simply as possible. It is sufficient for us to know that DailyReport instances use the allCustomers method to filter by categories. Naturally, the test should create only matching Customer objects:

```
public class DailyReportTest extends TestCase {
  private DailyReport report;
  private CRMPersistence persistence;
  private Calendar reportDate;
  private CustomerCategory catFortune100;
  protected void setUp() throws Exception {
    persistence = new DummyCRMPersistence();
    reportDate = Calendar.getInstance();
    report = new DailyReport(persistence, reportDate);
    catFortune100 = persistence.createCategory(
      "fortune 100");
  }

public void testAllContacts() throws Exception {
    Customer customer1 = persistence.createCustomer(
      "Customer 1", catFortune100);
    Customer customer2 = persistence.createCustomer(
      "Customer 3", catFortune100);
    Calendar dayBefore = (Calendar) reportDate.clone();
    dayBefore.add(Calendar.DATE, -1);
    customer1.addContact(dayBefore, "note 1");
    customer1.addContact(reportDate, "note 2");
    customer2.addContact(dayBefore, "note 4");
    List contacts =
      report.allContactsForCategory(catFortune100);
    assertEquals(1, contacts.size());
    // ...
  }
}
```

The only remarkable addition to our modified test is that the constructor of DailyReport now additionally demands a CRMPersistence object. We already know this pattern from the introduction of dummy and mock objects. Most important, the test class is now shorter. Some of the database-specific code and the complete tearDown() method are no longer needed.

Testing the error handling mechanism   The dummy class now allows us to test for correct behavior of our error handling mechanism. For this purpose, we configure the dummy object so that it throws the appropriate exception at the right moment (see Chapter

6, Section 6.7). This way, we can simulate any error, from network failure to a violation of database constraints.

Alternative: Mock object

An appropriate mock class would have been a good alternative to the DummyCRMPersistence class. But in view of the fact that it could have verified only the call of allCustomers(), we didn't think it would bring a benefit worth trying. This is certainly a question one can argue about.

If we want to expand a dummy database to the point that it becomes a lightweight database for testing purposes, we would generally have to put up with a larger development effort. The use of a *lightweight* or *in-memory database* (e.g., HsqlDB [URL:HsqlDb] and Cloudscape [URL:Cloudscape]) is more economical in most of these cases (see also Section 9.4, subsection Speeding Up the Test Suite).

| 9.3 | **Designing a Database Interface** |

One central issue in the approach just described is the design of the database interface. When using the test-first approach, it will be built gradually and can constantly be adapted to the real-world requirements of the higher layers. Nevertheless, in this evolutionary approach, too, we should be careful to observe consistent naming and uniform semantics of the supplied interface methods. The design of CRMPersistence was based on the following guidelines:

Basic assumptions in designing a persistence interface

- We distinguish between *independent* and *dependent* objects. Independent objects (i.e., Customer and CustomerCategory in our above example) get methods to create (createXXX), override (writeXXX), and delete (deleteXXX) in and from the persistence interface. Dependent objects (i.e., only CustomerContact in this example) are stored, overwritten, and deleted through their mother objects. We could also treat Customer as a dependent class, because its instances depend on the existence of the assigned category object. However, we decided not to allow navigation from the category to the customer and to permit no automatic deletion of all customer objects belonging to a category.

- *Query* and *retrieval* methods are added to the interface as needed (i.e., allCategories(), getCustomer(...), and allCustomers(...) in this example). These methods can return both independent and dependent objects.

- When an object is created, written, and deleted, then this will automatically create, write, or delete all dependent objects. We have to be particularly careful about recursion when implementing this property.

- All methods defined in the interface are wrapped by transactions. This means that both getter and setter access to persistent objects outside of transactions are allowed. It also means that the consistency and actuality of data is guaranteed only at the time when an interface method is used. This simplified assumption is sufficient for many applications and simplifies work with a persistence interface.

- All *checked exceptions* (see Glossary) occurring during storage are converted into a special exception type (i.e., CRMException in this case). In particular, this signals when consistency conditions in our persistent domain model are violated. For example, an attempt to delete a CustomerCategory object should fail when this category still contains persistent Customer instances.

- If necessary, the implementation takes care of maintaining the identity of an object. In this example, we don't insist on identity (==), but content ourselves with equality (equals(...)).

These basic assumptions have to match the requirements of our application. At times, both the design and the implementation of a persistence interface are more difficult due to special requirements. We will look at three typical difficulties in the sections that follow: transactions visible to the outside, ad hoc queries, and object-centered persistence.

Transactions

The transaction concept plays a central role in databases. So far, we have assumed that encapsulation of single persistence calls in transactions is sufficient. However, there are situations where transactions have to be available from the outside, for example, to execute several persistent actions in a transaction-protected manner. From the technical interface perspective, we could use an additional transaction interface in such cases. In the simplest case, we would use one single method:

```
public interface CRMTransaction {
   Object run() throws Exception;
}
```

In addition, CRMPersistence has to be extended by one (or several) methods to execute the transactions:

```
public interface CRMPersistence {
   ...
   Object executeTransaction(CRMTransaction transaction)
      throws CRMException;
}
```

In our application code, a transaction call would then look like this:

```
public Set allCustomersFirstCategory() throws CRMException {
   CRMTransaction t = new CRMTransaction() {
      public Object run() throws CRMException {
         Set categories = persistence.allCategories();
         CustomerCategory cat =
            CustomerCategory) categories.get(0);
         return persistence.allCustomers(cat);
      }
   };
   return (Set) persistence.executeTransaction(t);
}
```

The situation in a real-world implementation dealing with a database or another persistence framework can be easy or very difficult, depending on the availability of nested transactions and various transaction types. In contrast, the implementation in DummyCRMPersistence is very easy:

```
public Object executeTransaction(CRMTransaction transaction)
   throws CRMException {
   try {
      return transaction.run();
   } catch (CRMException crmex) {
      throw crmex;
```

```
    } catch (Exception ex) {
        throw new CRMException(ex.getMessage());
    }
}
```

The above interface includes the transaction's commit implicitly. Alternatively, we could offer a commit(), a rollback(), or even the creation of subtransactions in the transaction object (i.e., CRMTransaction in this example). This would allow us an even finer control of the transactional behavior.

Drawbacks of explicit transactions

However, we should not forget that making transactions visible means that the program code will be more complicated and inflated. This means that we should make transactions visible only if we cannot do without explicit transactions. It is often sufficient to extend the persistence interface by a few parameters or methods to avoid this additional complexity.

Ad Hoc Queries

Many applications are characterized by the fact that SQL code—mostly specialized and optimized queries—are spread over all parts of a program. This "decentralization" is often motivated by a need to optimize queries. From the designer's perspective, there are several drawbacks inherent in this approach. First, code of the business logic becomes dependent upon a specific technology (SQL database), a specific database, and a fixed schema. Second, code from an initially specific level, namely, the production of persistence, is distributed over numerous classes, packages, and layers, instead of concentrating it in one place.

Need for ad hoc queries

The separation of the persistence interface from the implementation introduced in this chapter prevents SQL queries from reaching the upper layers. Nevertheless, developers sometimes get to a point where they have to extend the persistence interface by a new query method for each new functionality. This is the reason why most persistence frameworks and object-oriented databases offer a way to build ad hoc queries against the database. We could give in to this pressure and extend our CRMPersistence interface by the following method:

```
Set executeSqlQuery(String queryString) {}
```

But we would let ourselves in for the drawbacks just described. In addition, we would spoil our option to easily test this method's client code. In the simplest case, we would have to verify SQL strings for correct syntax and semantics. For this reason, such an expansion should be used as a last resort.

Dedicated "query language"

A better and normally sufficient way is to build a very small query language and specialize it for our application. A very simple example is the method we already have: allCustomers(CustomerCategory category). Passing an example object, for example, an object with its attribute set so it serves as search parameter and wildcard, is a little more complex. We can expand this query language as needed—to include our own classes for searching value ranges and/or combinations and much more.

The benefit of such a program-specific query language is twofold: it is independent of any persistence mechanism and data schema, and it is independent in representing queries by use of the programming language. Compared to string-based languages like SQL, a program-specific query language improves testability and allows the compiler to remove many query input errors upfront. As long as we keep the query definition within the Java source we can even stick to a pure object-oriented description of it. In case we have to externalize the query definitions, in order to make them configurable for instance, we can build a simple textual parser as described in *Building Parsers with Java* [Metsker01].

Optimizing for performance reasons

Sometimes there is a requirement to optimize queries for a specific database, a specific schema, or a specific physical database layout for performance reasons. In my experience, it is sufficient to offer separate time-critical queries in the persistence interface to treat and optimize them separately, whereas the majority of all ad hoc queries is still created generically from the query language.

Object-Centered Persistence

So far in this chapter, we directed each access to the persistent storage medium over an interface (CRMPersistence). This approach has several drawbacks:

Drawbacks of a centralized persistence interface

- The implementing object must be passed to all objects that need to invoke persistence methods, which causes the number of method or constructor parameters to increase.

- In a large persistent domain model, the number of methods available in the interface would soon exceed the limit of clarity.

One approach to mitigate these drawbacks is to move part of the persistence methods towards the objects: writeXXX() and deleteXXX() become write() and delete() in class XXX. And if we enable write() to store newly created objects, we will no longer need the createXXX() method. On the other hand, we don't want to lose the independence of our persistent objects. Figure 9.2 shows a possible solution to this problem.

Two points are important in this design:

- The original interface CRMPersistence is split into two interfaces: CRMPersistence for access from the outside and InternalCRMPersistence for access by the persistent objects themselves.

- All independent persistent objects know their "internal" persistence implementation, to which they pass the write() and delete() invocations.

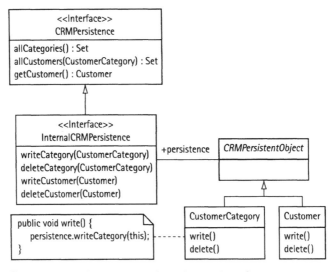

Figure 9.2 An object-centered persistence interface.

Scaling problems

There is one constraint left in this approach: the internal persistence interface can tend to become (too) big. In this case, the next scaling step consists of splitting the internal interface, normally into one interface for each independent object. Splitting the internal interface means that the implementation class should also be split, eventually leading to a much more complex design.

For this reason, we should stick to the principle that the simplest solution is the best. Consequently, evolutionary designers would begin with a centralized persistence interface, then swing round to object-centered persistence at some point in time, and eventually split both the internal interface and the implementation at a later stage. An interesting experience report about the evolution of a persistence framework can be found in Jim Little's text [Little01]. Therein Little describes how a complex architecture, which looked good on paper but was unusable in the real world, was migrated step by step into a simpler, yet superior design by applying an evolutionary and test-driven approach.

9.4 Testing the "Right" Persistence

So far we have seen that it is desirable and possible to free the persistence interface from dependence upon a specific persistence implementation. This means that we can simplify and accelerate the tests for the underlying code significantly.

However, we are not free from our obligation to test the actual implementation of the persistence interface. Of course, this means that we will encounter the same problems we had to deal with in our first naive version of `DailyReportTest` (see Section 9.1), with one exception. It is now sufficient to test the expected persistence functionality only once; we don't have to do the same things over and over again for all higher-level tests. Among other things, we have to test for the following:

- Can I create, modify, and delete objects?

- Will the query methods supply the correct results?

- Will violations of domain constraints be prevented?

- Does the transactional behavior work?

Let's look at a few examples from this catalog. The first example is a test for the creation of persistent customer objects, including the setUp() and tearDown() code parts:

Testing the
object creation

```
public class CRMDatabaseTest extends TestCase {
    private CRMDatabase database;
    protected void setUp() throws Exception {
        database = new CRMDatabase("jdbc:odbc:CRM");
    }
    protected void tearDown() throws Exception {
        if (database.isConnected()) {
            Iterator i = database.allCategories().iterator();
            while (i.hasNext()) {
                CustomerCategory each =
                    (CustomerCategory) i.next();
                this.deleteCategoryAndDependentCustomers(each);
            }
            database.shutdown();
        }
    }
    private void deleteCategoryAndDependentCustomers(
                CustomerCategory category) throws CRMException {
        Iterator i = database.allCustomers(category).iterator();
        while (i.hasNext()) {
            Customer each = (Customer) i.next();
            database.deleteCustomer(each);
        }
        database.deleteCategory(category);
    }
    public void testCustomerCreation() throws Exception {
        CustomerCategory cat = database.createCategory("cat");
        Customer customer1 =
            database.createCustomer("customer1", cat);
        Customer retrieved1 =
            database.getCustomer(customer1.getId());
        assertEquals(customer1, retrieved1);
        assertEquals(customer1.getName(), retrieved1.getName());
        assertEquals(customer1.getCategory(),
                    retrieved1.getCategory());
```

```
        Customer customer2 =
            database.createCustomer("customer2", cat);
        Customer retrieved2 =
            database.getCustomer(customer2.getId());
        assertEquals(customer2, retrieved2);
        Set allCustomers = database.allCustomers(cat);
        assertEquals(2, allCustomers.size());
        assertTrue(allCustomers.contains(customer1));
        assertTrue(allCustomers.contains(customer2));
    }
}
```

A prerequisite for this kind of testing is an empty database—in this example an ODBC database; empty in the sense that no Customer and CustomerCategory objects exist in the visible area. If we cannot guarantee this, then the effort will be much bigger. We can see that the tearDown() code is still relatively complicated, because we want to ensure that no "dead objects" from the tests will remain. If this code fails only once, it can mean that things have to be manually deleted from the database to get back to a controllable initial state.

In contrast, there is nothing really surprising about the test method testCustomerCreation(). It creates the required objects, fetches them again from the database, and verifies the attributes. The tests for deleting and overwriting are similar. The following test—this time omitting the setUp and tearDown—checks the allCustomers(...) query method:

Testing a
query method

```
public void testAllCustomers() throws Exception {
    CustomerCategory cat1 = database.createCategory("cat1");
    CustomerCategory cat2 = database.createCategory("cat2");
    Customer customer1 = database.createCustomer("customer1", cat1);
    Customer customer2 = database.createCustomer("customer2", cat2);
    Customer customer3 = database.createCustomer("customer3", cat1);
    Set cat1Customers = database.allCustomers(cat1);
    assertEquals(2, cat1Customers.size());
    assertTrue(cat1Customers.contains(customer1));
    assertTrue(cat1Customers.contains(customer3));
    Set cat2Customers = database.allCustomers(cat2);
    assertEquals(1, cat2Customers.size());
    assertTrue(cat2Customers.contains(customer2));
}
```

Nothing new, or is there? Much more interesting are unit tests to verify for correct error signaling, for example in the attempt to delete a `Customer-Category` object that is still in use:

Testing
constraint
violations

```
public void testCategoryDeletionWithCustomerFailure()
    throws Exception {
    CustomerCategory cat = database.createCategory("Category 1");
    Customer cust = database.createCustomer("customer1", cat);
    try {
        database.deleteCategory(cat);
        fail("CRMException expected");
    } catch (CRMException expected) {}
    database.deleteCustomer(cust);
    database.deleteCategory(cat);
}
```

This is another test case that corresponds to the pattern introduced in Chapter 4, Section 4.5. Note that we verify for correct continuation after the `CRMException` occurrence. Our last example provides for a rollback when `executeTransaction()` is used:

Testing a
transaction
interface

```
public void testExecuteTransactionRollback() throws Exception {
    CRMTransaction t = new CRMTransaction() {
        public Object run() throws CRMException {
            database.createCategory("cat1");
            // should fail and rollback:
            database.createCategory("cat1");
            return database.allCategories();
        }
    };
    try {
        database.executeTransaction(t);
        fail("CRMException should have been thrown");
    } catch (CRMException expected) {}
    assertTrue(database.allCategories().isEmpty());
}
```

Additional tests All tests shown in the preceding examples, except for the creation of a database instance, are independent of the type of the underlying implementation. Instead of directly connecting to an RDBMS via JDBC, we could alternatively use *object-relational mapping tools*, object-oriented databases, or persistence mechanisms based on serialization.

Depending on the implementation, we will need additional tests, for example to check for correct implementation of *caching* mechanisms. In addition, we haven't considered concurrent access to the database in several threads yet. Chapter 10, Concurrent Programs, includes suggestions for this type of concurrent test. The Web site accompanying this book includes a complete test suite for a simple and non-concurrent JDBC implementation of the persistence interface.

Approaches for Test Data Consistency

The approach selected above to provide a persistent test fixture was pretty simple: persistent objects were created in setUp() or in the respective test method. These objects can then be modified, deleted, fetched, or otherwise manipulated within the test. Finally, we ensured in the tearDown() method that all created objects will eventually be deleted. This approach works well when the addressed (logical) database is available exclusively for a unit test. Also, if the initial state is always an empty database, then deleting objects can often be accelerated by several drop table and subsequent create table invocations.

Multiuser database The situation is different when dealing with a database accessed by several developers, perhaps even concurrently. In this case, we have to ensure that, once a test run is completed, the database is put back into the previous state. We could extend the approach discussed here in this direction, for example by using specific IDs for specific test types, or by marking specific records as test records. In practice, all of this leads to a large number of linked dependencies, coordination problems among developers, increasingly complex tearDown code, and increasingly inconsistent databases. In fact, these databases would often have to be repaired manually or completely refreshed.

The four-databases approach [URL:Dbunit] describes difficulties arising in the cases we've discussed and suggests the use of four databases for different purposes and test types:

1. The **production database**, consisting of live data—no testing on this database.

2. Your **local development database**, which is where most of the testing is carried out.

3. A **populated development database**, possibly shared by all developers so you can run your application and see it work with realistic amounts of data, rather than the handful of records you have in your test database.

4. A **deployment database**, where the tests are run prior to deployment to make sure any local database changes have been applied.

A problem identified in the four-database approach relates to the synchronization of the data schemas. Database 2 serves for unit tests in our sense in that the prerequisite of a dedicated database is given.

Speeding Up the Test Suite

Using a lightweight database

Although their number is reduced, persistent test cases still take a long time. An approach that has been successfully used by the author is to run the persistent test cases against a lightweight or in-memory database during development and to switch to the real database only for integration tests. For example HsqlDb [URL:HsqlDb] can be run in several modes, two of which follow:

- **In-memory mode.** Holds the data submitted via SQL persistent as long as the connection is not being closed. This is useful to test classes which work on instances of `java.sql.Connection`.

- **Local mode.** Writes all data to a file and retrieves it from that file. This is much faster than building a real connection and retrieving data from it as long as the amount of data is small.

This method of improving the performance of persistent tests comes with a caveat, though: Using different databases for development and deployment can hide problems connected to different variants of SQL and different capabilities of the JDBC drivers used. You should therefore have a

Using
preconfigured
data

sufficient number of persistent tests using the deployment database of choice—at least once in a while.

Another way to speed things up is to start from a data repository offering preconfigured objects for all persistent test cases, instead of starting from an empty database. In this case, the attempt to reset all modified data to their initial state upon `tearDown()` will fail at the latest when some attributes of the preconfigured records change. Still, we can think of two variants:

- We envelop the test in a transaction that is started in `setUp()` and rolled back in `tearDown()`. Note, however, that this works only provided that

  - our database supports nested transactions, and we do not run any tests requiring a commit of the outermost transaction; or

  - when running tests on methods not protected by transactions.

  Optimistic locking strategies can lead to the problem that the final transaction commit fails under certain circumstances. Note that this type of error cannot be discovered in this way.

- At times, it may be faster to load the initial test state from a database dump or by use of an SQL script instead of creating the fixture object by object. On the other hand, it will then take more effort to adapt the script or constantly recreate the dump file.

JDBC Mocks

What can we do if our persistent test suite still runs too slowly? It is "too slow" when we run it less often than necessary because of the long wait—when we are not running it *at least* before each integration of modified sources into the total project. Why not use mock objects in this case, too?

By their nature, mock objects are implementation-specific; that is, we have to know exactly how the class `CRMPersistence` implements persistence. In our example, this means *direct* persistence (i.e., JDBC is addressed without detour over a persistence framework). A good point to use the mock approach could, therefore, be an additional constructor. Instead of the database URL, we give this constructor an instance of the `java.sql.Connection` type:

```
public class CRMDatabase implements CRMPersistence {
  public CRMDatabase(Connection connection)
    throws CRMException {
    ...
  }
  ...
}
```

Fortunately, most interfaces in the java.sql package can basically be "mocked" without major problems.

JDBC database access functions by the following scheme: the Connection instance uses createStatement() to create a Statement object. The latter, in turn, has several methods for SQL calls, such as executeQuery (String sqlQuery), which return ResultSet instances. Such a set of results can then be iterated to determine the result lines and the individual column values.

Complexity
of the
mock approach For this reason, one single MockConnection object is not sufficient to allow us meaningful testing. This connection dummy itself has to create MockStatement instances, and the latter have to create MockResultSets. This means that configuring a mock connection is anything but easy. We have to define which mock statements to supply in which order, when and how often a commit() should be sent, and so on. And we have to deal with a similar complexity for our mock statements and mock result sets. Moreover, the inter-object invocation sequence is very important for a correct implementation. For example, a ResultSet instance should no longer be used as soon as the creating Statement object was closed by close(). The following problems can result:

- The actual number and order of required statements, queries, commits, and the like changes often during a refactoring process. For this reason, the effort involved in adapting mock-based tests can be very high.

- The functionality of required mock objects is no longer trivial, causing a considerable development effort.

- Our confidence in having the required security for refactoring steps with our mock tests is hard to achieve due to the complex state-based semantics of the JDBC interface.

- We also have to validate dynamically generated SQL commands against the database.

Conclusion For all these reasons, the use of mock objects in the given case holds intricate dangers, questioning the sense of this venture. Our objective to speed up unit tests for persistence can often also be achieved by using a lightweight database as described in the preceding subsection, Speeding Up the Test Suite.

Those who still want to experiment with mock objects in the JDBC environment are referred to the package `com.mockobjects.eziba.sql` at [URL:MockObjects]. This package can relieve you from a considerable part of the effort involved in mock implementation. At [URL:MockJDBC], Steve Freeman uses an example to show how the mock classes of this package can help in the test-first development of a JDBC program.

Evolution of the Persistence Technology

Does it have to be SQL? Sharp readers will probably have noticed that we haven't yet asked the question about the sense of using an SQL database. In fact, many projects begin with the explicit specification that all persistent data should be in database XYZ of vendor ZYX.

On the other hand, if we can select a technology, then the use of a complex commercial database system from the outset will represent the best solution only in very few cases. Sticking tightly to the principles of the test-first development, the history of the persistence mechanism used typically looks more or less as follows:

- The first requirement to persistence often consists of simple configuration data that can best be saved to a file by using Java's `Properties` class.

- At a later point, we decide to store the state of the application as an object mesh. Java's serialization is suitable for this purpose.

- At some further point in time, a new user story requires frequent and targeted saving and reading of specific objects. For this reason, we select a freely available SQL database that does not involve much administration work and use JDBC to directly write our few classes to that database.

- As we progress, there will be more classes calling for persistence. Considering that manually mapping our objects to tables will be too expensive, we decide to look for an object-relational mapping tool.

- New requirements demand complex transaction behavior patterns, very high throughput rates, or absolutely safe recovery capabilities of the system. And now a costly and maintenance-intensive database system may appear justified.

Of course, some sort of turnoff from this road might be possible, such as using native Java databases or selecting a commercial OODBMS. The specifics of our project is the only important thing to keep in mind. As advocates of the test-first approach, we should be careful not to be put off by the common wisdom, You simply don't question the use of an RDBMS.

9.5 Interaction between Persistence Layer and Client

As described in Chapter 4 (Section 4.6) and in Chapter 7 (Section 7.2), it is normally not sufficient to test for the correct use of an interface through the client in one vein, and for correct implementation of an interface in another, at least from the theoretical perspective. In addition, we must closely examine the interplay of "neighboring" objects.

How many transaction tests are required? For example, objects of the classes `DailyReport` and `CRMDatabase` are neighbors *at runtime*. However, if we were to test the complete interaction between report instances and database instances, then we would be back where we began in this chapter: endlessly long integration tests with a setup and tear-down complexity that would wear us out.

For this reason, it makes sense to limit ourselves to a few interaction test cases to verify the basic interplay. More specifically, we would mainly do database read operations. To get the idea, look at the following code excerpt from the interaction test suite, which creates a real CRM database, populates it with some data, and hands it over to the `DailyReport` constructor:

```
public class CRMInteractionTest extends TestCase {
    private static CRMDatabase database;
    private static CustomerCategory category;
    private static Customer customer;
    private static Calendar today;
    ...

    private static void createScenario() throws CRMException {...
        today = Calendar.getInstance();
        database = new CRMDatabase(TEST_DB_URL);
        category = database.createCategory("fortune 100");
        customer = database.createCustomer("Customer 1", category);
        customer.addContact(today, "note 2");
        database.writeCustomer(customer);
    }

    private static void deleteScenario() throws CRMException {...}

    public void testDailyReport() throws Exception {
        DailyReport report = new DailyReport(database, today);
        List contacts = report.allContactsForCategory(category);
        assertEquals(1, contacts.size());
    }

    public static Test suite() {
        Test test = new junit.extensions.TestSetup(
            new TestSuite(CRMInteractionTest.class)) {
                protected void setUp() throws Exception {
                    System.out.println("test setup: setUp()");
                    createScenario();
                }
                protected void tearDown() throws Exception {
                    System.out.println("test setup: tearDown()");
                    deleteScenario();
                }
            };
        return test;
    }
}
```

TestSetup
decorator

This test class shows another option for how to accelerate certain tests. Our actual test suite is wrapped with a junit.extensions.TestSetup decorator in the suite() method. This decorator serves to accommodate those setup and tear-down operations needed only once for all tests of a suite. Because we want to limit our interaction tests to read operations in our specific case, we can build the testing scenario before the beginning of all interaction tests and tear down all test cases at once at the end.

Integrating
the test suite

There is one more thing we should remember: when implementing the suite() method in test classes, we must be careful to really use this method in the aggregate test suite and not inadvertently in the default implementation:

```
public class AllTests {
    public static Test suite() {
        TestSuite suite = new TestSuite("All CRM tests");

        ...

        suite.addTest(CRMInteractionTest.suite());
        // instead of: suite.addTestSuite(CRMInteractionTest.class);
        return suite;
    }
}
```

9.6 Summary

Persistence plays an important role in most programs. The creation of unit tests for persistence mechanisms is often accompanied by major problems, because both the execution speed and the large number of dependencies make the naive testing approach difficult.

Hiding the persistence layer behind an abstract interface allows us to separate the higher-layer tests from a concrete implementation and thus from a database. This simplifies our test cases and accelerates their execution by several orders of magnitude. Use of the real implementation normally verifies only the methods specified in the persistence interface, which should be kept as small as possible. In addition, we should always strive for the simplest persistence technology within the context of a specific project.

Mock objects can be used to test an implementation built on JDBC, but often require too much work to be worthwhile. A few interaction tests between the persistence mechanism and higher-level objects are meaningful to ensure a basically functioning communication.

Chapter 10

Concurrent Programs

Only a few years ago, the majority of software developers were able to concentrate on problems occurring when a program executed one single sequential command stream. Today, very few applications run sequentially; the catchword is *concurrent*.

Concurrency The principle of concurrency is based on the concept of things happening at the same time. Concurrency can be purely virtual, like the execution of a program on a computer with one single processor. But it can be actually present, when several processors or even several computers are involved.

Processes and threads We distinguish between *processes* and *threads*. Most operating systems seal off processes from one another, which means that processes have to communicate over explicit communication channels (e.g., pipes). In contrast, threads are "lighter"; they share a process and thus an address space, but they have their own *program counter* and their own stack. This means that threads represent the smallest unit for the allocation of computing time (i.e., *scheduling*). This chapter concentrates on threads, because they represent the standard mechanism for concurrency in Java.

Threads in Java Java makes it easy for the developer to create and start threads. This functionality is provided by the class `java.util.Thread`. In addition, Java offers possibilities for synchronization between threads, using the keyword `synchronized` and the methods `wait()` and `notify()`, located in the `Object` class. This chapter assumes that the reader has basic knowledge of these Java features. The basic concepts are discussed and explained in many introductory Java textbooks [Hyde99].

| 10.1 | **Problems Using Threads** |

As long as two threads simply run alongside each other, they won't cause us any trouble, at least no more so than usual sequential programs. Problems normally arise when several threads *try* to synchronize (e.g., to exchange information) or when they *have* to synchronize because several of them want to access the same data (i.e., the same objects).

Hidden threads   Many developers are not aware of (potentially) concurrent access by several threads. For example, all event processing of AWT occurs in a separate thread. And servlet instances also have to expect that several threads may invoke their service() method concurrently. Similarly, the danger in singletons is often overlooked when they are planted into a multi-thread environment, when they were originally not conceived for parallel access.

Design goals   The following goals should be kept in mind when designing multi-threaded applications:

- **Safety.** When a method of an object that is also visible in other threads is invoked, it maintains its semantics even when other threads access it (quasi) concurrently, and the object's consistency is not destroyed. To be on the safe side, we need to protect parts of the code against concurrent execution by several threads. Java uses the keyword synchronized for this purpose.

- **Liveness.** Each thread is given sufficient opportunity to continue running. Two typical situations jeopardize the liveness of threads:

  - When a **deadlock** occurs, two or more threads are waiting for one of them to release resources, so that all threads are blocked.

  - **Starvation** means that one thread no longer gets its turn to continue running. A thread is normally starved due to faulty priority-setting mechanisms.

Unfortunately, there are no universal rules on how to optimally achieve these goals for all concurrent programs. Doug Lea's [00] seminal work on concurrent programming in Java discusses many traps and patterns to avoid them. Naturally, we would like to be able to minimize the probability of these problems from occurring in the first place by using appropriate unit tests. For this reason, apart from the "normal" functionality, the following things should also be tested in (multi-)threaded programming:

Additional
test goals

- A thread starts and ends as expected.

- Two or more threads are synchronized as expected.

- The synchronization of threads does not lead to deadlocks.

- Objects used in several threads are *thread-safe*.

Nondeterminism

Testing programs with several threads is more difficult due to the fact that it is usually impossible in practice to run exactly the same program cycle a second time. The operating system's *scheduler* and the specific thread implementation of the JVM used determine when processor time is allocated to a specific thread. For this reason, certain error situations occur only under very specific or extremely rare circumstances. This means that we can never be really sure whether or not a faulty behavior was removed only because it has not occurred in the last few test runs.

Nondeterministic
testing strategies

When testing, we try to control this nondeterministic behavior by two methods:

- We let specific test cases run very frequently.

- We try to make the thread behavior *sufficiently deterministic* by targeted timing and additional synchronization.

We will use both techniques later.

Target Objects

As usual in unit tests, we always concentrate on small units. However, the ways in which threads can handle objects and how objects attempt to be thread-safe are inexhaustible. Among this enormous complexity, there are two types of objects that occur frequently, such that we want to concentrate our testing efforts on these objects:

- Objects offering *asynchronous services*. This means that their actual behavior runs in a separate thread, while other threads can trigger and request this service (see Section 10.2).

- Objects handling a synchronization function, for example, to transport data between threads (see Section 10.3).

Of course, there are mixed types between these two object types; they offer asynchronous services and synchronize the triggering of these services in one way or another.

<table>
<tr><td>10.2</td><td></td></tr>
</table>

10.2 | Testing Asynchronous Services

Asynchronous service objects come in many different flavors. Some start a single "worker thread," which handles all jobs consecutively when they are created. Others create a separate thread for each job. Still others have a fixed pool of threads, using them alternately to serve incoming requests. An important distinguishing feature is whether or not the triggering thread might be interested in the result of an asynchronous service job at one point in time.

Service without Result

Let's use an example to see the test-first development of a service object. In the beginning, there is usually a normal synchronous invocation, as requested by the following test:

```
public class MyServiceTest extends TestCase {
   public void testServiceInvocation() {
      MyService service = new MyService();
      assertFalse(service.hasFinished());
      service.execute();
      assertTrue(service.hasFinished());
   }
}
```

Motivation for an asynchronous service   Suppose that during the further course of the implementation, the runtime of the execute() method becomes suddenly longer than many callers would want it to be. This observation and the knowledge that we don't have to rely on a result of the service execution lets the implementation and thus our tests march towards asynchronous invocation. Here is the first attempt:

```
public void testServiceInvocation() {
   MyService service = new MyService();
   assertFalse("Not yet started", service.hasStarted());
   service.invokeAsynchronously();
   assertTrue("Started", service.hasStarted());
}
```

This test does not really force the service to run asynchronously (i.e., in another thread). For example, it would be conceivable to test for fast return of the invokeAsynchronously() method. But how fast would be fast enough? Due to a lack of stronger sanctions, we are pragmatic and look at the method's name as an obligation. Under this assumption, the implementation of the invokeAsynchronously() method looks like this in the simplest case:

```
public class MyService {
   private volatile boolean started = false;
   ...
   public void execute() {
      //service execution
   }
   public void invokeAsynchronously() {
      new Thread() {
         public void run() {
            started = true;
            execute();
         }
      }.start();
   }

   public boolean hasStarted() {
      return started;
   }
}
```

Nondeterministic test failure

At first sight, everything appears to be correct and the test runs faultlessly. But if we run it often, the test runner's bar will sporadically turn red.[1] This is due to the wrong assumption that our service thread will happily start running without delay after the invocation of invokeAsynchronously(). In reality, we cannot predict when the new thread created in invokeAsynchronously() will actually start running, and whether the line,

```
started = true;
```

will be reached before the main thread, namely,

```
assertTrue("Started", service.hasStarted());
```

starts. To reduce the probability that a single test functions accidentally, we manipulate the test suite so that it doesn't run once, but always 10 times—a concession to nondeterminism. Mind that this doesn't give us any guarantees either, but it is a pragmatic way to improve our chances:

```
public class MyServiceTest extends TestCase {
    ...
    public static Test suite() {
        TestSuite suite = new TestSuite(MyServiceTest.class);
        return new junit.extensions.RepeatedTest(suite, 10);
    }
}
```

Repeated tests

The class junit.extensions.RepeatedTest is a test decorator that can be built around any arbitrary suite or single test.

A first attempt to make the sequence of events more predictable is to insert a short sleeping phase into the test thread, which the service thread can use for its work:

```
public void testServiceInvocation() throws Exception {
    MyService service = new MyService();
    assertFalse("Not yet started", service.hasStarted());
    service.invokeAsynchronously();
```

---

1. The exact behavior depends on the operating system, the JVM you use, and sometimes the compiler's mood.

```
Thread.sleep(100);
assertTrue("Started", service.hasStarted());
}
```

Pseudo-determinism   This is sufficient for the present case to create a kind of "pseudodeterminism." The chance that the 100ms wait time will expire before the other thread gets going is small.

Now we should test whether or not a second attempt to restart the service will fail; after all, MyService instances are designated for one-time use:

```
public void testDoubleInvocation() {
   MyService service = new MyService();
   service.invokeAsynchronously();
   try {
      service.invokeAsynchronously();
      fail("RuntimeException expected");
   } catch (RuntimeException expected) {}
}
```

And here is a first implementation attempt that doesn't work:

```
public void invokeAsynchronously() {
   if (started) {
      throw new RuntimeException("MyService already started");
   }
   new Thread() {
      public void run() {
         started = true;
         execute();
      }
   }.start();
}
```

Once again, the unpredictable timing of the threads plays a role. The test shows that the service thread has not yet had a chance to set "started" to "true" upon the second invocation of invokeAsynchronously(). Consequently, we had to introduce an additional variable:

```
public class MyService {
  ...

  private boolean invoked = false;
  public synchronized void invokeAsynchronously() {
    if (invoked) {
      throw new RuntimeException(
        "MyService already started");
    }
    invoked = true;
    new Thread() {
      public void run() {
        started = true;
        execute();
      }
    }.start();
  }
}
```

In the method invokeAsychronously() before actually starting a new thread, we test that no service invocation has taken place yet and throw an exception in that case. Note that this method was now declared synchronized to prevent two threads from entering it at the same time. This "synchronized" is not being enforced by our tests though; we really begin to have doubts if all aspects of concurrent programming can be tackled by driving our development through tests only.

Service with Result

Delayed response   As long as we are happy with the fact that the service was started, our main task is met. However, the service is often started asynchronously only to be able to use the result of a lengthy calculation or information retrieved over a slow Internet connection *at a later point in time*.

There are many variations on how to allow the service thread to inform the requesting thread about the result. Doug Lea dedicates an entire chapter of his book to this issue.[2] The interesting thing from our perspective is

_____

2. [Lea00, chap. 4, p. 281].

that the test has to pause for some time before it can expect a result and check it for correctness.

Consider an asynchronous summation service (SumUpService); its result can be requested as String over the method getStringResult(). As long as there is no result yet, this method returns null. And here is the test:

```
public void testInvocationWithResult() throws Exception {
    int[] numbers = new int[] {1, 2, 3};
    SumUpService service = new SumUpService(numbers);
    service.invoke();
    Thread.sleep(1000);
    assertEquals("6", service.getStringResult());
}
```

Once more, we have used sleep(...) to give the worker thread a chance to complete the summation. In doing this, however, we encounter the problem that we don't know how long the calculation will really take. We can (normally) define an upper limit and expect termination of the service within this limit. This maximum value is normally higher than the average value and strongly dependent on the platform on which we are executing the tests. So our test may take much longer than it actually needs to.

Assert with timeout The helper class RetriedAssert can help us out of this dilemma.[3] It allows repeated verification of an assert condition up to a maximum wait time. This means that our test will change as follows:

```
public void testInvocationWithResult() throws Exception {
    int[] numbers = new int[] { 1, 2, 3 };
    final SumUpService service = new SumUpService(numbers);
    service.invoke();
    new utmj.threaded.RetriedAssert(2000, 100) {
        public void run() throws Exception {
            assertEquals("6", service.getStringResult());
        }
    }.start();
}
```

---

3. This and all other helper classes in this chapter are included in the package utmj.threaded, available from the Web site to this book.

The maximum wait time (2000ms in this example) and the request interval (100ms) are determined when the anonymous inner instance is created. Consequently, we know that our test will wait up to a maximum of two seconds for the result, but that it will continue at the latest after 100ms from the end of the calculation. This way to invoke assertions also works for most of the other procedures that an asynchronous service can use to notify its result. The RetriedAssert class is superfluous when the service itself offers a way to wait for the result, including notification within a maximum timeout interval.

Expected Exceptions in Split-Off Threads

Another test should verify the occurrence of an exception while the service is running. We know that the implementation of SumUpService cannot handle numbers greater than 1000, which means that it throws an IllegalArgumentException *during the service execution* in these cases. We wrote the following test to verify this situation:

```
public void testInvocationWithIllegalNumber() throws Exception {
    int[] numbers = new int[] { 1, 1001, 3 };
    final SumUpService service = new SumUpService(numbers);
    try {
        service.invoke();
        fail("IllegalArgumentException expected");
    } catch (IllegalArgumentException expected) {}
}
```

The test fails although the implementation of SumUpService suggests something else,[4] at least at first sight:

```
public class SumUpService {

    ...

    private void sumUp() throws InterruptedException {
        int sum = 0;
        for (int i = 0; i < numbers.length; i++) {
            int each = numbers[i];
```

---

4. Of course, we built the if condition into sumUp() for demonstration purposes only.

```
        if (each > 1000) {
            throw new IllegalArgumentException(
                each + " too big");
        }
        sum = sum + each;
    }
    result = Integer.toString(sum);
}

public void invoke() {
    new Thread() {
        public void run() {
            try {
                sumUp();
            } catch (InterruptedException ignore) {}
        }
    }.start();
}
```

Exceptions in subthreads are lost

A closer look shows the problem clearly: the invoke() method starts only the service thread. Exceptions occurring in this thread are not passed to the original thread.

Luckily, there is a helper class to solve this problem, too: utmj.threaded. ExceptionAssert. This helper class allows us to check for uncaught runtime exceptions in split-off threads; all others have to be caught eventually. The use of this class is similar to RetriedAssert:

```
public void testInvocationWithIllegalNumber() throws Exception {
    int[] numbers = new int[] { 1, 1001, 3 };
    final SumUpService service = new SumUpService(numbers);
    new utmj.threaded.ExceptionAssert(
        IllegalArgumentException.class, 2000) {
        public void run() {
            service.invoke();
        }
    }.start();
}
```

We pass the expected exception type as constructor parameter, including the maximum wait time. The test fails when this wait time has elapsed before this exception has occurred somewhere.

Unexpected Exceptions

We learned in the previous section how expected exceptions in split-off threads can be verified. But what about unexpected runtime exceptions?

In "normal" operation, each uncaught exception leads to a test error. Normally, we would also like to have this behavior for multi-threaded programs. And again, the utmj.threaded package offers us an appropriate test decorator, MultiThreadedTest, we can use to decorate the corresponding test suite:

```
public class SumUpServiceTest extends TestCase {
    ...
    public static Test suite() {
        TestSuite suite = new TestSuite(SumUpServiceTest.class);
        return new utmj.threaded.MultiThreadedTest(suite);
    }
}
```

Behind the scenes, both ExceptionAssert and MultiThreadedTest use the same trick: they create a subclass of java.util.ThreadGroup, which handles uncaught runtime exceptions by overriding the method uncaughtException(Thread t, Throwable e).

10.3 Testing for Synchronization

The special thing about the objects we tested in Section 10.2 was that they created their own threads to handle specific services in the background. The situation is different with objects that do not create threads themselves, but have methods that can be invoked by different threads. Such objects have to be *thread-safe,* which means that there are synchronization mechanisms to prevent threads from bumping into one another. In addition, we have to ensure that the synchronization does not lead to deadlocks or thread starvation. Another task of synchronization may consist of having a thread wait until a specific condition is true.

Example:
BoundedCounter

Consider a simple example: BoundedCounter, a counter with limits. The counter should support incrementing, decrementing, and requesting a number of the type long. In addition, there are upper and lower count limits. As soon as the counter reaches such a limit, then a thread that would potentially exceed the limit with its invocation would be stopped until another thread finishes its reverse count operation.[5]

Simple Test Cases

Let's try to do a test-first implementation of this class. We will first use a few single-threaded test cases:

```
public class SingleThreadBoundedCounterTest extends TestCase {
    private BoundedCounter counter;
    protected void setUp() {
        counter = new BoundedCounter(0, 3);
    }
    public void testCreation() {
        BoundedCounter counter = new BoundedCounter(0, 3);
        assertEquals(0, counter.getMin());
        assertEquals(3, counter.getMax());
        assertEquals(0, counter.count());
        counter = new BoundedCounter(1, 4);
        assertEquals(1, counter.getMin());
        assertEquals(4, counter.getMax());
        assertEquals(1, counter.count());
    }
    public void testCountUpToMax() {
        counter.increment();
        assertEquals(1, counter.count());
        counter.increment();
        assertEquals(2, counter.count());
```

---

5. Lea [00] uses this example often. A more complex variant of it (i.e., the class BoundedBuffer) is included in the source code to this book.

```
        counter.increment();
        assertEquals(3, counter.count());
    }
    public void testCountDownToMin() {
        counter.increment();
        counter.increment();
        counter.increment();
        assertEquals(3, counter.count());
        counter.decrement();
        assertEquals(2, counter.count());
        counter.decrement();
        assertEquals(1, counter.count());
        counter.decrement();
        assertEquals(0, counter.count());
    }
}
```

Note that the test cases of this suite go only up to the limit of the count range. Each attempt to count beyond the limits would eventually doom the counting thread, and thus our test, to wait forever, as per specification.

Concurrent Test Cases

The following test cases require starting and coordinating several threads. In contrast to the service objects used in the previous subsection, this case offers us the benefit that no thread is created in the background. This means that we control all threads, which gives us more control over our testing.

Consider the first test case: this test should verify that a thread is suspended as soon as it attempts to increment the counter beyond its maximum value. Basically, this test needs three threads, specifically, two threads to handle the BoundedCounter instance, and another one to verify specific conditions and to keep the actions in the right order.

sleep() as a synchronization means

One option to synchronize the order of actions in several threads is to use appropriate sleep times (i.e., Thread.sleep(...)), in each of these threads. However, the drawback of this concept is that calculating the sleep times is expensive and error-prone, especially in complex scenarios. In addition, we have to select much longer times than actually needed due to the scheduler's imponderabilities, the unknown runtime of single command sequences, and the different platforms on which we might want to run the tests. Therefore using sleep() statements in tests should be avoided.

One reviewer pointed out that there is another problem with naively inserting Thread.sleep into application code since it can change the program's behavior in the presence of an InterruptedException. All sleeps should therefore use the following pattern which properly resets the internal interruption state without introducing an exception throw:

```
try {
   Thread.sleep(delay);
} catch (InterruptedException ie) {
   Thread.currentThread().interrupt();
}
```

The class Concurrent TestCase   An elegant approach to replace sleep() invocations in the tests would again be the use of Java's built-in synchronization mechanisms. A simple way to control several threads exists in the class utmj.threaded.ConcurrentTestCase for testing purposes. We will consider the test case just formulated as source code to better understand this idea:

```
import utmj.threaded.*;
public class ConcurrentBoundedCounterTest extends
   ConcurrentTestCase {
   public void testCountBeyondMax() {
      final BoundedCounter counter = new BoundedCounter(0, 2);
      Runnable runnable1 = new Runnable() {
         public void run() {
            try {
               counter.increment();
               counter.increment();
               checkpoint("before increment");
               counter.increment(); // should wait
               checkpoint("after increment");
            } catch (InterruptedException ignore) {}
         }
      };
```

```
        this.addThread("thread1", runnable1);
        this.startAndJoinThreads(200);
        assertEquals(2, counter.count());
        assertTrue("before checkpoint",
                this.checkpointReached("before increment"));
        assertFalse("after checkpoint",
                this.checkpointReached("after increment"));
        assertTrue("deadlock", this.deadlockDetected());
    }
}
```

When deriving our test cases from ConcurrentTestCase, we have a way to add test threads by naming and implementing a Runnable object. There are various methods to start all threads. The variant used here—startAndJoinThreads(long timeout)—waits for a maximum of timeout milliseconds for all threads to end. Finally, we can pass a checkpoint—checkpoint(String name)—to check whether or not they have been passed—checkpointReached(String name)—and then verify whether or not a deadlock occurred in one of the threads—deadlockDetected(). Table 10.1 gives an overview of the methods available in ConcurrentTestCase.

The second test case should verify that a thread waiting since it reached the maximum value can start incrementing again in another thread after a decrement():

```
public void testThreeUpOneDown() {
    final BoundedCounter counter = new BoundedCounter(0, 2);
    Runnable runnable1 = new Runnable() {
        public void run() {
            try {
                counter.increment();
                counter.increment();
                checkpoint("before increment");
                counter.increment(); // should wait
                checkpoint("after increment");
            } catch (InterruptedException ignore) {}
        }
    };
    Runnable runnable2 = new Runnable() {
```

Table 10.1 *Concurrent TestCase—Important methods.*

Method	Description
Methods used in the main thread:	
`protected void addThread(String name, final Runnable runnable)`	Add a thread to the test case.
`protected void startThreads()`	Start all threads of the test case.
`protected void joinAllThreads (long millisecondsToWait)`	Wait (maximum `millisecondsToWait`) for all threads to end.
`protected void startAndJoinThreads (long millisecondsToDeadlock)`	Start all threads and wait for them to end.
`public boolean deadlockDetected()`	Determine whether at least one thread has not ended within the wait time of a join.
Methods used in an arbitrary thread:	
`public void synchronized checkpoint(String checkpointName)`	Pass a checkpoint.
`public boolean checkpointReached (String checkpointName)`	Determine whether a checkpoint was already passed.
`public synchronized void waitForCheckpoint (String checkpointName)`	Wait till a checkpoint is passed in another thread.
`public boolean hasThreadStarted (String threadName)`	Determine whether a specific thread was already started.
`public boolean hasThreadFinished (String threadName)`	Determine whether a specific thread has already ended regularly.
`public synchronized void waitUntilFinished(String threadName)`	Wait for the regular end of a specific thread.
`public void sleep(long milliseconds)`	Sleep and don't throw an `InterruptedException`.

```
        public void run() {
          try {
            waitForCheckpoint("before increment");
            sleep(50); // (1)
            counter.decrement();
          } catch (InterruptedException ignore) {}
        }
      };
      this.addThread("thread1", runnable1);
      this.addThread("thread2", runnable2);
      this.startAndJoinThreads(200);
      assertEquals(2, counter.count());
      assertTrue("after checkpoint",
        this.checkpointReached("after increment"));
      assertFalse("no deadlock", this.deadlockDetected());
}
```

We can see another possibility for synchronization in the runnable2 object, namely, waitForCheckpoint(String name) waits till another thread has passed a specific checkpoint. And yet, we cannot do without sleep(...) in this case either. Although we know from point (1) in thread2 that thread1 has left the checkpoint behind, we want to additionally make sure it has already sent the third increment() message. Unless we manipulate the BoundedCounter class, the only thing that can help us here is pseudodeterminism, by adding sleep calls.

Once we have added two appropriate test cases for the minimum value, the implementation of BoundedCounter looks like this:

```
public class BoundedCounter {
  ...
  public BoundedCounter(long min, long max) {...}
  public long getMin() {...}
  public long getMax() {...}
  public long count() {return count;}

  public synchronized void increment()
    throws InterruptedException {
    while (count == max) {
      this.wait();
```

```
        }
        count++;
        this.notify();
    }

    public synchronized void decrement()
        throws InterruptedException {
        while (count == min) {
            this.wait();
        }
        count--;
        this.notify();
    }
}
```

The class seems to be working well and, indeed, we managed to infiltrate synchronization and thread mechanisms into the program thanks to our test-first effort. But careful, there are still a few pitfalls.

Nondeterministic Test Cases

Experienced thread programmers can make out the flaws in the preceding implementation quickly: First, the notify() in decrement() and increment() can cause problems when more than two threads are working. It should be replaced by notifyAll() in both cases. Second, the method count() should be synchronized, because access to a variable of the type long may not be atomic. Is it possible now to find test cases that identify these two problematic implementations?

First, let's deal with the notify problem. For the problem to be noticed, at least one thread has to be waiting till it gets a chance to increment the counter and another one to decrement the counter. The following test attempts to bring this situation about in a 10 to 1 ratio:

```
public class NonDeterministicBoundedCounterTest
            extends ConcurrentTestCase {
    ...
    public void test10Inc1Dec() {
        final BoundedCounter counter = new BoundedCounter(0, 1);
        Runnable incRunnable = new Runnable() {
```

```
public void run() {
    try {
        counter.increment();
    } catch (InterruptedException ignore) {}
    }
};
Runnable decRunnable = new Runnable() {
    public void run() {
        try {
            for (int i = 0; i < 10; i++) {
                counter.decrement();
            }
        } catch (InterruptedException ignore) {}
    }
};
this.addThread("dec", decRunnable);
for (int i = 0; i < 10; i++) {
    this.addThread("inc-" + i, incRunnable);
}
this.startThreads();
this.joinAllThreads(1000);
assertTrue("deadlock", !this.deadlockDetected());
assertEquals(0, counter.count());
    }
}
```

Initially, the bar remains green while the test case is running. But when we repeatedly click Run, we get a failure now and then: junit.framework. AssertionFailedError: deadlock. What happened?

Considering that notify() brings only one single thread back to life, we can wake up a thread with continuation conditions that have not been met yet, depending on our luck and the scheduler's state. However, the outcome of the test is not predictable for each individual case. To provoke a failure with high probability, we have to run the test suite several times; 10 repetitions will do in this case:[6]

---

6. This number can fluctuate strongly, depending on JVM and computer equipment.

```
public class NonDeterministicBoundedCounterTest
      extends ConcurrentTestCase {
   ...

   public static Test suite() {
      TestSuite suite = new TestSuite(
            NonDeterministicBoundedCounterTest.class);
      return new junit.extensions.RepeatedTest(suite, 10);
   }
}
```

Now, the faulty test suite forces us to correct the class BoundedCounter:

```
public class BoundedCounter {
   ...

   public synchronized void increment()
      throws InterruptedException {
      while (count == max) {
         this.wait();
      }
      count++;
      this.notifyAll();
   }

   public synchronized void decrement()
      throws InterruptedException {
      while (count == min) {
         this.wait();
      }
      count--;
      this.notifyAll();
   }
}
```

A similar attempt to force synchronization of the count() method over a repeated nondeterministic test fails.[7] The reasons can be manifold: access to a long variable need not be atomic, according to the Java specification, but it can be, and in fact it is atomic on most processors and JVMs.

---

7. The source code for the test method testCount() is available from the book's Web site.

The problem could also occur when several processors are used, depending on the computer architecture and the operating system. In any event, I was not able to write a test that led to a faulty behavior of the method count(), even repeating it thousands of times. Nevertheless, most developers would probably make the following change:

```
public class BoundedCounter {
    public synchronized long count() {return count;}
}
```

10.4 Summary

This chapter showed how and to what limits the test-first approach can be used to develop multi-threaded programs. The normal behavior of asynchronous services and synchronization objects can be tested if the developers know the required patterns. This testing work is facilitated by specialized classes, like those included in the package utmj.threaded.

In contrast, testing for problems that occur only sporadically (e.g., deadlocks and poor synchronization) is difficult due to the inherent non-determinism. We managed to create a single test case that contributed to removing a faulty notify call. Nevertheless, we suspect that this was possible only because we identified the problem to be a standard error *in advance.*

However, the problem with these tests is not that they cannot discover all concurrency errors. What test is infallible? The problem is rather that these tests are (necessarily) based on many assumptions so they may lead us to believe we are on the safe side. A concrete JVM implementation variant can then demonstrate the absurdity of this false sense of security.

As bitter as it may be for the thoroughbred tester, many other things can often contribute more than expensive unit test suites to avoid concurrency errors:

- Studying the literature on concurrency and thread programming in Java [Lea00, Hyde99].

- Selecting the simplest thread model that will be sufficient for the specific case. More careful considerations often show that concurrency can be avoided.

- Isolating concurrency and synchronization in a few classes and methods, with frequent reviewing of these classes.

- Using multi-thread utility classes, for example, the package util.concurrent (see [URL:UtilConcurrent] and [Lea00]).

- Having all concurrency-related code reviewed by a concurrency expert.

- If you really want be as sure as possible that your chosen approach towards synchronization and multi-threading has no leaks or hidden pitfalls, there is no way around strict modeling with formal methods like Petri nets, temporal logic, finite state machines, and the like.[8]

Depending on the application, synchronization problems can also be discovered in extensive load tests, randomized insertions of Thread.sleep() and Thread.yield(), or by use of thread analysis tools (e.g. Sitraka's Threadalyzer [URL:Threadalyzer]). In addition, running these tests on multiprocessors (MPs) is often a quicker way to detect synchronization problems because MPs generate more thread interleavings. Some memory-model-based errors can only be seen on multiprocessor machines.[9]

The ConTest project An innovative and interesting path towards detecting race conditions, deadlocks, and other intermittent bugs in multi-threaded Java programs has been followed by IBM's research project *ConTest* [URL:ConTest]. Quoting from the Web site:

> ConTest transforms a Java program into a program that should behave in the same way but is more likely to exhibit concurrent bugs such as race conditions and deadlocks. This seemingly strange behavior is useful because finding bugs in the transformed application is easier. Every bug found in the transformed application is a bug in the original program. . . . You can just rerun your original tests but you are now more likely to find bugs. Contest . . . alleviates the need to create a complex testing environment with many processors and applications, and works by instrumenting the bytecode of the application with heuristically controlled conditional sleep and yield instructions.

---

8. A thorough summary of those techniques can be found in [Gomaa93].
9. See [Lea00], section 2.2 for a discussion of these issues.

Chapter 11

Distributed Applications

Distributed systems take concurrent applications a step further. The single components of an application not only run concurrently—they are also located in different places. Boger [01] defines distribution as follows:

What is distribution?

Distribution is the logical or physical spatial distance of objects in relation to each other. Two objects that cannot use the regular method invocation to communicate, but have to use mechanisms of the remote communication, are distributed in relation to each other. This is the case when they reside on different computers . . . but also when they reside in different address spaces on the same computer . . . .

Problems of distribution

In addition to the problems relating to concurrency (see Chapter 10), distributed systems introduce further requirements and problems. From a tester's perspective, the following are most important:

- *Finding other objects* **in the network (e.g., by using a "name service" that allows us to register objects under unique names).** In the testing context, this means that a client's behavior has to be considered even when the server object cannot be found.

- *Insecure communication.* The sender of a message has to be prepared that something may go wrong when sending the message or receiving a reply. Consequently, we should try to prevent the sending object from being able to take an undefined state or, more seriously, prevent deadlocks from occurring.

Transparency of
distribution

The theoretical objective here is to distribute objects as transparently as possible. This means that the actual location and invocation mechanism of a remote object should be hidden from the caller. In practice, however, distribution requires the explicit handling of potential communication problems. And other properties of local systems (e.g., automatic *garbage collection*) can reach their limits. For this reason, real transparency can only be achieved if local objects are treated like remote objects. Naturally, the significantly higher effort this involves is found to be a burden in most cases.

Distribution Mechanisms in Java

As a young programming language conceived for use in networked environments from the outset, Java offers more options to realize distributed applications. After all, distribution means that bits and bytes are moved from one process to another over a network. This communication can be implemented in various abstraction layers:

- From the Java perspective, the bottom layer is represented by **sockets**. A socket allows you to transmit uninterpreted data streams from one computer to another. All others build on this mechanism. Java's java.net package offers the infrastructure required for direct use of sockets.

- From the programmer's perspective, another abstraction is more suitable: sending messages to remote objects. This mechanism is called *Remote Method Invocation (RMI)* and is included in Java's java.rmi package. However, RMI is limited to Java[1] and you have to know the location of a remote object or the registry's location.

- Another way to abstract an object's location and the implementation language is *Common Object Request Broker Architecture (CORBA)*. CORBA offers standardized interfaces to most programming languages and a large number of services for object management, searching, authentication, and more.

- However, CORBA has lost a lot of its attractiveness since Sun introduced the Java-proprietary *Enterprise JavaBean (EJB)* standard. In

---

1. Well, not quite, because an RMI connection for IBM's VisualAge **for Smalltalk** is available.

addition to plain distribution, the EJB specification includes its own component model and considers other aspects like persistence, transactions, security, and scalability.

■ The *Jini (Java Intelligent Networking Infrastructure)* represents an infrastructure to provide, register, and find distributed services based on its specification [URL:Jini]. One integral part of Jini is *JavaSpaces,* a mechanism that supports distribution, persistence, and migration of objects in a network [Boger01].

RMI and EJBs are interesting representatives of their kind, thanks to their high abstraction level and their specialization for Java. For this reason, we will discuss below what unit testing can look like in the RMI and EJB environments. To follow the rest of this chapter you should know at least the basics of these technologies.[2]

11.1 RMI

RMI consists basically of two parts: an interface to address remote objects and an implementation of this interface. To deploy this implementation, JDK offers some additional helper classes, a tool to create local *stub objects* (rmic), and a name service to register objects (rmiregistry). The following discussion assumes a basic knowledge of RMI, found in the literature [Darwin01].

The following subsections show how to test-first develop a simple RMI server and the pertaining client.

The Server

The interface of our example server is very simple:

```
public interface MyRemoteServer {
    String callService();
}
```

---

2. There is plenty of introductory material on the Web, including online tutorials for both RMI [URL:RMITutorial] and EJB [URL:EJBTutorial].

For now, everything runs locally, so we write the first test without anticipating any remote invocation:

```
public class MyRemoteServerTest extends TestCase {
    public void testCallService() {
        MyRemoteServer server = new MyRemoteServerImpl();
        assertEquals("OK", server.callService());
    }
}
```

Interface instead of static methods

The next steps try to push toward a soft transition to a distributed system. First, we will deal with one of RMI's testability shortcomings—the static naming interface. We move the part of the interface we are interested in from java.rmi.Naming to an interface:

```
import java.rmi.*;
import java.net.*;
public interface MyNaming {
    void rebind(String name, Remote obj)
        throws RemoteException, MalformedURLException;
    void unbind(String name) throws RemoteException,
        NotBoundException, MalformedURLException;
}
```

And for now, we offer a mock implementation instead:[3]

```
import java.rmi.*;
public class MockNaming implements MyNaming {
    public void rebind(String name, Remote obj) {...}
    public void unbind(String name) {...}
    public void expectRebind(String name, Class remoteType) {...}
    public void expectUnbind(String name) {...}
    public void verify() {...}
}
```

Back to the server. To be able to address the server remotely, we have to adapt its interface to the RMI practices and define a name for the RMI binding:

---

3. This implementation is available at the Web site to this book.

```
import java.rmi.*;
public interface MyRemoteServer extends Remote {
    String LOOKUP_NAME = "MyRemoteServer";
    String callService() throws RemoteException;
}
```

We are now ready to rebuild the testing method, taking the new interface, MyNaming, into account. In this context, we also have to bear in mind that a static method should be used to start the server; we call it create-Server() in this example:

```
public void testCallService() throws Exception {
    MockNaming mockNaming = new MockNaming();
    MyRemoteServer server =
        MyRemoteServerImpl.createServer(mockNaming);
    assertEquals("OK", server.callService());
    mockNaming.verify();
}
```

So far, the Naming object is passed as parameter, but not used yet. So let's extend our test:

```
public void testCallService() throws Exception {
    MockNaming mockNaming = new MockNaming();
    mockNaming.expectRebind(
        MyRemoteServer.LOOKUP_NAME, MyRemoteServerImpl.class);
    MyRemoteServer server =
        MyRemoteServerImpl.createServer(mockNaming);
    assertEquals("OK", server.callService());
    mockNaming.verify();
}
```

Next, we add a test that checks for correct release of the server, while doing a refactoring at the same time:

```
public class MyRemoteServerTest extends TestCase {

    private MyRemoteServer server;
    private MockNaming mockNaming;
```

```
    protected void setUp() throws Exception {
        mockNaming = new MockNaming();
    }

    public void testCallService() throws Exception {
        mockNaming.expectRebind(MyRemoteServer.LOOKUP_NAME,
            MyRemoteServerImpl.class);
        server = MyRemoteServerImpl.createServer(mockNaming);
        assertEquals("OK", server.callService());
        mockNaming.verify();
    }

    public void testReleaseService() throws Exception {
        mockNaming.expectRebind(MyRemoteServer.LOOKUP_NAME,
            MyRemoteServerImpl.class);
        mockNaming.expectUnbind(MyRemoteServer.LOOKUP_NAME);
        server = MyRemoteServerImpl.createServer(mockNaming);
        ((MyRemoteServerImpl) server).release();
        mockNaming.verify();
    }
}
```

What's missing? A test with the real RMI. Let's first consider the MyNaming implementation by use of java.rmi.Naming:

```
import java.rmi.*;
import java.net.*;
public class RMINaming implements MyNaming {

    public void rebind(String name, Remote obj)
        throws RemoteException, MalformedURLException {
        Naming.rebind(name, obj);
    }

    public void unbind(String name) throws RemoteException,
        NotBoundException, MalformedURLException {
        Naming.unbind(name);
    }
}
```

And here is the test case for use of RMI:

```
public void testRealService() throws Exception {
   RMINaming naming = new RMINaming();
   server = MyRemoteServerImpl.createServer(naming);
   MyRemoteServer client = (MyRemoteServer) Naming.lookup(
      MyRemoteServer.LOOKUP_NAME);
   assertEquals("OK", client.callService());
   ((MyRemoteServerImpl) server).release();
}
```

The following implementation resulted from the three test cases just implemented:

```
import java.net.*;
import java.rmi.*;
import java.rmi.server.*;
public class MyRemoteServerImpl extends UnicastRemoteObject
implements MyRemoteServer {
   private MyNaming naming;

   private MyRemoteServerImpl(MyNaming naming)
      throws RemoteException {
      super();
      this.naming = naming;
   }

   public String callService() {
      return "OK";
   }

   public static MyRemoteServer createServer(MyNaming naming)
      throws RemoteException, MalformedURLException {
      MyRemoteServer server = new MyRemoteServerImpl(naming);
      naming.rebind(LOOKUP_NAME, server);
      return server;
   }

   public void release() throws RemoteException,
      NotBoundException, MalformedURLException {
```

```
                    naming.unbind(LOOKUP_NAME);
                }
            }
```

RMI deployment   To give the test suite a chance, two things must be in place: the corresponding stub for MyRemoteServerImpl must have been created (e.g., by using rmic), and the RMI registry must be running (e.g., by starting it with rmiregistry from the command line). The attentive reader will now be able to easily imagine how MockNaming can be extended to test for the expected behavior of the createServer() method in case of errors.

The Client

Testing the "remote client" involves two tasks:

- First, we test to see whether or not the client uses the name service correctly to find the remote server instance.

- Second, we test for correct use of the remote server objects, similar to the approach used for local objects.

To complete the first task, we add a lookup() method to the interface MyNaming introduced above:

```
import java.rmi.*;
import java.net.*;
public interface MyNaming {

    ...

    Remote lookup(String name) throws NotBoundException,
        MalformedURLException, RemoteException;
}
```

Then we expand MockNaming accordingly:

```
import java.rmi.*;
public class MockNaming implements MyNaming {

    ...
```

```
    public void expectLookup(String name, Remote lookup) {...}
    public Remote lookup(String name) {...}
}
```

With this extended material on hand, we can now proceed with the first test for the client:

```
public class MyRemoteClientTest extends TestCase {

    public void testLookup() throws Exception {
        MyRemoteServer remote = new MyRemoteServer() {
            public String callService() {
                return "";
            }
        };
        MockNaming namingClient = new MockNaming();
        namingClient.expectLookup(
            MyRemoteServer.LOOKUP_NAME, remote);
        MyRemoteClient client = new MyRemoteClient(namingClient);
        namingClient.verify();
    }
}
```

As a substitutional stub object, the test uses an anonymous instance of the MyRemoteServer interface. This technique can also be used to test the actual client behavior. The example below tests a simple callTwice() method, and includes refactoring of the test class:

```
public class MyRemoteClientTest extends TestCase {

    private MockNaming naming;
    protected void setUp() {
        naming = new MockNaming();
    }

    public void testLookup() throws Exception {...}

    public void testCallTwice() throws Exception {
        MyRemoteServer remote1 = this.createRemoteServer("Test");
```

```
        naming.expectLookup(
            MyRemoteServer.LOOKUP_NAME, remote1);
        MyRemoteClient client1 = new MyRemoteClient(naming);
        assertEquals("TestTest", client1.callTwice());
        MyRemoteServer remote2 = this.createRemoteServer("Xyz");
        naming.expectLookup(
            MyRemoteServer.LOOKUP_NAME, remote2);
        MyRemoteClient client2 = new MyRemoteClient(naming);
        assertEquals("XyzXyz", client2.callTwice());
    }

    private MyRemoteServer createRemoteServer(
            final String returnString) {
        return new MyRemoteServer() {
            public String callService() {
                return returnString;
            }
        };
    }
}
```

Note that two different servers are used here to avoid a trivial implementation of the client class. Of course, we could use a mock implementation for MyRemoteServer as an alternative to anonymous internal instances. Such a mock class could nicely use all of its strengths when we also want to test for error handling or to extend the interface.

Testing the error handling mechanism

Other tests have to deal with the client's behavior in the event of distribution problems. The following piece of code is an example, in that the client's reaction in case the server object is not registered:

```
public void testFailingLookup() throws Exception {
    naming.expectLookupThrowException(
    MyRemoteServer.LOOKUP_NAME, new NotBoundException("test"));
    try {
        MyRemoteClient client = new MyRemoteClient(naming);
        fail("NotBoundException expected");
    } catch (NotBoundException expected) {}
}
```

Suppose we had to deal with the simplest possible error handling mechanism in this case: NotBoundException is passed to the caller. For this test case, we had to extend the class MockNaming by the method expect-LookupThrowException(...). Similarly, we can test the client's behavior in the event the connection is interrupted. For this purpose, the server dummy must throw a RemoteException when callService() is invoked.

Testing with a real server

Finally, we want to test the client's interaction with a real server object:

```
public void testWithRealServer() throws Exception {
    MyNaming naming = new RMINaming();
    MyRemoteServer server = MyRemoteServerImpl.createServer(naming);
    MyRemoteClient client = new MyRemoteClient(naming);
    assertEquals("OKOK", client.callTwice());
    ((MyRemoteServerImpl) server).release();
}
```

Similar to the server test suite, this test case requires that the stubs for MyRemoteServer have been created and an RMI registry has been started.

Summary of RMI

Let's take a close look at what we actually ensured with our previous test cases. The following aspects were tested:

- Implementation of the callService() method in MyRemoteServerImpl.
- Implementation of callTwice() in MyRemoteClient.
- Correct registration of MyRemoteServerImpl instances in and release from the RMI registry.
- Correct use of lookup() in MyRemoteClient.
- Basic ability to address the class MyRemoteServerImpl over RMI.
- Basic ability of MyRemoteClient instances to cooperate with RMI stubs.

Deployment problems

However, our tests *do not cover deployment problems* in the network, including registry availability, avoiding name conflicts, setting the correct security manager, publishing stub classes on the Web, and many other aspects. These things should be covered in acceptance tests or specialized deployment tests. Note that the RMI invocation within the same JVM is sufficient for unit tests.

Concurrency problems

Another thing our previous example does not consider is test cases dealing with potential concurrency of remote method invocations. The good news is that this aspect is basically similar to the concurrency in local multi-thread applications (see Chapter 10). This is because the actual synchronization happens between the client and the server stub, or between the client skeleton and the server implementation, residing in the same address space.

11.2 | Enterprise JavaBeans

EJBs are Java components running in an *EJB container*. This container is responsible for the lifespan of the components and for transactional behavior, persistence, load distribution, and security. A good introduction to programming with EJBs has been done by Monson-Haefel [Monson01].

Problems when testing EJBs

Test-first development in micro-iterations works best when the unit tests are running in an isolated and fast way. But how are we supposed to run the test suite every 10 minutes or so, when the deployment of an EJB component can take several minutes? And how can we isolate a component's test when the behavior of this component depends on specific configurations in the *deployment descriptor*? The problems occurring in EJB testing are similar to those in testing persistent objects (see Chapter 9), only worse by one order of magnitude. What we find here is strong state-dependent behavior and inextricable dependencies on the configuration of the application server used. In addition, the deployment of the components takes too much time.

Using mocks for EJBs?

Considering all of the above, it doesn't come as a surprise that the attempt to replace an EJB container, or its interfaces, respectively, by dummy or mock objects for unit testing is doomed to fail.[4] The behavior of a container influences so many aspects that the effort involved in developing suitable dummies comes very close to developing a real container. In addition, the deployment descriptor of an EJB has a major impact on that EJB's behavior. For these reasons, we also have to simulate the deployment.

---

4. Unsuccessful attempts are frequently reported at [URL:YahooJUnit].

The above scenario suggests that EJBs should best be tested in the context of an EJB container (i.e., an application server). This means that all who hoped to find a simple solution for fast and isolated EJB unit testing in this chapter will be disappointed.

Just a Facade

Fortunately, the situation is not hopeless. We can at least reduce the number of necessary container tests to a minimum. To this end, instead of implementing the actual application logic directly in EJBs, we use a lower layer. The beans serve only as a *facade* of the actual business logic.

Generated EJBs Although it is not always possible, we can design our enterprise beans so that they directly map the business objects. This gives us a way to generate EJBs from these business objects. In this case, we have to test *only* the generator, but not the beans themselves. Whether or not programming a generator represents the simplest solution depends on the number of EJBs we have to create.

The Box Metaphor Peeters [01] includes a more detailed discussion of this approach. The Box Metaphor describes a set of rules on how EJBs as plain technology representatives can be separated from the core of an application. More specifically, each box consists of a vertical cross section of the actual business logic. To the outside, the box represents itself only by the interface of a facade. This interface (i.e., the EJB container in our case) has to be fully independent of the specific technology. The EJBs themselves represent the implementation of this facade. They are very simple, because they normally do nothing but delegate. If there are dependencies to entity beans, then these entity beans can usually be replaced by dummy implementations with little effort, because they are bare placeholders for data.[5]

Bipolar EJBs One expansion to this approach consists in implementing *bipolar* Enterprise JavaBeans [Peeters01]. A bipolar EJB is an EJB that can be instantiated as a local object. "Clients" of the facade do not have to know whether an instance lives locally or in the container. This is achieved by defining the EJB's *remote interface* as an extension to the facade interface. At runtime, a factory object selects the EJB form, which can be either local or remote. In this case, too, a generator can significantly reduce the effort involved in

---

5. Provided you stick to SUN's J2EE application patterns.

programming the two EJB forms. A similar direction is also taken by the *local interfaces* defined in the EJB 2.0 specification [URL:EJB].[6]

Testing Inside the Container

Nygard and Karsjens [Nygard00] describe how EJBs can be tested inside the container. They recommend creating the InitialContext object and the home instances used in the setUp() method. The beans are then no longer instantiated in the test itself, but rather in their own factory methods. Schematically, an EJB test class could then look like this:

```
public class MyEjbTest extends Testcase {
    private MyEjbHome home;

    protected void setUp() throws Exception {
        Context initial = new Initialcontext();
        Object homeRef = initial.lookup("MyEjb");
        home = (MyEjbHome) PortableRemoteObject.narrow(
            homeRef, MyEjbHome.class);
    }

    private MyEjb createMyEjb(String par) throws RemoteException{
        return home.create(par);
    }

    public void testXXXX() throws Exception {
        MyEjb ejb = this.createMyEjb("test");
        // testing code
    }
}
```

Testing in the server context　　There are times when test cases need the environment of the application server. In these cases, we cannot test from a remote client; we have to test within the server. Nygard [00] introduces a test runner servlet specifically for this purpose. This servlet runs on the application server and can

---

6. At the time of this book's writing, the final release of the EJB 2.0 specification has been available for only a couple of months; 2.0-compliant application servers have reached the market only recently.

trigger arbitrary test suites in the server.[7] An alternative is the use of Cactus [URL:Cactus], which also allows you to run unit tests from an application server. We will learn more about Cactus in the context of Web applications in Chapter 12, Web Applications.

EJB testing during the build process

In view of the fact that the problems we've discussed can turn the execution of EJB tests into a time-consuming venture, it might be a good idea to run these tests mainly during the build phase of your project. In addition, it would then also be desirable to deploy the EJBs not only on one single application server, but to test for the EJBs' interaction with all targeted application servers at the same time. This task is a good target for combining JUnit and Ant—a make tool written in Java [URL:Ant].

EJBs and Simple Design

EJBs are "hip." It is not unusual in current software projects that a customer's only specific idea of the software under development is to absolutely use EJBs. If this strategic reason is not given, then it is worth thinking twice about the necessity of a heavy technology like Enterprise JavaBeans.

EJBs and the "simplest possible" principle

From the perspective of an evolutionary development and design strategy, committing to EJBs at the beginning of a project is seldom justified. Vera Peeters [01] writes this:

> Using EJB is definitely not the simplest thing to do. So how do EJBs fit with ... the "Do The Simplest Thing That Could Possibly Work" principle? Well, to be honest, I think they don't. If you start developing a new system, chances aren't very high that you have a good reason to start using EJBs.

After a few iteration cycles, it may well be possible that some of the complex properties inherent in EJBs are really a good thing to have.[8] Before we are sure that this is so, however, we should spare ourselves the stress of deployment, additional complexity, and unavoidable test complications. Design principles like the Box Metaphor just introduced make it easier for us to take a specific technology to an independent level. I recommend this approach also for the introduction of all other technologies and

---

7. This also corresponds to the approach chosen by JUnitEE [URL:JUnitEE].
8. Look at the work of Maier [01] to see how EJB features are weighed against actual project requirements.

frameworks that don't make us confident about their benefits from the very beginning of a project.

Another reason one might be inclined to include EJBs in a test-first development project arises when using existing code. But here, too, extracting the technology from the domain code into a layer of its own may allow us to migrate from EJB to simpler means later.

11.3 Summary

This chapter discussed the use of unit tests in the development of distributed systems. The problems in distributed systems relate mainly to finding remote objects and properly handling connection errors, at least from the tester's perspective. We described RMI and EJB as they are currently the most popular Java distribution mechanisms.

In the case of RMI, a universal test-first development is possible by use of mock objects. However, deployment problems are hard to cover in local unit tests, so they have to be dealt with in additional deployment tests.

The use of EJB forces us to test the actual beans inside the EJB container. This approach involves an intermediate deployment process, slowing down the test cycle considerably. This problem can be reduced by moving the business logic to a separate layer. In addition, the introduction of this technology should be delayed until it becomes an imminent requirement in each specific case.

Chapter 12

Web Applications

The World Wide Web is the largest distributed application in the world. Currently, however, nonstandardized and inflexible HTML interfaces are the main technique used to access the wealth of components—Web sites—out there. Although these interfaces are relatively easy to use for humans, they are not suitable for building complex applications. One of the current efforts to improve this situation are so-called *Web services*. Web services are aimed at establishing a uniform infrastructure for the description and registration of Web-based services and for providing access to these components.

Web applications with Java

However, the big challenge in the development of a Web application is still the building and integration of local components, where *local* means "belonging to a single Web provider." There are currently many frameworks and libraries devised to make it easier for Java programmers to develop Web applications. For example, the large Apache[1] project *Jakarta* [URL:Jakarta] includes many small projects, considering the wide range of aspects involved in Web programming. The technical basis for all kinds of different efforts are still primarily *servlets* and *Java Server Pages (JSPs)*. Hunter and Crawford [01] and Pekowsky [00] provide two examples of textbooks introducing these technologies.

How this chapter is organized

The fact that, similarly to EJBs, servlets require the context of a server makes testing on unit level a costly venture. Fortunately, the servlet API is much more transparent and easier to isolate. This chapter attempts to

---

1. The Apache Software Foundation hosts and drives a lot of open source projects. It's best known for the Apache Web Server.

discuss testing in reverse order: we will first describe functional testing, then discuss interaction tests, and finally try a fine-grained test-first approach.

<table>
<tr><td>12.1</td></tr>
</table>

12.1 Functional Tests

The most intuitive way to test Web applications is to open your Web browser, type in the URL you want to visit, and then click off and verify that the application behaves as expected. This has nothing to do with automation, but still. . . . The next step is to use a specialized capture and replay tool that remembers your mouse movements, clicks, and keyboard hits during the first run to then automatically replay them. There is a wide choice of such tools on the market.

HttpUnit Similar options are supported (but directly in Java) by *HttpUnit*. In contrast to what the name suggests, HttpUnit has little to do with unit testing. HttpUnit is an open source Java API for accessing Web sites without a browser and is ideally suited for automated unit testing of Web sites when combined with a Java unit testing framework such as JUnit. HttpUnit, including extensive documentation, is free and can be downloaded from [URL:HttpUnit]. We can use this functionality for "remote controlling" arbitrary Web applications, but also to test these applications.

The following simple example shows how HttpUnit can be used for testing. Typically, functional tests are retrospective (as opposed to test-first); so we begin with the following simple servlet that is to be tested later:

```
import java.io.*;
import javax.servlet.http.*;
public class MyServlet extends HttpServlet {

    public void doGet(HttpServletRequest request,
                    HttpServletResponse response) {
        doPost(request, response);
    }

    public void doPost(HttpServletRequest request,
                    HttpServletResponse response) {

        try {
```

```
            String name = (String) request.getParameter("name");
            PrintWriter writer = response.getWriter();
            writer.println("<html><head><title>My Servlet" +
                            "</title></head>" +
                            "<body>Hello, " + name +
                            "!</body></html>");
            writer.close();
        } catch (Throwable ex) {
            ex.printStackTrace();
        }

    }
}
```

All this servlet does is insert the passed parameter name into a reply
page, Hello, <name>!. We test for simple access to the servlet, using an
HTTP GET request to a URL (e.g., http://servername/servlet/MyServlet?
name=Johannes):

```
import com.meterware.httpunit.*;
public class MyServletTest extends TestCase {
    private final String SERVLET_URI =
        "http://myserver/servlet/MyServlet";

    public void testGetRequest() throws Exception {
        WebConversation con = new WebConversation();
        WebRequest request = new GetMethodWebRequest(SERVLET_URI);
        request.setParameter("name", "Johannes");
        WebResponse response = con.getResponse(request);
        assertEquals("text/html", response.getContentType());
    }
}
```

Approach   The starting point is an instance of WebConversation, comparable to a
browser session. This object returns an instance of class WebResponse
when getResponse(WebRequest) is invoked. In this example, we create an
HTTP GET request (GetMethodWebRequest) with a parameter (setParame-
ter(...)). The response object can eventually be consulted for test verification. The first step tested only the content type of the returned page.
Let's add more verification items:

```
public void testGetRequest() throws Exception {
    WebConversation con = new WebConversation();
    WebRequest request = new GetMethodWebRequest(SERVLET_URI);
    request.setParameter("name", "Johannes");
    WebResponse response = con.getResponse(request);
    assertEquals("text/html", response.getContentType());
    assertEquals("My Servlet", response.getTitle());
    assertTrue(response.getText().indexOf("Hello, Johannes!") != -1);
}
```

We can see that the class WebResponse allows us to access both single html elements—getTitle()—and the full HTML text—getText()—of the response page.

Structural tests   While verifying the HTML code soon becomes unmanageable, the targeted access to tables, forms, and links allows us to verify exactly those elements of an HTML page that are important for correct functioning of the application. We can use HttpUnit to fill in information in Web forms, follow links, and use frames, cookies, and SSL. But it does not support browser script languages like JavaScript.[2]

To understand this better, we will extend the servlet by a form that can be used to change the parameter name and resend the request:

```
public class MyServlet extends HttpServlet {
    ...
    private final String SERVLET_URI = "MyServlet";
    public void doPost(HttpServletRequest request,
                       HttpServletResponse response) {
        try {
            String name = (String) request.getParameter("name");
            PrintWriter writer = response.getWriter();
            writer.println("<html><head><title>My Servlet" +
                          "</title></head>" +
                          "<body>Hello, " + name + "!");
            writer.println("<form name=\"form1\" action=\"" +
                          SERVLET_URI + "\">");
            writer.println("<input type=text name=\"name\"" +
                          value=\"" + name + "\">");
```

---

2. But there is a special test framework for it, JsUnit [URL:JsUnit].

```
        writer.println("<input type=submit name=\"button\" +
                    value=\"Change Name\">");
        writer.println("</form></body></html>");
        writer.close();
    } catch (Throwable theException) {
        theException.printStackTrace();
    }
  }
}
```

The following test specifically accesses the form elements and its children:

```
public void testGetRequest() throws Exception {
    WebConversation con = new WebConversation();
    WebRequest request = new GetMethodWebRequest(SERVLET_URI);
    request.setParameter("name", "Johannes");
    WebResponse response = con.getResponse(request);
    ...
    WebForm form = response.getFormWithName("form1");
    assertEquals("Johannes", form.getParameterValue("name"));
    assertEquals("Change Name",
                form.getSubmitButton("button").getValue());
}
```

Figure 12.1 shows what the page now looks like in the browser.

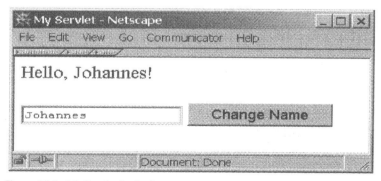

Figure 12.1 MyServlet in the browser.

Another test checks whether or not entering a new name and clicking the Change Name button works as desired:

```
public void testChangeName() throws Exception {
    WebConversation con = new WebConversation();
    WebRequest request = new GetMethodWebRequest(SERVLET_URI);
    request.setParameter("name", "Johannes");
    WebResponse response = con.getResponse(request);
    WebForm form = response.getFormWithName("form1");
    request = form.getRequest("button");
    request.setParameter("name", "Frank");
    response = con.getResponse(request);
    assertTrue(response.getText().indexOf("Hello, Frank!") != -1);
}
```

In theory, HttpUnit allows us to also verify the page layout, because we can use the method response.getDOM() to get a DOM-compliant tree representation of a page.[3] In practice, however, such detailed tests often prove to be too fragile to deserve automation.

Functional tests   To do the testing in the form shown here, we have to install the complete Web application on the server. This and the fact that we are testing only on the highest functional level shows clearly that these test cases are not unit tests, but functional tests on system level. As we proceed we will see how HttpUnit can also be used for "real" unit tests.

Project-specific test framework   There exist, meanwhile, a couple of other HttpUnit-like frameworks, for example, the Web Application Testing Framework [URL:WATF]. The drawback of using HttpUnit or a like tool as a functional testing tool is that it requires programming knowledge. As a potential alternative, we could use either a capture and replay tool or develop a project-specific framework allowing us to specify functional tests in textual form, for example, XML as in Canoo-Webtest [URL:Webtest]. This means that we could kill two birds with one stone:

- The customer or the tester can create test cases independently.

- We are totally free to define the degree of detail of the test case specification. This means that we can separate everything that will change

---

3. DOM stands for *Document Object Model* (see Glossary).

and has to be tested from what will not change so that we won't have to repeat these things in each new test case.

12.2 | Testing on the Server

To let our tests loose on single units (e.g., the servlet class itself) we need mechanisms to get hold of the parameter objects used there. The most important ones are the request (HttpServletRequest), the response (HttpServletResponse), and the configuration (ServletConfig).

Cactus   *Cactus* has been developed with the idea of automatic testing in mind; it offers a packaged and simple mechanism to automate server-side testing. Cactus is part of Apache's Jakarta project and extends JUnit by the ability to interface to servlet and JSP requests for a Web server. This means that we can manipulate the request object before a request and study the response object after the request's processing. Cactus can be downloaded from [URL:Cactus], including full documentation and installation instructions.

Let's see the basic approach by our above servlet example. Note that Cactus test cases run both on the client and the server. This particular kind of split personality is shown in Figure 12.2 and works like this:

- One part of the test case runs on the server; as usual, it is located in the testXXX() method.

- Another part of the test runs on the client; it is specified in the methods beginXXX(WebRequest theRequest) or endXXX(WebResponse theResponse).

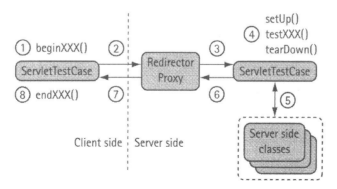

Figure 12.2   Test case running in Cactus.

- The client and the server communicate over a proxy servlet or a proxy JSP, respectively, which catches the invocations and starts the test case.

A translation of the above testGetRequest() test case for Cactus (in Version 2.3) looks like this:

```
import org.apache.cactus.*;
public class MyServletCactusTest extends ServletTestCase {
    public MyServletCactusTest(String name) {...}

    public void beginGetRequest(WebRequest theRequest) {
        theRequest.addParameter("name", "Johannes");
    }

    public void testGetRequest() throws Exception {
        MyServlet servlet = new MyServlet();
        servlet.init(config);
        servlet.doGet(request, response);
    }

    public void endGetRequest(WebResponse response) {
        java.net.HttpURLConnection connection =
            theResponse.getConnection();
        assertEquals("text/html", connection.getContentType());
        assertTrue(response.getText().indexOf("Hello,
            Johannes!") != -1);
    }
}
```

The principle of a Cactus test case   The principle is as follows: First, the method beginGetRequest() is executed on the client. The request object can be prepared in this method (e.g., by setting a parameter). The request is then sent to the server, where it is intercepted by a proxy. This proxy causes the method testGet-Request() to be invoked, where the servlet is instantiated, initialized, and doGet() is invoked. In our earlier example, we could also test for the session state. Once the response is returned to the client, the endGetRequest() method is invoked on the client; it has access to the response object and HttpURLConnection.

The WebResponse class of Cactus does not offer the same comfort as the WebResponse class of HttpUnit to check the returned page for correct structure. But we can use the HttpURLConnection object to instantiate an Http-Unit WebResponse so that there is a rudimentary way to integrate Cactus and HttpUnit:

```
public void endGetRequest(WebResponse response) throws Exception {
    java.net.HttpURLConnection connection =
        response.getConnection();
    com.meterware.httpunit.WebResponse httpUnitResponse =
        com.meterware.httpunit.WebResponse.newResponse(connection);
    assertEquals("text/html",httpUnitResponse.getContentType());
    assertEquals("My Servlet", httpUnitResponse.getTitle());
    assertTrue(httpUnitResponse.getText().indexOf(
        "Hello, Johannes!") != -1);
    com.meterware.httpunit.WebForm form =
        httpUnitResponse.getFormWithName("form1");
    assertEquals("Johannes", form.getParameterValue("name"));
    assertEquals("Change Name",
                    form.getSubmitButton("button").getValue());
}
```

Cactus can do more   Note that this example does not show the full set of functions available in Cactus. For example, we can access all methods of a servlet as well as the session object, cookies, and much more. In addition, Cactus supports Java server pages and the testing of JSP tag libraries. The package includes extensive documentation and many examples.

Drawbacks   Using Cactus to test Web applications has two main drawbacks. First, the application under test has to be deployed on an application server. This is time-consuming and slows down the testing-coding-testing cycle, similar to EJBs. Second, the test granularity is not as fine as we would like it to be for test-first development, because the starting point is always a servlet (or a JSP).

Benefit   The major benefit of Cactus is that the Web component is checked for proper functioning on a real application server. Unlike HttpUnit, using Cactus means that we are no longer acting on the level of functional black-box tests, but are actually running white-box integration tests.

| 12.3 | **Testing with Dummies** |

Neither of the two test approaches discussed so far in this chapter is particularly suitable for test-first development. The dependence of servlets upon other relatively complex interfaces makes it much more difficult for us to simply get going as in the development of other objects. On the top layer, we have the interfaces HttpServletRequest, HttpServletResponse, and ServletConfig. These interfaces, in turn, point to other interfaces, namely HttpSession, ServletContext, and RequestDispatcher.[4] With a little effort we should be able to replace this handful of interfaces with dummy objects.

Let's plunge into a new example. Assume that a login servlet should meet the following specification:

- When invoked by a GET request, the servlet returns the login page in HTML form.

- Clicking the Login button on the login page causes the same servlet to be invoked by use of the HTTP POST method. Next, the name and password should be checked against a user database. If this is successful, then the user is directed to another URL; if it was unsuccessful, the user is taken back to the login page.

Testing the GET method   Let's first deal with the GET request. A first test should check whether or not the page returns correct HTML with a request to enter the password:

```
import utmj.servlet.*;
public class LoginServletTest extends TestCase {
    public void testGet() throws Exception {
        LoginServlet servlet = new LoginServlet();
        DummyServletConfig config = new DummyServletConfig();
        servlet.init(config);
        DummyHttpServletRequest request =
            new DummyHttpServletRequest();
        DummyHttpServletResponse response =
            new DummyHttpServletResponse();
        servlet.doGet(request, response);
```

---

4.   The servlet API Version 2.2 is our reference point here.

```
        DummyWebResponse webResponse = response.getWebResponse();
        assertTrue(webResponse.getText().indexOf(
            "Enter name and password to log in.") != -1);
        servlet.destroy();
    }
}
```

`utmj.servlet`
To simulate the servlet environment, we use simple dummy objects from the package utmj.servlet, which can be downloaded from the companion Web site to this book.[5] Our decision in disfavor of mock objects originates from habit and is a matter of taste.[6] We can see that the behavior of a servlet engine is simulated in this way: first instantiate the servlet, then initialize it, and finally destroy it at the end of the test. The class DummyWebResponse is a specific subclass of HttpUnit's abstract WebResponse class. This is necessary because HttpUnit does not make its specific subclasses public.

We are now ready to complete our test and do a refactoring at the same time:

```
import com.meterware.httpunit.*;
import utmj.servlet.*;
public class LoginServletTest extends TestCase {
    private LoginServlet servlet;
    private DummyHttpServletRequest request;
    private DummyHttpServletResponse response;
    private String getAction(WebForm form) {...}
    private String getMethod(WebForm form) {...}

    protected void setUp() throws Exception {
        servlet = new LoginServlet();
        servlet.init(new DummyServletConfig());
        request = new DummyHttpServletRequest();
        response = new DummyHttpServletResponse();
    }
```

---

5. An approach similar to our dummy objects can be followed by using ServletUnit, a simulated servlet container which comes with HttpUnit.

6. Suitable servlet mock objects are included in the mock object package at [URL:Mock-Objects].

```
protected void tearDown() throws Exception {
    servlet.destroy();
}

public void testGet() throws Exception {
    servlet.doGet(request, response);
    DummyWebResponse webResponse = response.getWebResponse();
    assertTrue(webResponse.getText().indexOf(
        "Enter name and password to log in.") != -1);
    WebForm form = webResponse.getFormWithName("loginForm");
    assertEquals("action",
        LoginServlet.SERVLET_URI, this.getAction(form));
    assertEquals("method", "post", this.getMethod(form));
    assertEquals("name input field",
        1, form.getParameterValues("name").length);
    assertEquals("password input field",
        1, form.getParameterValues("password").length);
    assertEquals("password input type",
        "password", this.getInputType(form, "password"));
    assertNotNull("login button",
        form.getSubmitButton("loginButton"));
    }
}
```

To test the `action` and `method` attributes and the input type of the parameters, we had to write helper methods. Actually, we would expect the existence of these helper methods in HttpUnit's `WebForm` class.[7]

Testing the POST method But let's continue in our example; we will now test the POST request behavior. The user database is accessed over an interface to verify the name and password:

```
public interface UserDatabase {
    boolean verify(String name, String password);
}
```

At least two test cases are now required: (a) one with a final, and (b) one with an invalid name-password combination. First the valid combination:

---

7. Perhaps one of our readers feels like participating in the further development of Http-Unit?

```
public void testPostValidUser() throws Exception {
    UserDatabase mockDb = new UserDatabase() {
        public boolean verify(String name, String password) {
            assertEquals("myname", name);
            assertEquals("mypassword", password);
            return true;
        }
    };
    servlet.getServletContext().
        setAttribute("userDatabase", mockDb);
    request.addParameter("name", "myname");
    request.addParameter("password", "mypassword");
    servlet.doPost(request, response);
    DummyRequestDispatcher dispatcher =
        ((DummyServletContext) servlet.getServletContext()).
        getRequestDispatcher();
    assertEquals("Forward path",
        LoginServlet.FORWARD_URI, dispatcher.getPath());
    assertTrue("Forward called", dispatcher.forwardCalled());
    assertNotNull("Session created", request.getSession(false));
}
```

Notice that several things are happening here. At the beginning of the test, we build a mock object of the type UserDatabase on the fly. We then insert this database as an attribute into the servlet context. The verification at the end consists of three parts: verifying the RequestDispatcher path, invoking the forward method, and creating an HttpSession instance.

The entire dummy functionality is already included in the utmj.servlet package. On the other hand, building our own mock objects would surely be justified, because at least their basic functionality would remain the same for all servlets and could be reused.

Our second test case with an invalid password is very similar to the first one in that we also do some refactoring to remove duplicate code:

```
import utmj.servlet.*;
public class LoginServletTest extends TestCase {
    ...
```

```java
private void assertRequestDispatcher(String expectedPath) {
    DummyRequestDispatcher dispatcher =
        ((DummyServletContext) servlet.getServletContext()).
            getRequestDispatcher();
    assertEquals("Forward path",
        expectedPath, dispatcher.getPath());
    assertTrue("Forward called", dispatcher.forwardCalled());
}

private UserDatabase createMockDatabase(
    final String expectedName,
    final String expectedPassword,
    final boolean verify) {
    return new UserDatabase() {
        public boolean verify(String name, String password) {
            assertEquals(expectedName, name);
            assertEquals(expectedPassword, password);
            return verify;
        }
    };
}

private void setMockDatabase(String expectedName,
        String expectedPassword, boolean verify) {
    UserDatabase mockDb = this.createMockDatabase(
        expectedName, expectedPassword, verify);
    servlet.getServletContext().
        setAttribute("userDatabase", mockDb);
}

public void testPostUnvalidUser() throws Exception {
    this.setMockDatabase("wrongname", "wrongpassword", false);
    request.addParameter("name", "wrongname");
    request.addParameter("password", "wrongpassword");
    servlet.doPost(request, response);
    assertRequestDispatcher(LoginServlet.SERVLET_URI);
    assertNull("No session created", request.getSession(false));
}
```

```
public void testPostValidUser() throws Exception {
    this.setMockDatabase("myname", "mypassword", true);
    request.addParameter("name", "myname");
    request.addParameter("password", "mypassword");
    servlet.doPost(request, response);
    assertRequestDispatcher(LoginServlet.FORWARD_URI);
    assertNotNull("Session created", request.getSession(false));
}
}
```

Toward the end, the test case testPostUnvalidUser() verifies whether or not a forward is sent to the servlet itself and to ensure that no session instance was created. Note that the redundancy in both test methods was not entirely removed, because the author believes that this makes the test logic easier to understand.

The servlet implementation looks like the following:

```
public class LoginServlet extends HttpServlet {
    public final static String SERVLET_URI = "LoginServlet";
    public final static String FORWARD_URI = "something.jsp";

    private void forwardTo(HttpServletRequest request,
        HttpServletResponse response, String path)
            throws IOException, ServletException {
        RequestDispatcher dispatcher = this.getServletContext().
            getRequestDispatcher(path);
        dispatcher.forward(request, response);
    }

    private UserDatabase getUserDatabase() {
        return (UserDatabase) this.getServletContext().
            getAttribute("userDatabase");
    }

    private boolean verifyPassword(HttpServletRequest request)
        throws ServletException, IOException {
        UserDatabase database = this.getUserDatabase();
        String name = request.getParameter("name");
        String password = request.getParameter("password");
```

```
        return database.verify(name, password);
    }

    protected void doGet(HttpServletRequest request,
                         HttpServletResponse response)
        throws ServletException, IOException {
        response.setContentType("text/html");
        PrintWriter writer = response.getWriter();
        // write HTML login page...
        writer.close();
    }

    protected void doPost(HttpServletRequest request,
                          HttpServletResponse response)
        throws ServletException, IOException {
        if (this.verifyPassword(request)) {
            request.getSession();
            this.fowardTo(request, response, FORWARD_URI);
        } else {
            this.fowardTo(request, response, SERVLET_URI);
        }
    }
}
```

Benefit   The important thing is that this servlet is not quite ready to run in a browser, because the "real" implementation of UserDatabase is missing. This means that testing with HttpUnit is ruled out. In fact, we managed to enable a test-first approach here, although by use of relatively complex dummies.

12.4 | Separating the Servlet API from the Servlet Logic

The above tests for the doPost method required some relatively expensive preparation, because we had to create a mock user database and pack it into the servlet context, and we set specific parameters in the request object. In addition, our validation steps made a detour: from servlet (to DummyServletContext, further to DummyRequestDispatcher, from DummyHttpServletRequest to DummyHttpSession).

Test configuration and validation are complex

The larger the number of parameters and helper objects required, the more difficult becomes the development and adaptation of our test cases. If we find that the test case configuration and/or validation makes us lose track of things, then this is a sign that the design includes too many dependencies. In the case discussed here, the structure of the servlet API is the first thing to blame, because it couples the servlet itself to request, response, configuration, context, and—over detours—to the dispatcher. However, we should not use this as an excuse to passively tolerate the design flaws of this API.

Moving the servlet API

One way to minimize the dependence of our servlet logic upon the servlet API and thus make the servlet more testable is to move all API functions that the servlet needs to do its internal logic to a separate interface. For our sample login servlet, such an interface could look like this:

```
import javax.servlet.http.*;
public interface ServletInvocation {
    String getName();
    String getPassword();
    UserDatabase getUserDatabase();
    HttpSession createSession();
    void forwardTo(String uri);
}
```

The name ServletInvocation suggests that a new instance is created for each servlet invocation This approach avoids the concurrency problems inherent in servlet objects.[8] The interface in the form shown here is specialized to the LoginServlet. But experience has shown that a large number of methods needed in all servlets or at least in one group of servlets evolves quickly.

To be able to replace the ServletInvocation interface by its mock counterpart in our tests, we need a corresponding "factory":

```
import javax.servlet.*;
import javax.servlet.http.*;
public interface ServletInvocationFactory {
```

---

8. One of the most common errors in servlet programming is the use of variable instance variables within the servlet class.

```
ServletInvocation createInvocation(
    HttpServletRequest request,
    HttpServletResponse response,
    ServletContext context);
}
```

The interface and class mesh under development, including the pertaining implementations, now looks as shown in Figure 12.3. If we now put the factory into `ServletContext`, then each `doPost()` invocation initially creates the invocation object and then proceeds with the normal servlet logic. The test cases for the servlet itself are now much clearer thanks to the use of the mock factory and mock invocation. We need a few additional tests for the real `ServletInvocation` implementation. The practical realization of this concept is an ideal exercise for all readers.

Alternative approaches   Moving functions of the servlet API into a separate object is only one variant of the idea, How do I make the controller logic of the servlet independent of the servlet API, so that it is better testable? This principle has also been generically implemented in servlet frameworks, such as Apache's Turbine [URL:Turbine] and Struts (discussed later in this chapter).

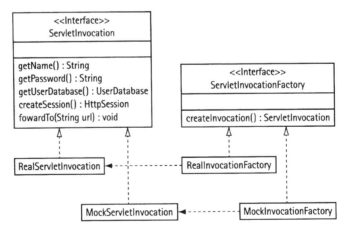

Figure 12.3 ServletInvocation.

12.5 | Testing the HTML Generation

The "Builder" design pattern

The doGet method of our sample login servlet could also gain in testability if we were to use the *Builder*[9] design pattern instead of directly creating HTML code. More specifically, we would have to introduce an interface, PageBuilder, and a corresponding factory. The builder interface could look like this:

```
public Interface PageBuilder {
    void addTitle(String title);
    void addText(String text);
    void startForm(String name, String method, String action);
    void addInput(String type, String name, String value);
    void endForm();
    void createHtml(OutputStream stream);
}
```

The builder can be replaced by a MockPageBuilder in the usual way for testing purposes. In addition to better testability, this would ensure total independence of the page layout, just what we like to have for our unit tests.

Model View Controller

This friendly approach towards testing has little significance in the real world, because the servlet itself is seldomly used to create HTML today. The main reason is that the *Model View Controller (MVC)* approach, known from GUI development, has become popular in Web application development. The purpose of this pattern is to make the actual application objects (model) independent of their representation (view) and access logic (controller). MVC is described in many publications [Lewis95].

In Web applications, views are often programmed as *Java Server Pages (JSPs)*, and controllers as servlets, and models as normal Java classes or specialized wrapper beans. One of the reasons for this division is that the layout of a Web page, represented in the JSPs, can potentially be defined and modified by nondevelopers.

---

9. The description of this pattern—and others—is easier to understand in the work of Alpert et al. [98] than in the seminal work of Gamma et al. [95].

Java Server Pages

Java code in JSPs

As the name suggests, JSPs are nothing more than HTML pages using special tags to embed Java code or to access the attributes of Java beans. If we strictly follow the MVC division, then we will hardly find any Java code in a JSP that would have to be tested. The logic for the flow control dwells in the servlets, while the special logic resides in the models, where it can be tested. What really remains in the JSPs is code to access bean attributes, to pass through a loop, and to display/hide parts of pages. The very few things that could go wrong here are normally not tested in unit tests, but rather in functional tests. At that point, we can use HttpUnit or a similar tool to validate HTML pages.

Those who think they cannot do without unit tests for a JSP have to take the roundabout route over a Web server, and perhaps Cactus. An interesting attempt would be the integration of a JSP compiler (e.g., Jasper), which is integrated in Apache's servlet engine Tomcat [URL:Tomcat], into a dedicated JSP test framework. However, this idea has never been realized to my knowledge.

JSP Custom Tags

The small amount of Java code required in JSPs can be further reduced if we implement so-called *JSP custom tags*. These user-defined tags allow us to embed arbitrary functionality into a JSP, while maintaining the HTML or XML syntax, and without the slightest Java knowledge.

User-defined tags are supplied to the application server in a tag library. Creating such a library is pure programming work. The classes and interfaces needed are available in the package `javax.servlet.jsp.tagext`. Creating unit tests for your own tags means you have to do some mocking for a few interfaces and classes. A detailed description of this approach would go beyond the scope of this book; there are many sources, including Message 29405 at [URL:YahooXP], and the KaCoMa project [URL:KaCoMa], which is designed to be a tutorial for beginners of custom tag libraries and unit testing of corresponding software.

Struts

With *Struts* [URL:Struts], there exists a widely used Web application framework based on the Model 2 approach, which is a variation of the classic MVC paradigm. Struts provides its own controller component and integrates with other technologies to provide the model and the view. For the model, Struts can interact with any standard data access technology, including Enterprise Java Beans and JDBC. For the view, Struts works well with JSPs, XSLT, and other presentation systems. When using Struts some of the standard testing problems we discussed in this chapter are no longer an issue since we don't have to fuss around with the basic Servlet mechanism any longer. However, Struts is no test-first paradise either, which provoked the development of StrutsTestCase [URL:StrutsTest], an extension of `junit.framework TestCase`.

12.6 | Summary

This chapter described testing of servlet-based Web applications on three different layers:

- Functional tests, using HttpUnit, involve only those pages of a Web application that can be addressed over HTTP.

- White-box integration tests on the server, using Cactus, participate in the execution of servlets and JSPs, and allow access to the internal objects of the servlet API.

- Server-independent tests, using dummy and mock objects, allow test-first development of servlets.

Function tests for a Web interface are required in all of these cases, whereas there is a choice of different testing technologies. To create expensive integration tests, like those supported by Cactus, it appears worthwhile to wait until we actually hit recurring deployment and integration problems. However, this optimistic waiting means that there is a reassuring test suite handily available for the single servlets.

In addition, this chapter introduced an approach on how to separate a servlet's logic from the servlet API to improve testability. Finally, we discussed several ways to generate HTML and how to test this code.

This chapter showed that test-first development is also possible for Web applications. Once more, we noticed that the use of mock objects can contribute to decouple classes and thus to improve the design.

Chapter 13

Graphical User Interfaces

Readers who have gotten this far probably noticed that the "special cases" discussed in the second part of this book are nothing more than the same issue in recurring variations: the structure or interface design of a ready-to-use framework, a tool, or an API hampers the testing of the actual functionality.

Unclear testing criteria

Graphical user interfaces (GUIs) are no exception in this respect, because their implementation relies on the use of AWT or Swing, as well as additional components (e.g., Java2D). This situation is topped by an important aspect we already saw in connection with Web applications: A "good" user interface not only has to have clearly testable properties, it is also subject to unclear evaluation criteria, such as ergonomics, intuitive use, and esthetics, or in short *usability* [Nielsen94]. In contrast to what's required by the test-first approach, these criteria cannot be specified in advance. For this reason, it is not surprising that the test-first development of a GUI cannot cover all desirable aspects.

Nevertheless, we as test-first representatives are not left empty-handed in this issue either, as we will see in this chapter.

13.1 The Direct Way

The first idea that a deeply rooted test-first enthusiast will naturally follow is the direct way: why not develop a GUI exactly like all other classes, namely in small steps and with corresponding test cases before writing the application code? Many test-first critics are doubtful about this—a good reason to prove the opposite in a detailed example.

We will use the development of a simple user interface for a product catalog as our case study. The product catalog itself can be addressed over the following interface:

Domain model
```
public interface ProductCatalog {
    void addProduct(Product product);
    void removeProduct(Product product);
    Set getProducts();
    Set getAvailableCategories();
}
```

This interface is slim and allows us to add and remove a product and to output all products and all permitted product categories. This means that, to develop the GUI, we don't need a fully functioning implementation, including persistence and other trinkets. In fact, the simplest conceivable implementation will be sufficient, and with SimpleProductCatalog, we have it already (in the codebase on the Web site). But there is still a dependence upon the Product class and the product Category class:

```
public class Product {
    public Product(String pid) {...}
    public String getPID() {...}
    public Category getCategory() {...}
    public void setCategory(Category category) {...}
    public String getDescription() {...}
    public void setDescription(String description) {...}
}

public class Category {
    public Category(String name) {...}
    public String getName() {...}
}
```

Separating the logic from the interface
Encapsulating the entire specialist logic in a separate domain model—ideally in an interface—represents important heuristics: the GUI classes should contain as little logic as possible. This means that the correct coupling between user interface and specialist logic is the only functionality

that remains to be tested. In addition, encapsulation of the logic in interfaces rather than in classes contributes to independence and facilitates testing. Thus, improved testability is an additional argument in favor of using the MVC pattern (see also Chapter 12, Section 12.5).

Figure 13.1 shows the design of our graphical user interface for adding and deleting products. Our goal is to create a product editor (Product-Editor) and to ensure the following things:

Testing goals
- All important elements of the interface are in place, and they are correctly initialized and visible.

- All products available from the catalog are displayed in the list.

- Selecting a product from the list and subsequently clicking on *Delete* removes the product from the catalog and from the list.

- Clicking *Add* opens a dialog for the user to add a product.

The exact pixel representation of the interface is not to be tested. Although this would be possible, experience has shown that the layout of an interface is subject to frequent changes. For this reason, the test cases targeted to details would have to be modified often, such that it wouldn't be worth automating them. A visual inspection of the interface within the acceptance tests is better suited to this task.

Creation testing
But let's get down to work now. In the first step, we want to test that the editor is properly created and displayed:

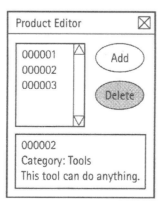

Figure 13.1 The desired Product Editor layout.

```
public class CatalogEditorTest extends TestCase {
   public void testCreation() {
      CatalogEditor editor = new CatalogEditor();
      editor.show();
      assertTrue(editor.isShowing());
      assertEquals("Product Editor", editor.getTitle());
   }
}
```

Our implementation is clearly shorter than the test code:

```
import javax.swing.*;
public class CatalogEditor extends JFrame {
   public CatalogEditor() {
      super("Product Editor");
   }
}
```

One reviewer commented here that the lines,

```
editor.show();
assertTrue(editor.isShowing());
```

check for nothing else but correct functioning of the class javax.swing.
JFrame. This is correct, but these lines serve a purpose: they enable us to
derive the editor from JFrame. Someone with no idea about Swing would
not (be able to) opt for this solution. This shows once more that a known
goal, namely to create a Swing application, influences both the design and
the implementation.

When running the first test, we notice a small flaw: the editor window
remains open after the test. So let's add a dispose() to the test and make
sure that it's called even when the test fails:

```
public void testCreation() {
   try {
      CatalogEditor editor = new CatalogEditor();
      editor.show();
      assertTrue(editor.isShowing());
      assertEquals("Product Editor", editor.getTitle());
```

```
      } finally {
         editor.dispose();
      }
   }
```

Display testing   Next, we will deal with testing the product list, including the known
refactoring in setUp() and tearDown():

```
public class CatalogEditorTest extends TestCase {
   ...

   private CatalogEditor editor;
   protected void setUp() {
      editor = new CatalogEditor();
      editor.show();
   }
   protected void tearDown() {
      editor.dispose();
   }

   public void testCreation() {
      assertTrue(editor.isShowing());
      assertEquals("Product Editor", editor.getTitle());
   }

   public void testProductList() {
      assertTrue(editor.productList.isShowing());
   }
}
```

To obtain access to the list widget productList within the test, we have
to make it available in an instance variable, either *protected* or *package
scope*. As an alternative, we could search the component tree for the
matching widget. We will see this approach later when testing with JFC-
Unit (see Section 13.2).

The implementation is straightforward, totally ignoring the esthetics of
the visible layout:

```
public class CatalogEditor extends JFrame {
   JList productList = new JList();
   public CatalogEditor() {
```

```
        super("Product Editor");
        getContentPane().add(productList);
    }
}
```

Link testing   Now let's test whether the product list really fills with products from the catalog. We need to make a design decision for this purpose: a Product-Catalog instance is passed to the editor within the constructor. The simple SimpleProductCatalog will do for testing here:

```
public class CatalogEditorTest extends TestCase {
    ...
    private ProductCatalog catalog;

    protected void setUp() {
        catalog = new SimpleProductCatalog();
        catalog.addProduct(new Product("123456"));
        catalog.addProduct(new Product("654321"));
        editor = new CatalogEditor(catalog);
        editor.show();
    }

    public void testProductList() {
        assertTrue(editor.productList.isShowing());
        ListModel model =
            (ListModel) editor.productList.getModel();
        assertEquals(2, model.getSize());
    }
}
```

Testing for getSize() alone is relatively weak. We could think of a helper method, which compares the content of a ListModel with the content of a Collection. For the moment, however, we are brave and contented with simple things, leading to the following implementation:

```
public class CatalogEditor extends JFrame {
    JList productList;
    public CatalogEditor(ProductCatalog catalog) {
        super("Product Editor");
```

```
    productList =
        new JList(catalog.getProducts().toArray());
    getContentPane().add(productList);
    }
}
```

This test tells us nothing about how the single products should be represented. And the implementation relies entirely on the toString() method in Product. By the way, this is a general weakness of the approach described here: we are merely testing the model of the graphical components and not what is really displayed. The reason is that the Swing widgets (i.e., the JList class in this case) don't let us access the actual representation.

Delete button testing   Let's see how products are deleted, the Delete button test is easy:

```
public class CatalogEditorTest extends TestCase {
    ...

    public void testDeleteButton() {
        assertTrue(editor.deleteButton.isShowing());
        assertEquals("Delete", editor.deleteButton.getText());
    }
}
```

and so is the implementation:

```
public class CatalogEditor extends JFrame {
    ...
    JButton deleteButton;

    public CatalogEditor(ProductCatalog catalog) {
        super("Product Editor");
        productList =
            new JList(catalog.getProducts().toArray());
        getContentPane().add(productList);
        deleteButton = new JButton("Delete");
        getContentPane().add(deleteButton);
    }
}
```

For this reason, we want to proceed to the actual Delete function, or actually to the corresponding test:

```
public class CatalogEditorTest extends TestCase {
    ...

    private ListModel getListModel() {
        return (ListModel) editor.productList.getModel();
    }

    public void testDeleteProduct() {
        editor.productList.setSelectedIndex(0);
        editor.deleteButton.doClick();
        assertEquals(1, getListModel().getSize());
        assertEquals(new Product("654321"),
            getListModel().getElementAt(0));
        assertEquals(1, catalog.getProducts().size());
        assertTrue(catalog.getProducts().contains(
            new Product("654321")));
    }
}
```

Note that both the ListModel and the catalog itself have to be tested, where the number of products alone is not sufficient this time. The test in this form only makes sense provided that Product.equals() has been previously implemented, namely, when the equality of two products is determined by their product IDs.

We quickly dare a first implementation attempt:

```
public class CatalogEditor extends JFrame
    implements ActionListener {
    ...
    private ProductCatalog catalog;

    public CatalogEditor(ProductCatalog catalog) {
        super("Product Editor");
        this.catalog = catalog;
        productList =
            new JList(catalog.getProducts().toArray());
        getContentPane().add(productList);
```

```
      deleteButton = new JButton("Delete");
      deleteButton.addActionListener(this);
      getContentPane().add(deleteButton);
   }

   public void actionPerformed(ActionEvent e) {
      deleteButtonClicked();
   }
   private void deleteButtonClicked() {
      Product toDelete =
         (Product) productList.getSelectedValue();
      catalog.removeProduct(toDelete);
      productList.setListData(
         catalog.getProducts().toArray());
   }
}
```

This solution gets by without separate implementation of the List-Model interface. But the experienced Swing programmer's hair stands on end; he or she wants a "neat and tidy" ListModel. We want that too, but because the code will *communicate* better, rather than because it will make the code shorter.

ListModel introduction   For this reason, we will turn our attention away from the editor and concentrate on a ProductsListModel instead. And because we are right in the swing of it,[1] let's take bigger steps. Our first test focuses on creating things:

```
public class ProductsListModelTest extends TestCase {
   public void testCreation() {
      ProductCatalog catalog = new SimpleProductCatalog();
      catalog.addProduct(new Product("123456"));
      catalog.addProduct(new Product("654321"));
      ProductsListModel model =new ProductsListModel(catalog);
      assertEquals(2, model.getSize());
      assertEquals(new Product("123456"), model.getElementAt(0));
      assertEquals(new Product("654321"), model.getElementAt(1));
   }
}
```

---

1. countPuns++

Sort order testing
Considering that the test requires lexicographic sorting of the products, while the catalog supplies an (unordered) Set, we realize that everything is harder than expected:

```java
public class ProductsListModel extends AbstractListModel {
    private ProductCatalog catalog;
    private List sortedProducts;

    public ProductsListModel(ProductCatalog catalog) {
        this.catalog = catalog;
        sortedProducts = new ArrayList(catalog.getProducts());
        Collections.sort(sortedProducts, new Comparator() {
            public int compare(Object o1, Object o2) {
                Product p1 = (Product) o1;
                Product p2 = (Product) o2;
                return p1.getPID().compareTo(p2.getPID());
            }
        });
    }

    public Object getElementAt(int index) {
        return sortedProducts.get(index);
    }

    public int getSize() {
        return sortedProducts.size();
    }
}
```

Deleting from
the model
Our next testing step is targeted to delete products from ListModel:

```java
public class ProductsListModelTest extends TestCase {
    ...

    private ProductCatalog catalog;
    private ProductsListModel model;
    protected void setUp() {
        catalog = new SimpleProductCatalog();
        catalog.addProduct(new Product("123456"));
        catalog.addProduct(new Product("654321"));
```

```
      model = new ProductsListModel(catalog);
   }

   public void testDeleteProduct() {
      model.deleteProduct(0);
      assertEquals(1, model.getSize());
      assertEquals(new Product("654321"),model.getElementAt(0));
      assertEquals(1, catalog.getProducts().size());
      assertTrue(catalog.getProducts().contains(
         new Product("654321")));
   }
}
```

It is no coincidence that this test case is very similar to the delete test in CatalogEditorTest. It should occasionally cause us to consider whether or not the old test has become pointless by the new one. The interface decision was taken in favor of delete(int index), because we can easily determine the selected index from JList. This makes the implementation pretty easy:

```
public class ProductsListModel extends AbstractListModel {
   ...

   public void deleteProduct(int index) {
      Product toDelete = (Product) sortedProducts.get(index);
      sortedProducts.remove(toDelete);
      catalog.removeProduct(toDelete);
   }
}
```

Embedding the model

And now back to the editor to embed the ProductListModel:

```
public class CatalogEditor extends JFrame implements ActionListener {
   ...

   public CatalogEditor(ProductCatalog catalog) {
      super("Product Editor");
      ProductsListModel model =
         new ProductsListModel(catalog);
```

```
        productList = new JList(model);
        ...
    }

    public void actionPerformed(ActionEvent e) {
        deleteButtonClicked();
    }
    private void deleteButtonClicked() {
        int deleteIndex = productList.getSelectedIndex();
        ((ProductsListModel) productList.
          getModel()).deleteProduct(deleteIndex);
    }
}
```

Isn't this wonderful? All tests are running! It's about time we take a look at all of this "for real." All we need first is a main() method and a rudimentary layout:

```
public class CatalogEditor extends JFrame implements ActionListener {
    ...

    public CatalogEditor(ProductCatalog catalog) {
        super("Product Editor");
        createWidgets(catalog);
    }

    private void createWidgets(ProductCatalog catalog) {
        getContentPane().setLayout(new FlowLayout());
        setSize(150, 150);
        ProductsListModel model = new ProductsListModel(catalog);
        productList = new JList(model);
        getContentPane().add(productList);
        deleteButton = new JButton("Delete");
        deleteButton.addActionListener(this);
        getContentPane().add(deleteButton);
    }

    public static void main(String[] args) {
        SimpleProductCatalog catalog = new SimpleProductCatalog();
        catalog.addProduct(new Product("1000001"));
```

```
        catalog.addProduct(new Product("2000002"));
        CatalogEditor editor = new CatalogEditor(catalog);
        editor.show();
    }
}
```

Unfortunately, visual testing has an unpleasant surprise in store for us: Although all tests are running, clicking the Delete button once does not make the selected product disappear! How could this happen?

Liar View bug pattern The answer is that we were taken in by the Liar View bug pattern [Allen01]: although the model behind JList is updated, the view itself is not informed about it. The correct thing to do would be to inform all ListDataListeners registered with ProductsListModel about a successful deletion. So let's extend a corresponding test case:

```
import javax.swing.event.ListDataEvent;
public class ProductsListModelTest extends TestCase {
    ...
    private boolean intervalRemovedCalled = false;
    public void testDeleteProduct() {

        ListDataListener listener = new ListDataListener() {
            public void intervalAdded(ListDataEvent e) {}
            public void intervalRemoved(ListDataEvent e) {
                intervalRemovedCalled = true;
            }
            public void contentsChanged(ListDataEvent e) {}
        };

        model.addListDataListener(listener);
        model.deleteProduct(0);
        assertTrue(intervalRemovedCalled);
        assertEquals(1, model.getSize());
        assertEquals(new Product("654321"),model.getElementAt(0));
        assertEquals(1, catalog.getProducts().size());
        assertTrue(catalog.getProducts().contains(
            new Product("654321")));
    }
}
```

Similar to examples in other chapters, we are using a *poor-house mock object*, that is, an anonymous class. The implementation needs one small addition:

```
public class ProductsListModel extends AbstractListModel {
    ...
    public void deleteProduct(int index) {
        Product toDelete =
            (Product) sortedProducts.get(index);
        sortedProducts.remove(toDelete);
        catalog.removeProduct(toDelete);
        fireIntervalRemoved(this, index, index);
    }
}
```

Now, the visual test works as expected. And just to make sure nobody can say we are careless, let's see a few functionality chunks in express testing.

Correct Enable status Chunk 1: Test to ensure that the Delete button is *enabled* only when a product is selected:

```
public void testDeleteButton() {
    assertTrue(editor.deleteButton.isShowing());
    assertEquals("Delete", editor.deleteButton.getText());
    assertFalse(editor.deleteButton.isEnabled());
    editor.productList.setSelectedIndex(0);
    assertTrue(editor.deleteButton.isEnabled());
    editor.productList.clearSelection();
    assertFalse(editor.deleteButton.isEnabled());
}
```

Product details Chunk 2: Test to ensure that the product detail view works correctly:

```
public void testProductDetails() throws Exception {
    assertTrue(editor.productDetails.isShowing());
    assertEquals("", editor.productDetails.getText());
    Product product =
        (Product) getListModel().getElementAt(0);
```

```
        product.setCategory(new Category("Records"));
        product.setDescription("The best of Kenny Haye");
        editor.productList.setSelectedIndex(0);
        assertProductDetails(product);
        editor.productList.setSelectedIndex(1);
        assertProductDetails(
            (Product) getListModel().getElementAt(1));
        editor.productList.clearSelection();
        assertEquals("", editor.productDetails.getText());
        editor.productList.setSelectedIndex(0);
        assertProductDetails(product);
    }
    private void assertProductDetails(Product product)
        throws IOException {
        BufferedReader reader = new BufferedReader(
            new StringReader(editor.productDetails.getText()));
        assertEquals("PID: " + product.getPID(),
                    reader.readLine());
        assertEquals("Category: " +
                    product.getCategory().getName(),
                    reader.readLine());
        assertEquals(product.getDescription(),
                    reader.readLine());
        assertNull(reader.readLine());
    }
```

This test case already considers deselection of a product and sequential selection of multiple products. The test in this form hasn't been built in one go, but piece by piece. It also shows that visually controlling the components from time to time can be useful to find new test cases.

Let's have another look at the current implementation state of Catalog-Editor:

```
import java.awt.*;
import java.awt.event.*;
import javax.swing.*;
import javax.swing.event.*;
public class CatalogEditor extends JFrame
        implements ActionListener, ListSelectionListener {
```

```
JList productList;
JButton deleteButton;
JTextArea productDetails;
public CatalogEditor(ProductCatalog catalog) {
   super("Product Editor");
   createWidgets(catalog);
}
private void createWidgets(ProductCatalog catalog) {
   getContentPane().setLayout(new FlowLayout());
   setSize(150, 150);
   addProductList(catalog);
   addProductDetails();
   addDeleteButton();
}
private void addProductList(ProductCatalog catalog) {
   ProductsListModel model =
      new ProductsListModel(catalog);
   productList = new JList(model);
   productList.setSelectionMode(
      ListSelectionModel.SINGLE_SELECTION);
   productList.addListSelectionListener(this);
   getContentPane().add(productList);
}
private void addProductDetails() {
   productDetails = new JTextArea();
   getContentPane().add(productDetails);
}
private void addDeleteButton() {
   deleteButton = new JButton("Delete");
   deleteButton.setEnabled(false);
   deleteButton.addActionListener(this);
   getContentPane().add(deleteButton);
}
public void actionPerformed(ActionEvent e) {
   deleteButtonClicked();
}
private void deleteButtonClicked() {
```

```
      int deleteIndex = productList.getSelectedIndex();
      ((ProductsListModel) productList.getModel()).
        deleteProduct(deleteIndex);
    }
  public void valueChanged(ListSelectionEvent e) {
    if (productList.getSelectedValue() == null) {
      clearProductSelection();
    } else {
      selectProduct(
        (Product) productList.getSelectedValue());
    }
  }
  private void clearProductSelection() {
    deleteButton.setEnabled(false);
    productDetails.setText("");
  }
  private void selectProduct(Product product) {
    deleteButton.setEnabled(true);
    productDetails.setText("");
    productDetails.append("PID: " +
      product.getPID() + "\n");
    productDetails.append("Category: " +
      product.getCategory().getName() + "\n");
    productDetails.append(
      product.getDescription() + "\n");
  }
}
```

We find nothing that could be a big surprise for Swing programmers, perhaps with the only exception of gradually losing patience as the layout still leaves a great deal to be desired. However, one important piece of functionality is still missing: the Add button. First, the button itself in a trivial test:

```
public void testAddButton() {
  assertTrue(editor.addButton.isShowing());
  assertEquals("Add", editor.addButton.getText());
}
```

Opening a dialog And now let's see what's behind it. The problem we have to deal with here is that another dialog should open for the user to enter new product data. But how can we test such a thing?

Here is our answer: not at all in the test suite for `CatalogEditor`! In this case, we are only interested in having the editor somehow get a hold of a new product instance:

```
public void testAddProduct() {
    editor.setProductCreator(new ProductCreator() {
        public Product create() {
            return new Product("333333");
        }
    });

    editor.addButton.doClick();
    assertEquals(3, getListModel().getSize());
    assertEquals(new Product("333333"),
        getListModel().getElementAt(1));
    assertEquals(3, catalog.getProducts().size());
    assertTrue(catalog.getProducts().contains(
        new Product("333333")));
}
```

This approach deserves a closer look. We have decided to move the creation of a new product to a `ProductCreator` interface. It allows us to use a dummy implementation for testing purposes. Another trick is the PID we have actually chosen, which means that we concurrently test for correct sorting of the list.

To keep it happy, the test requires a considerable amount of code:

```
public class CatalogEditor extends JFrame
    implements ActionListener, ListSelectionListener {

    ...
    JButton addButton;
    private ProductCreator productCreator;
    private void createWidgets(ProductCatalog catalog) {

        ...
        addAddButton();
    }
    public void actionPerformed(ActionEvent e) {
```

```
            if (e.getSource() == deleteButton) {
               deleteButtonClicked();
            } else {
               addButtonClicked();
            }
         }
         private ProductsListModel getProductsListModel() {
            return ((ProductsListModel) productList.getModel());
         }
         private void addAddButton() {
            addButton = new JButton("Add");
            addButton.addActionListener(this);
            getContentPane().add(addButton);
         }
         private void addButtonClicked() {
            Product newProduct = productCreator.create();
            getProductsListModel().addProduct(newProduct);
         }
         protected void setProductCreator(
            ProductCreator creator) {
            productCreator = creator;
         }
      }
      public class ProductsListModel extends AbstractListModel {
         ...
         private void sortProducts() {
            Collections.sort(sortedProducts, new Comparator() {
               public int compare(Object o1, Object o2) {
                  Product p1 = (Product) o1;
                  Product p2 = (Product) o2;
                  return p1.getPID().compareTo(p2.getPID());
               }
            });
         }
         public void addProduct(Product newProduct) {
            sortedProducts.add(newProduct);
            sortProducts();
            catalog.addProduct(newProduct);
         }
      }
```

We can see that two classes had to be modified. The test chunk was actually too big for one single iteration. But everything seems to have gone well.

Liar View number two! Nope! Actually, the Liar View bug pattern we saw before sneaked in again: a corresponding test is still missing in `ProductsListModelTest`. To make sure our readers won't sink into a testing monotony, we will turn the tables this time—we will give only the bug fix and leave it up to the readers to write a matching test as an exercise:

```
public void addProduct(Product newProduct) {
    sortedProducts.add(newProduct);
    sortProducts();
    catalog.addProduct(newProduct);
    int index = sortedProducts.indexOf(newProduct);
    fireIntervalAdded(this, index, index);
}
```

Things unfinished Let's stop the development of this graphical product catalog editor at this point.[2] The following remains to be done or tested:

- A `ProductCreatorDialog` class that implements the `ProductCreator` interface is missing.

- We have to build this dialog class into our `CatalogEditor`.

- What happens if `ProductCreator.create()` returns `null`, that is, when the Cancel button is pressed in `ProductCreatorDialog`?

These requirements do not produce new test-first problems, so we can confidently leave them up to the experienced reader. Besides, nobody has to be ashamed of using a "visual" test to actually discover additional test cases or errors and to then translate them back into JUnit test cases. To work with an example based on this approach, we recommend our readers delete a product and then look at the buttons and product details. You will see that several things are wrong!

---

2. The code available from our Web site includes the complete example.

Brief Summary

As with our test-first development of servlets (see Chapter 12, Section 12.3), we have gotten to a point where the full functionality of the graphical editor is not yet available on a functional level, because a certain component (i.e., ProductCreatorDialog in this case) is still missing. But still, we can test the behavior depending on this in unit tests.

However, the layout of the product catalog editor is still unsatisfactory. The current layout is anything but pretty (Figure 13.2). Theoretically, we could check everything by automated testing. For example, [URL:WakeGUI] also tests for the relative position of widgets to each other. However, such test cases are often very unstable, because the layout of a GUI normally changes more often than its functionality. For this reason, we should carefully consider whether or not this type of test automation would better be implemented as part of the functional test suite. On the one hand, this would mean using different testing tools; on the other hand, we would get direct feedback from the users.

We will content ourselves with a (slightly) improved and refactored implementation of the layout at this point. This improved version takes us a step closer to the desired layout, as shown in Figure 13.3:

```
public class CatalogEditor extends JFrame
    implements ActionListener, ListSelectionListener {
    ...
    private void createWidgets(ProductCatalog catalog) {
```

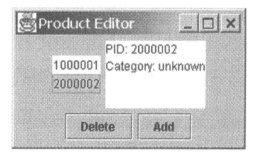

Figure 13.2 A "rudimentary" layout.

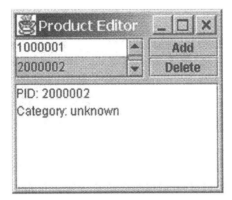

Figure 13.3 The improved layout.

```java
        buildProductDetails();
        buildProductList(catalog);
        buildAddButton();
        buildDeleteButton();
        buildLayout();
    }
    private void buildLayout() {
        getContentPane().setLayout(new BorderLayout(5,5));
        setSize(300, 300);
        JPanel buttonPane = new JPanel();
        buttonPane.setLayout(new GridLayout(2,1));
        getContentPane().add(new JScrollPane(productDetails),
            BorderLayout.SOUTH);
        getContentPane().add(new JScrollPane(productList),
            BorderLayout.CENTER);
        buttonPane.add(addButton);
        buttonPane.add(deleteButton);
        getContentPane().add(buttonPane, BorderLayout.EAST);
    }
    private void buildProductDetails() {
        productDetails = new JTextArea();
        productDetails.setPreferredSize(
            new Dimension(50,100));
    }
```

```
private void buildProductList(ProductCatalog catalog) {
    ProductsListModel model =
        new ProductsListModel(catalog);
    productList = new JList(model);
    productList.setSelectionMode(
        ListSelectionModel.SINGLE_SELECTION);
    productList.addListSelectionListener(this);
}
private void buildDeleteButton() {
    deleteButton = new JButton("Delete");
    deleteButton.setEnabled(false);
    deleteButton.addActionListener(this);
}
private void buildAddButton() {
    addButton = new JButton("Add");
    addButton.addActionListener(this);
}
}
```

Keeping the GUI Clear

The basic principle to facilitate GUI testing or to even make it almost superfluous is to keep all logic out of the GUI classes. In the preceding example we still had two kinds of logic within those classes:

- Interdependencies between two or more GUI elements, for example, selecting an item in the product list had to enable the Delete button.

- The GUI widgets are actually wired to the underlying models, for example, the product list model.

Humble Dialog

If we could eliminate the first point by extracting the interdependency logic into a class of its own, we could argue that the actual wiring is mere delegation, which is not really worthwhile testing. This is exactly the approach that Michael Feathers [02b] describes in *The Humble Dialog Box*. He presents a test-first technique to extract all user interface logic from the GUI class itself into a "smart object," which collaborates with an abstract view and can thus be developed and tested independently. The actual "humble" view implementation does nothing more than provide simple, delegating getter and setter methods.

<table>
<tr><td>13.2</td><td>

Short Detours

</td></tr>
</table>

The path we have taken so far in this chapter has a few hidden problems:

Problems
with the
above approach

- All GUI widgets important for the tests have to be made visible in non-private instance variables or over corresponding getter methods. This conflicts with the style propagated so far, which tells us that instance variables should always be private, and access methods should only be offered if they are used by clients of that class.

- The GUI component does not "operate" over the actual event mechanism, but uses special methods of the widgets. The drawback is that certain error types will not be revealed, for example:

  - Even invisible and `disabled` components can be addressed in the unit test.

  - Errors originating from the Swing thread problem[3] will slip through.

The first point, visible variables, is connected to the non-public class properties discussed in Chapter 8, Section 8.2. As mentioned in that section, there are pros and cons about the question as to whether or not "internal things" should be made visible for testing purposes only. In any event, it means that we are coupling the tests to internal things of the implementation, making it more fragile. Although moving the widget creation and the widget referencing to a dedicated class can solve the visibility problem, it often does not lead to the simplest design.

The second point is actually a limitation of the mightiness and thus effectiveness of the test cases. For this reason, we will discuss two approaches to solve this point in the following sections.

---

3. Most method calls of the Swing components are not thread-safe, so that they have to be passed explicitly to the AWT thread over `SwingUtilities.invokeLater(Runnable)` for handling, unless they are invoked from the event-handling code.

JFCUnit

Swing-based testing   JFCUnit is an open source project aimed at creating a framework for unit testing of Swing applications. You can download the latest version from [URL:JFCUnit] and actively contribute to the product's further development. JFCUnit provides support for the following:

- Locating `java.awt.Window` instances (e.g., frames and dialogs) opened by the code under test.

- Locating Swing components within the component tree of a window based on type, name, or other properties.

- Sending targeted events in the AWT event handling thread, clicking a button or selecting a JTree subtree, for example.

- Handling thread-safe testing of components.

The process of creating a JFCUnit test suite does not differ much from programming a normal suite. First of all, we have to derive our test classes from `junit.extensions.jfcunit.JFCTestCase`. This gives us access to a helper class that supplies methods for finding components and triggering events. Internally, JFCUnit takes care of switching between the test thread and the AWT event thread.

To understand this better, we will translate the above test case, `testDeleteProduct()`, into a JCFUnit test case:

```
import javax.swing.*;
import junit.extensions.jfcunit.*;
public class CatalogEditorJFCTest extends JFCTestCase {
    public CatalogEditorJFCTest(String name) {...}
    private JFCTestHelper helper;
    private ProductCatalog catalog;
    protected void setUp() {
        helper = new JFCTestHelper();
        catalog = new SimpleProductCatalog();
        catalog.addProduct(new Product("123456"));
        catalog.addProduct(new Product("654321"));
        new CatalogEditor(catalog).show();
    }
```

```
protected void tearDown() {
   helper.cleanUp(this);
}
public void testDeleteProduct() {
   CatalogEditor editor =
      (CatalogEditor) helper.getWindow("Product Editor");
   JList productList =
      (JList) helper.findComponent(JList.class, editor, 0);
   AbstractButtonFinder deleteButtonFinder =
      new AbstractButtonFinder("Delete");
   JButton deleteButton = (JButton) helper.findComponent(
      deleteButtonFinder, editor, 0);
   JListMouseEventData listClick =
      new JListMouseEventData(this, productList, 0, 1);
   helper.enterClickAndLeave(listClick);
   MouseEventData deleteClick =
      new MouseEventData(this, deleteButton);
   helper.enterClickAndLeave(deleteClick);
   ListModel listModel = productList.getModel();
   assertEquals(1, listModel.getSize());
   assertEquals(new Product("654321"),
               listModel.getElementAt(0));
   assertEquals(1, catalog.getProducts().size());
   assertTrue(catalog.getProducts().contains(
      new Product("654321")));
}
}
```

First, we instantiate JFCTestHelper in setUp(), then we create and display the product editor under test. The method cleanUp(...) in tearDown() removes all remaining windows and dialogs from the desktop. However, the actual events happen in testDeleteProduct(): the starting-point into a JFCUnit test case is normally from the main window of an application (i.e., ProductEditor object in our example). Next, we determine the productList and deleteButton widgets as subcomponents of the editor, and then feed them with the product selection and mouse clicking events. Note that we adopt the actual `assert` commands virtually as they are from `ProductEditorTest` of the corresponding test.

Differences to the first implementation

One important difference to the test approach discussed in the previous subsection is that we search for specific widgets by their types, names, or labels, instead of having to rely on the visibility in the class. Another important difference is that we do not call any methods directly from the widgets, but rather set those events in the event queue that will be triggered from within the GUI in the real world. Note that creating events with all their data is much more complex than a simple method invocation.

Benefits and drawbacks

The testing approach with JFCUnit has benefits and drawbacks. One major benefit is that the tests are very close to the actual events on a GUI. This means that we can test the behavior in several open windows and dialogs and discover Swing-typical multi-thread errors at the same time. The drawback is that the test cases have to make detours to access the actual components and widgets. Therefore, a JFCUnit test case is too heavy for the role of fine-grained unit test, but it is ideally suited for interaction and integration tests. Note that the current release—0.3 beta—supports only the most important Swing features; unusual things like drag and drop are not yet included.

The AWT Robot

From JDK 1.3 up

Since JDK 1.3, Java offers a class explicitly conceived for GUI testing: `java.awt.Robot`. Instances of this class offer ways to simulate mouse and keyboard actions, including the following commands: `mouseMove(...)`, `mousePress(...)`, `mouseRelease(...)`, `keyPress(...)`, and `keyRelease(...)`. However, this interface is on too low an abstraction level for unit tests. For example, mouse movements have to be positioned on exact pixels and each touch of keys has to be determined individually. The `Robot` class was mainly designed for the development of pure Java solutions in the capture and replay approach.

It is also feasible to use an AWT robot to build a test framework similar to the abstraction level of JFCUnit. This relieves the user from routine work like positioning the mouse pointer over a specific component or pressing several keys to enter a character string. Abbot is such a tool.

Other Tools

Abbot   Abbot [URL:Abbot] is a GUI testing tool built on `java.awt.Robot` that works on two levels of abstraction:

- Functional testing, by writing Swing test cases in a script language which can then be invoked from within JUnit.

- Programmatic unit level testing.

Jemmy   Another Swing GUI testing tool has been developed by Sun's Netbeans team. *Jemmy* [URL:Jemmy] is technically similar to JFCUnit since it emulates events being posted to the AWT event queue.

13.3 | Summary

This chapter showed how you can use the test-first approach to create graphical user interfaces (GUIs). Currently, the testing community uses mainly two variants:

- Fine-grained unit tests, by directly addressing components and widgets.

- JFCUnit for interaction tests that simulate the actual GUI operation.

- Either of the two approaches reaches its limits when trying to realize certain layout standards and nonspecifiable properties like ergonomics or esthetics.

In practice, many teams create user interfaces by use of special tools (GUI builders). Such tools can speed up the GUI implementation and open the way for a twofold approach: using the GUI builder to create the GUI's layout and developing the connection to the logic layer in the test-first approach.

Chapter 14

The Role of Unit Tests in the Software Process

Software development process and methodology represent a controversial area. The number of influences that drive the decision for one process or another methodology are innumerable. We as developers often don't have the last word and, when the time for discussion is over, must get along with whatever has been decided on. This is no reason, though, not to develop test-first from then on. If you need arguments for why unit testing in general and test-first in particular are also very good ideas in non-XP projects, this chapter is for you. If you are already working in an environment where test-driven programming is accepted practice, you might want to skip ahead to the next chapter.

This chapter's target and audience

This chapter describes the role of unit tests in a software engineering environment. It shows how and at what cost automated unit tests based on the test-first approach can be integrated into a documented software process, and to what extent they are already integrated in commercial software engineering processes, such as the Rational Unified Process (RUP) [Kruchten99]. Such considerations concern corporate managers, project managers, and developers dealing with such processes and interested in the systematic introduction of unit tests.

When are heavyweight processes meaningful?

Heavyweight and document-oriented processes are less flexible than agile processes [Fowler01], and XP belongs to the latter. Small project teams developing software for a single customer often regard such software engineering processes as outdated. However, the use of such processes is meaningful, for example, when developing a combined hardware/software system. Late availability of the target hardware demands for early definition and "freezing" of requirements in general and interfaces in particular. In addition, the discipline of such management-oriented processes is necessary to coordinate large distributed project teams, teams working on a new standard product, for example. And finally, there are areas where defined software engineering processes are formally required by the customer, such as development projects for government agencies.

Cost-benefit considerations   Developing and introducing a different work method into a large development department usually means high investments. For this reason, a cost-benefit analysis should be conducted before decisions are made about the use of automated unit tests. The cost-benefit ratio depends largely on the structure of the process used. This chapter first introduces different process structures—sequential, incremental, and evolutionary structures—and then studies costs and benefits in relation to the respective structure. Finally, we will discuss the use of automated unit tests in popular commercial process models.

14.1 Activities in the Defined Software Process

A defined development process consists of a structured sequence of activities, with intermediate results and eventually the product.

Activities and Products

Figure 14.1 shows an example outlining general activities and results of a software process. We have intentionally not selected one of the processes discussed in the following sections; instead, we will use a simplified example, a small company developing customer-specific GUI components.

Sample process   The development is done as follows: The first step describes the functions of the component, the programming interface, and the user interface. This description is reviewed by the customer prior to beginning the implementation. The next step involves the design of the class model, the tests, and the implementation of the component. The component is tested first internally and later by the customer, where it is integrated into the customer's software. Finally, the finished component is deployed and the project is completed.

Basic terms   We also use this example to explain a few basic terms: A process consists of a set of steps or *activities*. The realization of an activity is described

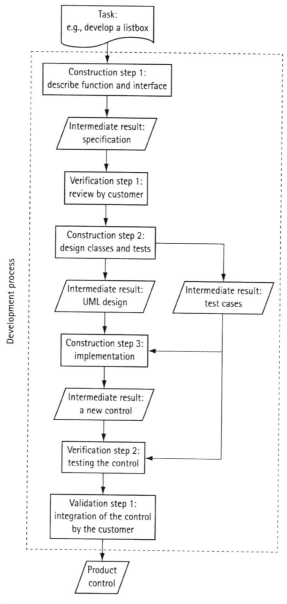

Figure 14.1 Activities, intermediate results, and products in the development process.

in the process and leads to a defined result. The rectangles in Figure 14.1 are activities, such as, Describe function and interface. The result of an activity is either a product (i.e., something that will be delivered to the project customer) or an internal, intermediate result (e.g., a project document or a software model).

Intermediate products Defined intermediate results allow us to determine the project's progress. These intermediate results are shown by parallelograms in Figure 14.1. Such intermediate results are often standardized documents. One example of such a document is the Specification. The benefit of text documents is that we can print and read them, which makes them very suitable for later review. In RUP [Kruchten99], intermediate results are software models (like UML Design in Figure 14.1) or executable programs (like the component after the implementation phase in Figure 14.1). Executable intermediate results can represent a more reliable proof of a project's progress than paper-based documentation. Of course, this is only true if we are dealing with finished and tested parts of the product and not with GUI prototypes that can be quickly created by a developer with the appropriate tools.

Product quality The objective of a software process is to create a high-quality software product. High quality means that the product meets the documented requirements and the (often) undocumented needs and expectations of customers and users. A variety of activities contribute to the creation of a high-quality product.

Construction Activities

Activities like the definition, design, and implementation of requirements serve to build the product's functionality. Errors occur in the course of these activities. The verification and validation steps described further in the sections that follow serve to remove these errors.

Avoiding errors The cheapest and best way to achieve high quality is to avoid errors in the constructive steps. There are various means to this end. Document templates help the project team members to fully document all requirements. Sound knowledge—and more important, the practice—of software engineering methods helps avoid systematic errors. And finally, the test-first approach contributes to avoiding errors because it improves the design quality.

Verification

Verification helps to determine whether or not the results of an activity meet the documented *requirements*. More specifically, we can determine whether or not a design reflects all documented requirements or the product implements all specified functions correctly. Various testing and reviewing techniques are normally used in the verification phase.

Test types   A *test* means that we run the software in a defined way, while watching or recording the results and evaluating the correctness of these results. There are different types of tests:

- *Function tests* verify that the software implements a specified function correctly, whether or not it is possible to add rows and columns to a table, for instance.

- *Benchmark tests* measure the performance of a system (defined hardware and software) and compare it with a reference, namely, an existing system or a given value. For example, a benchmark test for a graphic program determines how long it takes to load a 3D scene on a specific computer.

- *Load tests* verify whether or not the software works properly and efficiently under various operating conditions (e.g., a different number of parallel users). A variant of the load test is the *stress test,* which checks for the behavior of the software under extreme conditions, for example, a very large number of parallel users or under very limited computer resources.

- *Robustness tests* verify whether or not the software can react to errors without crashing, say, due to faulty inputs or exceptions or insufficient storage capacity.

- *Installation tests* verify whether or not the software can be properly installed under different conditions.

Review   A *review* means that a group of reviewers examines the result of an activity, such as a documented requirement or an important class definition. Such a group can consist of various members, including corporate managers, customer representatives, users, or developers. If a structured review process is followed (e.g., *inspections* [Gilb93]), then a review can often find errors more economically than tests. One reason this is so is that a reviewer finds an error when reading a document or source code at the location where the error was caused—when a reviewer sees a wrong variable assignment in the source code, for instance. In contrast, when a test finds a symptom, the developer has to go through a time-consuming debugging process to find the cause [Humphrey95]. Another positive side effect of reviews is the transfer of knowledge. Through their work as reviewers, project members learn new parts of the project. One reviewer remarked that reviewing the JUnit assertions together with an analyst or customer has helped tremendously to discover missing and wrong test cases.

Using pair programming for reviews

In addition to various testing types, XP also includes a very efficient form of reviewing. In pair programming (see Chapter 1, Section 1.2), developers review their developing work alternately and mutually. Pair programming reduces the number of errors and distributes knowledge about the code across the project team.

Verification techniques check for correct implementation of the software process and whether or not the specified result was produced in each phase. The developers have completed their work successfully if a software product passes the verification phase successfully. This means that unit tests are a verification measure. They ensure that the developer has correctly implemented all methods supplied by the component in its public interface.

Validation

Unfortunately, successful verification is no guarantee for the successful use of a software product, because the specification may not necessarily describe the customer's real wishes. For this reason, we need validation as an additional step. Validation serves to determine whether or not the product meets the user's requirements. Validation includes using the software within the target environment, in a pilot project or a beta test program in the case of standard products. Validation should also be used as early as possible.

Early feedback

For example, an early and very effective form of validation consists of agreeing on a common understanding of the requirements between the project team and the customer. The software process models discussed next use a set of techniques—scenarios, prototypes or storyboards—to this effect.

Quality Assurance

One might assume that quality assurance is an issue already covered by the verification and validation activities just mentioned. In the real world, this would be too optimistic a stance. Just because there is a written development process does not mean that it will be observed by the project members. Good intentions of doing the verification and validation activities are often defeated by short deadlines or the general lack of sexiness of such activities in the project routine. When project members do not see the process as being appropriate, for whatever reasons, they will move slowly but surely away from what's on paper toward a chaotic way of working, so that the pretty development process deteriorates to "shelfware."

Quality assurance is used to prevent this from happening and to ensure that both developers and corporate managers see how and at what level of quality the actual software process flows. Figure 14.2 shows the tasks involved in quality assurance.

Quality assurance supports the project manager in planning a project, particularly when planning suitable verification and validation measures and when adapting processes to the project requirements.

Process monitoring Quality assurance monitors the process, comparing the actual process with what is documented. In particular, quality assurance checks whether or not activities (e.g., project meetings, document reviews, tests) are actually taking place and that the intermediate results and the final product resemble what was defined in the process. Although this may sound like watching and knowing better, a good project involves all team members in the planning phase, and the process is based on their realistic approach. Ideally, quality assurance is the team's conscience, reminding everybody of their good intentions. Monitoring a process includes collection of data—about compliance with the deadlines, number of errors found during verification activities, and similar things. This data provides information about how appropriate and efficient the process really is.

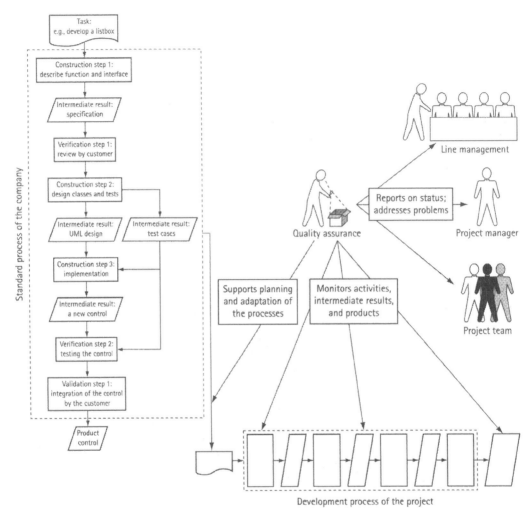

Figure 14.2 Quality-assurance tasks.

Quality assurance involves both the project team and corporate managers. It prepares the collected data for presentation and updates the project team about the efficiency of reviews and (system) tests, number of reported problems to be removed, deviation from the planning milestones, and the like. In addition to pure information, quality assurance

Sanctions also deals with significant deviations from the process. Assume, for example, that quality assurance finds that a certain member of the team does not develop tests for his or her modules. The quality assurance process involves such steps as discussion of the problem with the developer, talking about the motivation for tests (perhaps based on this book), and asking the developer to create the tests. If the developer does not react to encouragement and persuasion, quality assurance has to report the problem to the project manager, because the product's quality is at stake, and the project manager will have to solve the problem together with the team member.

In addition, quality assurance assumes an unpopular policing function. If problems cannot be removed within the project (e.g., when the project manager thinks that there is actually no time to be wasted for testing), then management should be informed. This very unpleasant task is crucial for a company to prevent a faulty product from being delivered due to time shortage, thereby aggravating the customer.

Should quality assurance be institutionalized?
If only for this reporting to the line management, it would be beneficial to assign quality assurance to staff outside the regular project hierarchy; in particular, this would ensure that the project manager can't silence them when they come up with bad news. Many of the new development models, (like RUP and XP discussed further in the sections that follow) do not mention quality assurance explicitly as a role. Instead, they allocate these tasks to the project manager, a "coach," or the customer on site. Even a strong standard like CMMI [CMU00] explicitly allows quality assurance to be assumed by all project members jointly, without specifically appointing a quality manager, especially in organizations with an open communications culture. However, CMMI recommends in such cases that quality assurance should be implemented by qualified staff according to a well-defined plan rather than just hoping for the best.

Unit tests are relevant for some of the activities introduced above. Creating unit tests by the test-first principle is a constructive quality measure, because it improves our design. Conducting unit tests is also a verification measure. The activities and results of unit tests are part of the development process and thus subject to quality assurance.

14.2 | Process Types and Testing Strategies

Sequential, incremental, and evolutionary models
With the process models used today, we can distinguish between different types, each requiring different testing strategies. Historically sequential models have been the first process models. They run tests at the end of the development project. In contrast, modern incremental and evolutionary

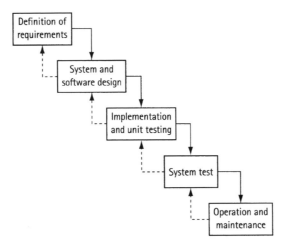

Figure 14.3 The waterfall model [Boehm76].

development models require early integration and early testing of software pre-versions.

Sequential Models

Waterfall model   Early process models were based on a sequential structure. The first and best known of these models is the *waterfall model* [Royce70, Boehm76], shown in Figure 14.3.

The waterfall model is a sequential model because each of its activities takes place at a specific point within the process for the entire product. In a sequential model, all requirements are written and itemized within the requirement definition activity. At the end of the activity, the requirements are reviewed, coordinated, and specified. Similarly, the system and software design activity moves the design of the system architecture forward to the fine-grained design stage. Subsequently, the entire software is implemented, integrated, and tested. Finally, the software is used in its production environment, and later maintained and further developed.

In sequential models, the integration of various modules and test runs takes place at the end of the corresponding phase, including the following partial activities:

Partial activities   ■ **Unit test.** The units (i.e., classes or modules) are tested individually after the implementation.

- **Integration and integration test.** The software is built successively from the individual components, as described in the design. Each partial system formed in this phase is then also tested.

- **System test.** The entire system is tested on the basis of the requirements; in other words, the specified functionality is tested just as intensely as the software's nonfunctional properties, such as efficiency, robustness, and so on.

- **Acceptance test.** The software is validated, for example by testing it in the production environment at the customer site. The acceptance test represents the formal acceptance of the software by the customer.

Error removal costs Errors found during testing lead to regression within the process, as indicated by the dashed lines in Figure 14.3. For example, if one of the tests finds an implementation error, then the implementation has to be corrected. Regressions within the process will be increasingly expensive, depending on how far back the cause of error is located within the process. For example, if a problem is due to a faulty requirement, then the requirement and the design based on it, as well as the program elements concerned, have to be modified and tested again.

The linear structure of sequential models is plausible and facilitates planning and communication of a project. Each activity of a project leads to a defined intermediate result, normally in the form of a document (e.g., a requirement specification) during the early phases. Sequential models are found in many areas of our lives (e.g., in (building) architecture) where the technical process is well mastered. However, experiences gained in the past decades have shown that a sequential approach is seldom suitable for software development.

Problems with sequential models The use of sequential models has led to problems in many software projects. This is mainly due to late integration and late testing of the software. Inconsistencies, misunderstandings, and quality problems often remain undiscovered till the end of a project, when the integration fails or testing exposes poor quality. Once problems have been found, work on the project has to start all over again, requirements have to be corrected, the design has to be modified, and large parts of the implementation have to be revised. This can mean that a project completed at "90%" is suddenly back where it all started [Royce90].

Incremental Models

Reducing the integration risk Incremental models are used to improve the technical manageability of projects and avoid the risk of a "big bang" integration at the end of a project [Jacobson99, Kruchten99, Stapleton97]. Figure 14.4 shows the structure of such a process.

In incremental processes, the system is built in a series of steps or *increments.* Figure 14.4 shows an example with three increments. To manage the project as a whole, incremental processes start with a coarse requirement definition for the entire project. A plan for the entire project describing all increments is based on this requirement definition. In addition, an architecture for the entire system is developed at the beginning of the project. It ensures that all increments can be realized and integrated into the entire system.

Example for gradual extension Each increment creates an extension of the system, building on the previous step. One example for such an approach is the creation of a time entry system in three steps. Step 1 is a core system that reads data from input terminals, writes data consistently to a database, and produces basic reports about staff work hours. This core system is already mature enough to be tested and used. Step 2 adds functions to exchange data with the

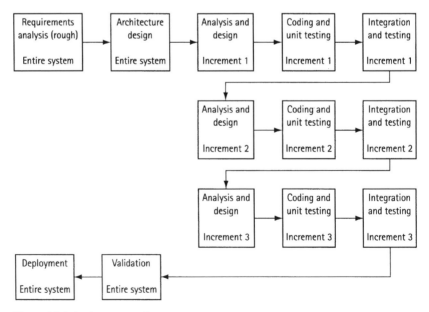

Figure 14.4 An incremental process.

project planning and billing system; it also represents a testable and usable system. Step 3 is the entire system, essentially step 2 extended by a GUI for manual input and time corrections.

Mini waterfall
Each single step is realized in an independent sequential process, often called a *mini waterfall*. The requirements are written in detail, a design is created, and new classes are implemented and tested in unit tests for each increment. Subsequently, the new classes are integrated into the entire system, followed by integration and system tests.

The incremental development approach has the following implications on the testing strategy:

- All tests, from the unit test to the system test, run at the end of each increment. This means that testers are needed throughout the project, in contrast to sequential processes, where they are needed only at the end.

- Considering that each system step contains the results from all previous steps, many tests are iterated. This means that the tests of step i become so-called regression tests in steps $i+1, \ldots, n$.

Limits of incremental models
Similar to sequential processes, incremental processes require a basic understanding of the requirements for the entire project at the beginning of the project. Although the incremental approach is more flexible to change compared to sequential models, incremental models are not suitable for projects based on unclear or unknown requirements. An evolutionary approach is more appropriate for such projects.

Evolutionary Models

Evolution through iterative approximation
Evolutionary processes start with a vision of the product under development. However, the requirements are not known and cannot be gathered (by interviews or analysis of existing systems) at reasonable cost.[1] In this situation, requirements can be stated only by realizing part of the product vision and the subsequent collection of feedback. This means that new preversions of the product are created iteratively, each covering an increasingly

---

1. This is more often the case than you would expect. Unfortunately, these findings are often gained only at the end of a project.

larger part of the vision. By using each pre-version in practice and implementing customer or endorser feedback, the product's pre-versions gradually approximate the customer's requirements.

Iteration plan

Although evolutionary development does not enable us to foresee the result of a project at the beginning, we have to plan each iteration. This plan describes the goals of each iteration (e.g., development of a central data repository component) and addresses project risks (e.g., technical feasibility in the chosen architecture). Each single iteration is implemented according to a suitable process model (e.g., a mini waterfall model), then the result is verified and feedback is collected. This evolutionary approach was described by Boehm [88] in a formal meta model—the *spiral model.*

During the past years, many scientists and consultants have dealt with the question of how to practically use an evolutionary model with its frequent requirement and design changes. They have developed techniques to prevent the design and code from becoming unusable at some point in time due to constant changes. For this purpose, software developers need permission to change and improve the design of an existing (and runnable!) system, which conflicts with the principle, Don't fix it if it ain't broke. In his famous book, Martin Fowler [99] used the term *refactoring* (see Chapter 1, Section 1.2) to describe how such design and code renovations can be realized, provided we run a sufficient number of unit tests.

The following rules apply to testing in the evolutionary process:

- Exactly as in the incremental model, all tests, from the unit test to the system test, run (at least) at the end of each iteration.

- After each refactoring step, the areas concerned—and often the entire system—have to be additionally tested; otherwise, there might be a risk of destroying some runnable functionality.

Agile software processes

In the past few years there has been a rapidly growing interest in evolutionary models in the form of *agile methodologies,* which have stirred up interest all over the software landscape. Under the motto "agile," 17 representatives of modern, lightweight software methodologies joined efforts to formulate a common manifesto, the *Manifesto for Agile Software Development* [Fowler01]. The processes (XP, Crystal, SCRUM, and Adaptive Software Development) proposed by the advocates of agile methodologies are evolutionary. The actual content of this manifesto concerns the process culture rather than the process itself. The basic notion is that the trained and motivated team, cooperating with the customer, comes first. Documents and tools are used only where they prove useful. The idea that a product can be fully specified in a document in advance is abandoned. Dramatic changes to the orientation of a project are seen as a characteristic of an increasingly dynamic business environment.

Continuous Integration

The trend away from sequential models towards incremental and evolutionary process models avoids late software integration. Following the thought through, we arrive at the idea to always keep the software in an integrated state, as XP requires. *Continuous integration* means integrating even small changes into the system, daily or even several times a day.[2]

Requirements of the building and testing processes

Continuous integration translates into extreme requirements of the testing process. The system must not become inconsistent from integrating a changed class. This means that testing is necessary after each integration. It also means that automated regression tests are required, because no test team can constantly test their software. In addition, both the tests and the build procedure have to be very efficient. As far as the build is concerned, this results in the requirement for incremental compilation and a good library concept. As for the test, fast tests automated in the programming language with testing frameworks are the only feasible option (e.g., no GUI tests where time-consuming operation sequences are simulated). For example, CruiseControl [URL:CruiseControl] is an open source tool that attempts to solve exactly these problems.

14.3 | Costs and Benefits of Automated Unit Tests

Early error discovery saves money

The main benefit of tests is to prevent and find errors. Errors found during the development phase mean cash money. The removal of an error found during the development is much cheaper than removing the same error when the software has already been delivered. Errors found after delivery

---

2. Fowler and Foemmel discuss the advantages and realization of continuous integration extensively at [URL:ContIntegration].

lead to unhappy customers, standstill of equipment or business processes, difficult and expensive error localization, and complex problem tracking and remove processes, and eventually to new delivery and installation of the software.

In addition to the enormous savings potential of early error identification, unit tests offer more benefits. Unit tests created by the test-first approach have a strong positive influence on the design. Moreover, unit tests are local, therefore the cause of errors is normally found *in* the tested class. If an error occurs in the system test, then localizing the error in the entire system is much more expensive. And additional costs (e.g., traveling expenses, standstill of business processes, penalties, etc.) have to be expected if the software is already in productive use.

Hard facts
The benefit of unit tests can be explained by the numbers: Studies conducted by IBM [Subramaniam99] observed that an error found during the coding or unit testing phase is cheaper by a factor of 10, compared to when it is found in the system test. This factor rises to 100 for errors found as late as during the software's productive use.

Test automation costs
At the other end of this enormous benefit are the costs for creating and updating tests. These costs are higher for automated than for manual tests. In contrast, the costs for test runs are much higher in manual testing. Figure 14.5 shows that automated tests pay off if they are repeated many times. From a specific number of n iterations, the costs for the n-th manual test run are higher than the costs of the n-th automated test run, plus one-time costs for creating the automated test.

Costs arising from test reworking
Another cost factor in automation is the cost for test reworking. When the functionality or the public interface of a class changes, then we also have to adapt our test cases. This means that, in reality, the cost for test automation is not constant; it depends on the (hard to foresee) rate in which the software changes.

Despite the difficulties in estimating the exact costs, we can state the following:

- In continuous integration (see the end of Section 14.2) automation of most test cases is a must; after all, these tests run several times daily. Chapter 2 showed this by a small example calculation.

- In incremental process models without continuous integration, the costs for automation have to be weighed against the costs for the test runs. It is recommended to collect experience by initially automating

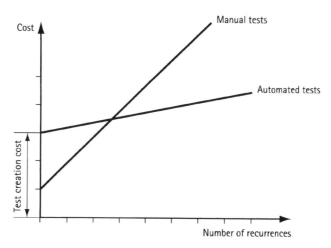

Figure 14.5 Comparing the costs of manual versus automated testing.

the most important basic tests, the so-called *smoke tests*,[3] which check basic application cases (e.g., starting and ending) of the software.

■ In sequential models, the development is followed by a time-limited integration phase. For this reason, unit tests are needed less often, and the benefit of automation becomes questionable. Often, automating unit tests is uneconomic in strongly sequential processes. Neverthe-less, automated tests have to be created for critical components that cannot be tested manually, important internal calculation compo-nents for example. In such a case, it is recommended to use a testing framework.

14.4 | Commercial Process Models

This section discusses the integration of unit tests based on commercial process models. The proprietary *Rational Unified Process (RUP)* is one rep-resentative of incremental models. We will be using *Extreme Programming* as an example for evolutionary (and agile) processes next, because it repre-sents the home of the testing approach discussed in this book.

---

3. The program is additionally put through a "smoke test," a relatively simple check, to see whether the product starts to smoke when being switched on.

Rational Unified Process

2500 pages of process description The Rational Unified Process (RUP) is a commonly used incremental process [Kruchten99]. This process is available in two variants. One publicly available version in the form of a book [Jacobson99] is called *Unified Software Development Process;* it was defined by the OO gurus, Jacobson, Booch, and Rumbaugh in 1999. In contrast, the actual RUP is a commercial product of Rational Software Corporation. The process definition of RUP is a hypertext document describing the workflow details in an overwhelming volume of about 2500 pages; it includes templates and offers tools for integration into the development flows.

Two-dimensional process structure The structure of RUP comprises two dimensions (Figure 14.6). The time dimension divides the project duration of RUP into various phases. Being an incremental model, RUP begins with a total planning phase, called *inception* in RUP lingo. This phase identifies all functional requirements and creates a coarse project plan. The next phase *(elaboration)* describes the most important requirements in detail; they form the basis to elaborate an architecture allowing us to realize all increments. The system is then incrementally created during the subsequent implementation phase *(construction)*. Each increment uses a small sequential process—a mini waterfall. The *transition* phase begins when all increments have been integrated into the system and tested. Next, the system is validated within its

Inception
Elaboration

Construction
Transition

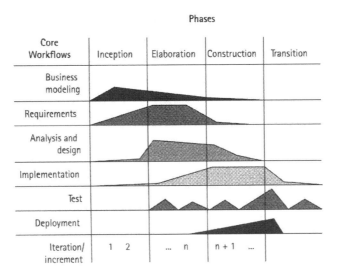

Figure 14.6 Structure of the Rational Unified Process.

production environment, and remaining errors are removed. Eventually, experiences are collected and process improvements are planned.

Core workflows The second dimension of the process description is the content dimension. This dimension describes *core workflows,* forming the mini-waterfall process used for each increment. The latter begins with the (optional) *business modeling,* where existing processes or systems are modeled and used as a basis for the new development. Based on the business requirements, the *requirements* workflow develops the requirements of the software. This basis is used for the *analysis and design* workflow to develop software models, where RUP is closely related to using the *Unified Modeling Language (UML)* [OMG-UML]. The subsequent workflows implement the increment based on the design, and then integrate it into the previous increments and test it.

Figure 14.6 also shows that the parts of each single workflow are not identical in each iteration. The first iterations strongly focus on gathering the requirements, while later iterations concentrate more and more on implementation and testing.

Supporting workflows In addition to the workflows for the mini waterfall, RUP also describes supporting management workflows, such as *configuration and change management, project management,* and *environment.* Although quality assurance is missing in RUP, experience has shown that RUP can be easily combined with classic quality assurance procedures, at least when the quality staff is trained for the notations and workflows of RUP.

Testing strategy in RUP The testing strategy in RUP consists of unit tests, integration tests, and system tests, similar to those described for other models. The universal systematics with regard to creating and documenting tests is of particular interest; it is based on the close relationship of RUP to UML and especially to *use cases.*[4] The starting point for a test is the scenarios, which are either,

- use cases that describe step by step how a user operates the system; or

- *interaction charts* representing the scenarios selected from a use case in UML by gradually describing the interaction between objects in the system.

---

4. A pragmatic and down to earth discussion of use cases can be found in *Writing Effective Use Cases* [Cockburn00b].

To test these scenarios, we need various elements:

Testing
vocabulary
in RUP

- **Testing procedures**, which are derived from the scenarios. A testing procedure describes a sequence of steps undertaken during a test. These steps are the scenario as described in the use case or interaction chart. For this purpose, we describe input data and the expected results.

- **Test cases** in RUP describe the combined input and output data to be tested in the testing procedure rather than the steps of the testing itself, in contrast to the terminology used in the rest of this book. These realization steps are documented in a testing procedure. A testing procedure can be used to run various test cases.

- **Test scripts** automate testing procedures. These scripts can be developed by use of a testing tool or testing framework, as described in this book.

Figure 14.7 shows how all these things interrelate. Uniform trackability from the use case to the testing procedure and the test script is particularly meaningful for requirement-driven system or acceptance tests, because it ensures that the requirements are properly tested.

For unit tests, however, this redundant documentation represents the maximum step, which we would create only in very rare cases, and it is not necessary in RUP. For central classes (e.g., classes that implement a protocol), we could also derive the automated unit test from an interaction chart for that class. In RUP, running unit tests produces a test result (e.g., in the form of a test log), like the one created by xUnit. First, we want to improve *halted tests* (i.e., tests that stopped due to errors in the test script)

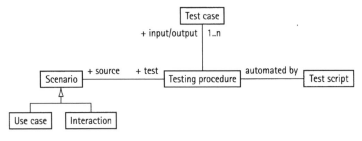

Figure 14.7 Relations between the RUP's testing artifacts.

until all tests terminate successfully. And finally, the test results are evaluated; the goal here is to have all tests functioning at 100% at the end of the iteration.

Regardless of the volume of additional documentation created, it is important to note that unit tests are an integral part of RUP and very well suited to its incremental development approach.

Extreme Programming

Basics for flexibility

XP is an evolutionary model, encouraging the customer toward a change in direction. The flexibility needed for this approach is essentially based on the support of refactoring, which can be used to clean up the design once the changes have been implemented (see Chapter 1, Section 1.2). To prevent extensive restructuring work to the point where integration of the software becomes extremely difficult or impossible, XP requires continuous integration. There must be a test for each functionality to ensure that restructuring does not destroy a previously implemented functionality. For this reason, test automation is a conditio sine qua non in XP as many tests have to run often.

User stories

In addition to unit tests, XP defines acceptance tests based directly on the customer's requirements. The requirements are formulated by the customer and written in the form of *user stories*, which describe various aspects of the system under development. A user story is a short description of a system function or property that fits on an index card. The details of each user story are collected later in customer interviews. There are acceptance tests for each story, checking whether or not the story has been realized correctly to meet the customer's acceptance criteria for the described system property.

Acceptance tests as automated acceptance criteria

For these acceptance tests, full automation is required in XP, too, although it is more difficult to achieve than with unit tests. For example, if a user story describes the look and feel of a screen representation, a report, or a file, then helper routines have to be developed or tools have to be used to check such representations (see also Chapter 1, Section 1.2, subsection, Test Types in XP). Acceptance tests are an automated variant of a customer's acceptance criteria.

XP versus RUP

When XP was first documented [Beck00a], it seemed obvious that it was some kind of countermovement to something as document-centric as RUP. It was not so much what the RUP said should be done or not be done, but the Taylorist view that could clearly be felt behind the scenes.

However, there quickly appeared voices who argued that XP can be considered an instance of the RUP process framework if you only take away enough of the optional parts of RUP [Martin01]. Meanwhile, with the growing support of lightweight, agile methodologies in the software engineering community, the interpretation of RUP has changed in order to show that it is—and has always been—an agile methodology framework [Larman01]. Now there even exists an XP-Plugin to the Rational Unified Process [URL:RupXpPlugin].

14.5 Will Automated Unit Tests Fit in My Process?

Both the waterfall model and the processes described earlier involve unit tests in one way or another. The benefit of local error removal can be equally achieved in all models. If the process supports test-first development, then we have the additional benefit of a strong design improvement.

Differences In contrast, there are differences in the automation cost-benefit ratio. Automation pays off increasingly the more often we can repeat test cases as regression tests. For this reason, the benefit is lowest in strongly sequential models, such as the waterfall model, but these models are retreating, mainly due to the high risk involved in late integration. Undoubtedly, people will empirically determine the limits of automation for the different variants of incremental and evolutionary models. With continuous integration, as requested by all agile processes, and test-first programming, full automation of unit tests is a must.

Bottom line Unit tests and the test-first approach can be used meaningfully in the modern process models we've discussed. Although they have actually come into fashion thanks to XP, their use is by no means limited to XP.

Chapter 15

Loose Ends and Opportunities

The last chapter of any book bears a great deal of responsibility, because various reader groups meet again in this chapter. All those who read from cover to cover wish an overall summary including suggestions for further approach. Those who read selected chapters would like to learn here what they didn't have time to read in detail. And all those who read only the last chapter want to see the core statement of this book presented on half a page. Let's begin with an executive summary.

Summary of the book

Testing is—still—a neglected area in the software development discipline, and many developers like to close their eyes to it. The truth is that the programming level is ideal for the use of automated unit tests, not only to reduce the number of bugs, but also to facilitate the developer's work. Contrary to what some may think, test cases do not slow down the programming process; they accelerate it, because they catch errors early and they facilitate refactoring of an existing program, or even make it possible in the first place. This opens up a chance for continual extension of your application, without falling into the feared "maintenance trap."

The *test-first approach* is a continuation of the test automation idea. This approach requires the creation of test cases before creating the actual application code. This means that tests assume a new, additional task: they considerably influence the design of an application and are thus *the* control instrument of an evolutionary design. In contrast to the widely used approach that tries to design as many details of a system as possible in advance, the test-first approach puts us in a position to further develop the fine design of a system in micro-iterations in a few minutes.

However, working by the test-first approach is by no means easy, and it requires each developer to rethink, especially in the beginning. Before you feel comfortable with this new way of programming, you have to learn basic steps and get over a few psychological hurdles. This book dealt with these initial problems and a large number of advanced issues and testing techniques. Where necessary, we represented the theoretical basics, and the reader's attention was drawn to questions that cannot be generally answered. Chapter 14 discussed the question of how test-first development can be integrated into the software processes commonly used today, probing each single technique with regard to its contribution to the whole—the development of software.

Despite all techniques and special cases discussed in this book, a large part is based on simplified assumptions:

Simplified assumptions

- With the test-first approach, we begin from zero; that is, there is no software we can build on or adapt.

- At the beginning of a project, the development team masters at least the basics of test-first programming.

- The team is the master over the entire code; there are no interfaces to other projects.

In fact, only very few projects meet all of these conditions. For this reason, the author puts the following ideas and approaches up for discussion.

15.1 Unit Testing for Existing Software

Only very few teams have to start a new software development project from scratch. A successful project is normally in the maintenance mode most of its life span. If we want to introduce a new technique such as unit tests or even test-first development to such a project we will have to deal with a few difficulties:

Difficulties in testing existing code

- The existing code base was most likely developed without much thought of testability, making subsequent creation of unit tests difficult.

- A refactoring effort required to improve testability (and the design) cannot be safely done when there are no tests. But because there are no tests due to poor testability, we get stuck in a chicken and egg problem.

- The quality of existing classes is not known. Test cases checking merely the existing and not the actually desired functionality risk lashing down errors in the program.

- The older the code base, the higher the probability that it contains a lot of unused functionality. Naturally, we don't want to implement test cases for such a functionality.

So no wonder Kent Beck [00a] considers testing one of the most frustrating areas for a development team that migrates to XP. Beck recommends resisting the temptation to create subsequent unit tests for all existing code. Depending on the project size, this would mean that the team would be tied down for weeks or even months without delivering additional functionality for the customer.

Testing on demand   Another approach is more promising and above all less risky: while new system parts are totally subject to a test-first development, the test cases for existing classes are added one by one as needed:

- As soon as legacy code has to be changed, for example, due to a new requirement or a program error, unit tests are written *around that code.* From now on, it is even possible to do refactoring to legacy code.

- Every time a problem emerges in legacy classes, no matter how small it may be or how easily it can be fixed, a corresponding test is added.

- Whenever untested classes are used, the code that checks the expected functionality in the legacy code should be added first.

If you follow these recommendations, the first thing you will notice is that the development speed will slow down. However, after some time, the testing coverage will achieve a satisfactory result even with the old code base, and the differences between old and new code are getting smaller. Another positive effect is that exactly those parts of the program that are run or changed often are those heavily tested.

Testing around Legacy Code

As plausible as this step-by-step approach may sound, it has one big draw-back: writing unit tests around legacy code is as easy as creating tests before the implementation only in rare cases. Often we find the old code base is so bad that only concurrent refactoring enables us to create unit tests at all. Michael Feathers [02a] discusses the issue and some techniques to tackle it in *Working Effectively with Legacy Code*.

It is, however, impossible to formulate a universal recipe for how to solve the problem in a specific case. Most of these cases require a sound mixture of caution and instinct to secure the most problematic parts of leg-acy code by test cases and to make them accessible to refactoring or to a complete replacement. Nevertheless, there are a few proven heuristics:[1]

Heuristics for subsequent testing

- First of all, we have to identify the component we can use to knot our test cases around. The better the object-oriented design in the old code, the easier it will be to identify an isolated and small unit. If this is not possible, if we can't find a separable unit in the worst case, we have to rely on a complete suite of function (or acceptance) tests.

- Test cases should be written only for the parts of the identified compo-nent that are actually used in other parts of the program. When in doubt, a static code analysis can provide additional—but not abso-lute—security.

- When creating test cases, we should initially concentrate on a unit's behavior visible from the outside. In this respect, existing current design documents could be helpful, but may point in the wrong direc-tion if outdated.

- The implementation of fine-grained white-box unit tests for existing code is worthwhile only provided that it is of high quality and in a sta-ble condition, which is normally the case only after some refactoring work.

- Refactoring without the safety net of unit tests is risky so that we should do it only in pairs. However, some restructuring steps are relatively unproblematic or can even be executed with corresponding tools, such

---

1. The following summary corresponds essentially to discussions at [URL:YahooXP] and [URL:WikiUTFLC].

as extracting a method, renaming a method, or deleting wrong comments. Here again, we should be careful to move forward only in very small steps.

- Encapsulation of the old components into a facade facilitates unit testing for new system parts and allows subsequent replacement of this unit by a new development.

- The easiest way to write unit tests is to write them for the low-level functions of the old code base. Sometimes, we can conquer legacy from below.

- It may happen that existing code is in such a bad state that only complete rewriting promises lasting success. In this case, we should invest sufficient time and energy into the creation of acceptance tests and encapsulation into a facade.

Bottom line   Creating subsequent unit tests is a tricky and challenging business, mainly due to the fact that testability was not a criteria in the design of that code. This means in some cases that enormous efforts are required to turn existing software into a permanently maintainable condition. In the worst case, frustration about later testing causes the entire testing approach to collapse. These risks and investments should be weighed against the cost of a complete or partial new development. More often than initially expected, a redevelopment from scratch turns out to be the cheaper variant.

No "testless" changes!   A team that is nevertheless entrusted with the task of maintaining "testless" software should mainly avoid one thing: simply getting straight down and going without first building a reassuring net of test cases. If the customer remains stubborn, insisting on "quick changes," then there is still the option of just not telling them about these indispensable quality measures.

15.2 | Introducing Unit Tests to the Development Team

We all know that a book is suitable only to a limited extent to convey applicable knowledge, and even less to change people's behavior. An organization or a project manager determined to introduce test-driven development faces the question of how the introduction of unit testing into the work process of the development team will actually work. The smartest approach depends strongly on the general development approach of an organization. In this respect, we distinguish between the *craftsmanship* approach and the *organizational* approach.

The Craftsmanship Approach

Apprentice, master, and journeyman

In his book entitled S*oftware Craftsmanship,* Pete McBreen [01] propagates the transition from *software engineering* to *software development as a craft.* In traditional craftsmanship, the abilities and reputation of the individual "master" play a decisive role in winning contracts. Quality and durability of a product are in the center, while training new craftsmen functions by the proven principle of apprentice, journeyman, and master. Extreme Programming and the other agile processes (see Chapter 14, Section 14.2) can be viewed as typical software development methods by the craftsmanship approach.

Teaching by good example

In the case of the craftsmanship development approach, a development team of manageable size will include an experienced developer, a master or journeyman, who will train the other team members by supporting them in their attempt at walking in a test-first environment and ensuring on the basis of his or her authority that all developers will correctly apply unit tests. If the team additionally uses programming in pairs, then the developers will mutually support each other in learning and continuous application of unit tests. The most important goal is to get a self-regulation mechanism going: short iterations→find slipped-through errors in tests →adapt and improve the testing practice.

Where do the masters learn?

A technique that allows coordination of such a craftsmanship approach across project borders is the so-called *communities of practice* [Cohen01]. Here, the master programmers form a community that meets regularly to exchange experiences and problems. This makes the realization of the test-first approach in various teams more uniform and more efficient, because a master programmer can obtain support from his or her peers in solving problems.

The Organizational Approach

In many larger development organizations, however, you won't find exclusively motivated teams, instructed in new technologies by a charismatic master programmer. In these cases, hierarchical management structures and formalized processes normally control the events. These rigid structures mostly have a negative impact on the team's commitment and willingness to learn.

Such a case requires an organizational approach to introduce the test-first development method to ensure meaningful use of the technique. Such an approach is more expensive and clearly more unpleasant than the craftsmanship approach. But sometimes it is the only way to get both the management and the developers onboard. An organizational flow to introduce unit tests could look as follows:

Six-step program to introduce new process practices

1. **Feasibility study, including cost-benefit analysis.** The current development process should be used to determine whether and how unit tests can be integrated into the process before a decision in favor of introducing unit tests is made. If an integration is basically possible, then costs and benefits of unit tests should be compared, similarly to our evaluation in Chapter 14. In this respect, costs also include expenditures for steps following the process introduction.

2. **Management decision and support.** Based on the study in step 1, the manager in charge of the development organization (e.g., the head of the development department) decides on the introduction of unit tests. This manager will select a project for the introduction of unit tests, including a separate budget and manager for the project. The next steps will be taken within the scope of this project.

3. **Adaptation of the development process.** The implementation of the unit tests will be built into the existing process description. Changes concern the description of activities, integration of new intermediate products (e.g., test cases, test results), modified role description, and modified tool environment.

4. **Implementation of pilot projects.** Next, the changed process should be checked for its practical suitability, before it becomes the new standard. This means that experiences with the changed approach should be collected from a representative set of projects. The members of the pilot projects have to be trained in theory and practice. Following a general introduction, one promising method is coaching by an experienced test-first expert. Regular reviews are necessary to bring the quality of the created test suites to the required level.

Within a closed frame of a pilot project, we recommend the craftsmanship approach described earlier, even if the formal steps described are necessary on an organizational level.

5. **Adaptation of the process based on the results.** The process documentation is revised based on the experiences gained from the pilot projects. The resulting software process is reviewed and approved. This means that the unit tests have become an official part of the development process.

6. **Rollout of unit tests within the organization.** This is the step where the remaining developers of the organization participate in training programs about the test-first and unit testing issues. From now on, each new project will use unit tests. The important thing is that each project has at least one staff member who has already gained practical experience and is able to act as coach for the project team.

Of course, the six-step plan introduced above can also be used for other process improvements [Kaltio00]. The important thing is, here too, that there is only one change per cycle, because major changes in one shot will most likely fail or not be permanent. In any event, the introduction of unit tests in large organizations should be active and take place within a separate project. Otherwise, the test-first idea might land where many good ideas have been stranded before: in aging file cabinets and remote archives.

15.3 | What's Missing?

When I started this book project, I had hoped to be able to cover all important unit-testing problems in one book this size. My research work during writing and the large number of comments obtained from the reviewers have shown that I was wrong. Each technical discipline we dealt with in a separate chapter led to a new problem that would have deserved another chapter.

Issues that fell through the selection funnel include unit tests in the context of XML and XSLT, Web services, SOAP, asynchronous messaging, numerous JUnit expansions, object-oriented databases, and many more. The fact that the number of uncovered testing problems increases rather than decreases is mainly due to SUN themselves, as they continually rig out Java with new APIs and components. Therefore, a fat paper file full of ideas has to wait for another book.

However, there are still questions that remain unanswered because I lacked either experience, theoretical material or understanding—and sometimes all three things. I want to address two of these loose ends very briefly:

- Test-first development with simple design and continuous refactoring works best when the complete code is created and changed within one single team. As soon as code gets out, we have to provide for additional documentation, for example, in the form of DBC contracts, and a more stable interface policy. Although extensive test suites are still required, they assume a different (additional) task.

- The question of whether the more important role of unit tests in test-driven development is quality assurance or design control remains unanswered. And using the test-first approach to improve the design is merely based on empirical experience and is not scientifically substantiated. This also holds true for many—if not all—other software development approaches.

The test-first approach is not a fully explored terrain, even at the end of this book. I look forward to intensive and fruitful discussions with you, readers, and to reading many more books about this topic.

Part III

Appendices

Appendix

Notes to JUnit

| A.1 | **Frequently Asked Questions (FAQs)** |

This short list of frequently asked questions was originally based on the FAQs contained in the JUnit documentation. The official JUnit FAQ list [URL:JUnitFAQ] has completely changed meanwhile. The following questions will be answered:

- How do I implement a test case for a thrown exception?

- How do I organize my test case classes?

- How do I run setup code once for all my test cases?

- I get a `ClassNotFoundException` when I use `LoadingTestRunner`. What can I do?

- Why do I get exception `XYZ` when using a graphical test runner, but not in the textual test runner?

- "`assert`" has been a keyword since JDK 1.4. Isn't there a conflict with JUnit's `assert` method?

- How do I best integrate JUnit with my favorite development environment?

How Do I Implement a Test Case for a Thrown Exception?

Catch the exception and if it isn't thrown, call the fail method. Fail signals the failure of a test case. Here is an example:

```
public void testIndexOutOfBoundsException() {
    Vector v= new Vector(10)
    try {
        Object o= v.elementAt(v.size());
        fail("ArrayIndexOutOfBoundsException expected");
    catch (ArrayIndexOutOfBoundsException expected) {
    }
}
```

Alternatively, you can use the ExceptionTestCase class:

1. Make your test case class a subclass of junit.extensions.Exception-TestCase.

2. Write the test ignoring exceptions:

```
public void testIndexOutOfBoundsException() {
    Vector v= new Vector(10);
    v.elementAt(v.size());
}
```

3. Create the test case:

```
Test t = new ExceptionTestCase(
    "testIndexOutOfBoundsException",
    ArrayIndexOutOfBoundsException.class);
}
```

Chapter 4, Section 4.5 includes extensive instructions for testing of error cases and exceptions.

How Do I Organize My Test Case Classes?

This question was answered in detail in Chapter 3, Section 3.3, Organizing and Running Tests.

How Do I Run Setup Code Once for All My Test Cases?

junit.extensions.
TestSetup

Wrap the top level suite in a subclass of TestSetup. Here is a sample All-Tests.suite() method:

```
public static Test suite() {
    TestSuite suite = new TestSuite();
    suite.addTest(...);
    ...
    TestSetup wrapper= new TestSetup(suite) {
        public void setUp() {
            oneTimeSetUp();
        }
    };
        return wrapper;
}
```

A practical example can be found in Chapter 9, Section 9.5. Kent Beck argues that the need for a one-time setup is often a sign of a design in need of improvement (see [URL:YahooJUnit], Message 2789), especially when the test cases depend on one another.

I Get a `ClassNotFoundException` When I Use `LoadingTestRunner`. What Can I Do?

Exclude list

LoadingTestRunner uses its own class loader implementation to reload your code by default upon each test run. But this class loader does not include any standard classes and no classes from JAR files. You can specify a list of packages excluded from the default class loader so that they will be reloaded only once. This list is defined in the file `excluded.properties` in the `junit.runner` package. In the original file that comes with JUnit Version 3.8, all JDK-owned packages are excluded:

```
#
# The list of excluded package paths for the TestCaseClassLoader
#
excluded.0=sun.*
```

```
excluded.1=com.sun.*
excluded.2=org.omg.*
excluded.3=javax.*
excluded.4=sunw.*
excluded.5=java.*
excluded.6=org.w3c.dom.*
excluded.7=org.xml.sax.*
excluded.8=net.jini.*
```

If you are using libraries as JAR files, you have to add the packages included in these files to the *exclude list*. To this end, you either change the original file in junit.jar or you create your own file of junit.jar in the class path. In this way, your version will be loaded instead of the original file.

Why Do I Get Exception XYZ When Using a Graphical Test Runner, But Not in the Textual Test Runner?

Normally LoadingTestRunner is to blame. You can either adapt the exclude list as described in the preceding FAQ, or you can disable the Reload option. Considering that the Java class loading behavior causes very difficult problems, in rare cases only disabling the Reload option or using the textual test runners helps.

"assert" Has Been a Keyword Since JDK 1.4. Isn't There a Conflict with JUnit's Assert Method?

assertTrue()   assert(...) was deprecated in JUnit Version 3.7. All calls should be replaced by assertTrue(...).

How Do I Best Integrate JUnit with My Favorite Development Environment?

Probably the most rudimentary form of integration is to simply make junit.jar available in the class path. This works in all cases, but starting a test runner may be more complex. Eclipse [URL:Eclipse] even comes with its own, seamlessly integrated JUnit test runner.

In addition, Ward Cunningham's Wiki includes a separate page about JUnit and IDEs [URL:WikiJWI]. This pages refers to tips, tricks, and problems relating to JUnit in connection with Forte, NetBeans, Kawa, Microsoft-Tools, JBuilder, VisualAge, and Emacs. You can find a TogetherJ integration at [URL:ExtremeJava].

A.2 JUnit Expansions

The number of expansions and add-ons developed and maintained for JUnit has grown continuously. Some of them were introduced in Parts I and II of this book.

A current list of these additional tools is maintained on the JUnit Web page at [URL:JUnitExt]. The following list is not complete, but it includes the most important additional tools available at the time of writing this book. To spare the reader from having to look up references in the bibliography, we directly list the URLs in this appendix.

JUnitX and XPTest

Testing private properties

JUnitX offers a way to access `private` or `protected` variables, methods, and classes in test cases. The tool builds on the latest JUnit version and uses the Java reflection mechanism.

XPTest combines and integrates JUnit and JUnitX in the UML modeling tool TogetherJ. This also allows automatic creation of test cases by using the pattern mechanism of TogetherJ.

URL: *www.extreme-java.de/*

Daedalos JUnit Extensions

Testing resources

The JUnit extensions of Daedalos allow you to define testing resources that are initialized only once. This can speed up some test suites.

URL: *www.daedalos.com/EN/djux*

JFCUnit

Swing testing   This expansion allows testing of Swing user interfaces. Chapter 13, Section 13.2, introduced JFCUnit in an example.

URL: *http://jfcunit.sourceforge.net/*

JUnitPP

JUnitPP expands JUnit by a test data repository, some command line arguments, a built-in iteration counter, and multi-threading from the command line.

URL: *http://junitpp.sourceforge.net/*

Mock Objects

Mock library   This library offers both an extensive base of generic mock objects and some specialized packages, for example, for testing of JDBC connections and servlets. The concept of mock objects was described in Chapter 6.

URL: *www.mockobjects.com/*

MockMaker

Mock generation   *MockMaker* is a tool that serves to create source code for mock objects and builds upon the mock objects library. The tool starts from an interface and generates classes allowing both the specification of the expected behavior and return of predefined function values.

URL: *http://mockmaker.sourceforge.net/*

EasyMock

Classless
mock objects
This package allows you to define simple mock objects directly in the test code, without the need to write your own mock classes. The underlying *Java proxy mechanism* is available from JDK Version 1.3 and higher.

> URL: *www.easymock.org/*

JXUnit

Data-centered
testing
JXUnit allows you to separate test data from the test logic by dumping the test data into XML files. This is more interesting for functional test suites than for fine-grained unit tests.

> URL: *http://jxunit.sourceforge.net/*

Joshua

Distributed
test run
Joshua was designed for the distributed execution of regression tests, based on Jini and JavaSpaces, in addition to JUnit.

> URL: *http://cs.allegheny.edu/~gkapfham/research/joshua/*

JDepend

Dependency
metrics
JDepend makes its way hand over hand through a set of Java class files and Java source directories and for each package, determines metrics on dependencies upon other packages. Properly interpreted, the figures provide hints

about expandability, reusability, and maintainability of a package. You can test automatically for permitted tolerances of specific measurement values in JUnit test cases.

URL: *www.clarkware.com/software/JDepend.html*

Jester

Mutation testing

Jester uses the *mutation testing* approach to offer a completion to conventional coverage analyses. This type of testing is based on targeted changes to the application code and subsequent checks to determine whether or not the original test suite detects these changes as errors. This means that you can identify code parts run within the suite, but with effects not verified in the tests. Chapter 8, Section 8.3, classified this approach into the classic coverage analysis.

URL: *http://jester.sourceforge.net/*

HttpUnit

Web
function tests

HttpUnit is a framework to address external Web sites in a Java program. One possible use in combination with JUnit is to run automated Web function tests. Chapter 12, Section 12.1, introduced this use in an example.

URL: *http://httpunit.sourceforge.net/*

JUnitEE

Test runner
servlet

This package uses a test runner servlet to run server-side test suites. One possible use is testing EJBs (see Chapter 11, Section 11.2).

URL: *http://junitee.org*

Canoo WebTest

XML-based
Web tests

Canoo WebTest is a free open source tool for automated testing of Web applications. It calls Web pages and verifies the results, giving comprehensive reports on success and failure. The test scripts are specified in XML as ANT tasks and use HttpUnit behind the scenes.

URL: *http://webtest.canoo.com/*

Cactus

Server-side
testing

Cactus is another tool that allows you to run server-side tests. In contrast to JUnitEE, this tool uses proxy servlets, which establish the connection to client test cases. Chapter 12, Section 12.2, introduced Cactus in theory and practice.

URL: *http://jakarta.apache.org/cactus/*

JUnitPerf

Performance
testing

JUnitPerf represents a collection of "test decorators" you can use to check performance and scalability.

URL: *www.clarkware.com/software/JUnitPerf.html*

J2MEUnit

Small-format
testing

Java 2 MicroEdition was designed for devices with scarce storage and resources. This means that the virtual machine may not support reflection, making it necessary to adapt JUnit. A JUnit port for this platform, *J2MEUnit* is available.

URL: *http://j2meunit.sourceforge.net/*

Test Mentor Java Edition

Commercial JUnit replacement

To my knowledge, Silvermark's *Test Mentor* is the only commercial software that supports the same test approach as JUnit and can even run JUnit test cases. In addition, this product offers a large number of additional functions, including graphical tools for test creation and documentation, management generic test modules, and test result management on XML basis.

URL: *www.silvermark.com/Product/java/stm/index.html*

Appendix B

Unit Tests with Other Programming Languages

<table>
<tr><td>B.1</td><td></td></tr>
</table>

B.1   Smalltalk

The dispute between Java advocates and Smalltalk supporters on the benefits and drawbacks of static versus dynamic typing will probably never come to an end. However, it is uncontested that a large number of ideas and novelties originated from the Smalltalk environment, including XP and the xUnit testing framework. For this reason, it is not surprising that the test-first culture is widely used in the Smalltalk world and that *SUnit*—the predecessor of JUnit—is widely supported.

Support of numerous Smalltalk dialects

SUnit has meanwhile become a *camp Smalltalk project;* that is, it is revised and expanded in regular intervals. Version 3.0 is available for most Smalltalk environments. More than a dozen variants, including variants for Dolphin, Gemstone, Squeak, VisualAge for Smalltalk, and VisualWorks, can be downloaded from [URL:SUnit]. All of these variants are based on the same code base; only the graphical test runners are specific to a particular dialect.

Creating Test Cases with SUnit

Basically, creating test cases is similar to JUnit. Test case classes are derived from TestCase; setUp and tearDown are available, and all parameterless methods beginning with "test" are automatically grouped into a test suite.

Let's look at a simple test case that tests for adding two elements to a list (OrderedCollection):

```
testTwoElements
    |list|
    list := OrderedCollection new.
    list add: 'first'.
    list add: 'second'.
    self assert: list size = 2.
    self assert: (list at: 1) = 'first'.
    self assert: (list at: 2) = 'second'.
```

The test runner that comes with the product (this example uses the version for VisualAge for Smalltalk) is unpretentious but absolutely sufficient in terms of functions (Figure B.1). There is a wide choice of test runner variants available online—surely one for each taste.

Differences to Java

Do test cases in SUnit look like those in JUnit? The answer can be, largely Yes, because the basic testing approach is the same in both languages. However, there are a few differences:

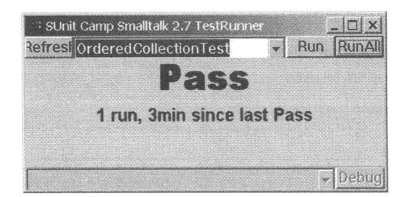

Figure B.1 The SUnit test runner.

Dynamic typification
- Smalltalk's lack of static typing reduces the required code quantity, in test methods also, but this may be compensated for by tests for the correct type of an object.

Mighty reflection
- The mightier reflection mechanism and easy access to classes of the development environment open up additional automation options. For example, when the test runner encounters a failure or error, it offers you a way to let the debugger or class browser jump directly to that position within the code.

Dummy implementations
- Smalltalk lets you create dummy and mock objects with little effort, because you don't have to implement all methods of an interface— only the ones used. The simplest dummy objects in Smalltalk are blocks.

No private methods
- Because all methods are public in Smalltalk, you don't have to use all kinds of tricks to test them.

Inheritance on the class side
- Since classes are real objects, living in an inheritance hierarchy in parallel to the objects, it is easy to implement a large number of features (e.g., *parametrized test suites*).

Programming in the debugger
- So-called "programming in the debugger" is commonly used in Smalltalk: you set break points in methods you haven't implemented yet and then start the tests and complete the actual functionality in the debugger. This allows you to work comfortably, especially in test-first development.

Evaluation

Attention: subjective!
It doesn't come as a surprise that the test-first approach found its supporters initially in the Smalltalk world. Working in the mighty Smalltalk environments for a while makes you feel that you are "somehow slowed down" in Java. It seems that the large number of detours required in Java strikes you even more. What a pity that Smalltalk still has not found its way out of its niche even after 20 years. A few weeks (or more) of Smalltalk experience would be a good thing for Java developers who try to rid themselves of the usual preconceived opinions.

B.2 | C++

Progressing in the unit testing framework for C++, called *cppUnit,* is disproportionate to the widespread use of the language. There was only a pre-alpha version available at Sourceforge [URL:CppUnit] when this book went to press. One cause behind the slow progress of the testing framework for C++ is the lack of standardization for this language—in the area of user interfaces and library formats, for example. In particular, it seems obviously difficult to support different compilers by one common framework.

Compiler support   While cppUnit offers only rudimentary support for C++ compilers under UNIX and Borland C++, it concentrates heavily on the support of Visual C++, the de facto standard compiler for Windows. Installation and operation instructions, as well as a graphical test runner, are available for only this compiler. Accordingly, the following description is based on Visual C++ 6.0 and cppUnit Version 1.6.2.

Installation

Once you have downloaded and unpacked the tar file, there are two class libraries available:

- The actual framework classes, including a text-based test runner, are in the cppUnit-1.6.2/src/cppUnit directory.

- cppUnit-16.2/src/msvc6/testrunner contains a graphical test runner based on Microsoft Foundation Classes (MFC) [Kruglinski98].

The directories mentioned above include preconfigured Visual C++ project files and workspaces for both components, simplifying the translation and generation of corresponding libraries. Just load the workspace and use *Rebuild All* to start the compilation.

cppUnit-1.6.2/examples includes examples for using cppUnit. The projects *CppUnitTestMain* and *CppUnitTestApp* include regression tests for the cppUnit framework itself.

Setting Up a Test Project

The example projects show how a workspace for your own test projects should look like. When setting up such a test project, you can proceed as follows:

1. Create a new and empty workspace.

2. Add cppUnit by selecting Project→Insert Project into Workspace to add the file cppUnit.dsp to your workspace.

3. Create your new project by selecting File→New→Projects to add a *Win32 Console Application* to the workspace. You have to select the Add to current workspace option in the *New Project Dialog*.

4. Adapt your *Project Settings*. There are a few things to do here. The include path for cppUnit has to be typed in the well-hidden Settings tab, C/C++→Preprocessor→Additional include directories. In addition, you have to enable support for *Run-Time Type Information (RTTI)* [Schildt98]. To enable RTTI, select the appropriate checkbox in the tab, C/C++→C++ Language. Next, go to the tab, Link→General to add the unit test library to the Object/library modules list. This is cppunitd.lib for the default debugging configuration. And finally, a piece of information that's missing in the installation instructions: select the Debug Multithreaded DLL option in the tab, C/C++→Code Generation→Use run-time library.

Creating Test Cases

Now that you have overcome the wiles of installation, you can create your test cases. cppUnit defines analog classes similarly to JUnit. Note that all classes are defined in the name space, CppUnit; in other words, that the descriptors known from JUnit have to be preceded by the prefix, Cpp-Unit::. This means that the class CppUnit::TestCase is the basis for creating test cases. The following listing shows the declaration of a test case, AppendTest, in a C++ header file, corresponding to the Java test case StringBufferTest from Chapter 2, Section 2.3:

```
class AppendTest : public CppUnit::TestCase
{
    char *s;
public:
    AppendTest();
    virtual ~AppendTest();

    void setUp();
    void testAppendString();
    void testEmptyBuffer();
}
```

As in Chapter 2, Section 2.3, we are running two tests, where one (testEmptyBuffer) tests for correct determination of the length of an empty string and the other (testAppendString) tests for correct appending to an empty string. The corresponding methods look like this:

```
AppendTest::AppendTest() : TestCase()
{}
AppendTest::~AppendTest()
{}
void AppendTest::setUp() {
    s = new char[100];
    *s = '\0';
}
void AppendTest::testEmptyBuffer() {
    CPPUNIT_ASSERT(strlen(s) == 0);
}
void AppendTest::testAppendString() {
    strcat(s, "Ein String");
    CPPUNIT_ASSERT(strcmp(s, "Ein String") == 0);
    CPPUNIT_ASSERT(strlen(s) == 10);
}
```

Running Your Tests

To run your tests, you need a test runner and a test suite consisting of the test cases you want to run, as in JUnit. Unfortunately, C++ lacks a reflection mechanism, so that cppUnit cannot automatically collect all methods beginning with "test." Although cppUnit uses the C++ mechanism Runtime Type Information, this mechanism merely allows you to determine type IDs and type names, but doesn't let you find classes and methods by names. This means that the syntax used to build a test suite is somewhat more complex in cppUnit, compared to Java, because cppUnit requires a pointer to the method itself, in addition to the test method's name:

```
static CppUnit::Test *suite() {
   CppUnit::TestSuite *ts = new CppUnit::TestSuite;
   ts->addTest(
      new CppUnit::TestCaller<AppendTest>("testAppendString",
         &AppendTest::testAppendString));
   ts->addTest(
      new CppUnit::TestCaller<AppendTest>("testEmptyBuffer",
         &AppendTest::testEmptyBuffer));
   return ts;
}
```

The class TestCaller allows you to run each single test case. The template argument, AppendTest, is used to state the name of your test case class, allowing you to run the fixture. Subsequently, you run the test by means of the pointer to the test method (e.g., &AppendTest::testEmpty-Buffer).

Finally, to run the test suite, you need a test runner. A text-based test runner is part of the cppUnit project:

```
int main( int argc, char* argv[] )
{
   CppUnit::TextTestRunner runner;
   runner.addTest(AppendTest::suite());
   runner.run();
   return 0;
}
```

This returns the following output for the preceding test suite:

```
..
OK (2 tests)
```

An error is reported as follows:

```
.F.
!!!FAILURES!!!
Test Results:
Run: 2   Failures: 1   Errors: 0
There was 1 failure:
1) test: testAppendString line: 34 C:\
cppunit-1.6.2\src\demo\demo\AppendTest.cpp
"strlen(s) == 9"
```

All these things can be done in a much nicer way if you use the graphical test runner (Figure B.2). To use the graphical test runner, you have to add the test project as MFC-based Win32 application. As demonstrated in the cppUnitTestApp example, the test runner project should also be added to the workspace. In addition to the library, cppunitd.lib, you have to add the libraries, testrunnerd.lib and testrunnerd.dll.

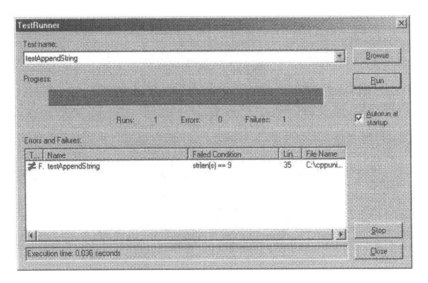

Figure B.2 A graphical test runner.

Overall Impression

The package does not appear to be fully mature yet. In addition, limitations of the language—such as lacking compatibility between the implementations, missing reflection, and the good old juggling with pointers and storage management—make testing much more laborious, compared to Java, let alone Smalltalk.

<table>
<tr><td>B.3</td></tr>
</table>

B.3 The Rest

The test-first approach can basically be used in any programming language that allows you to quickly toggle between code writing and code running as you work away on your project. For this reason, it is not surprising that JUnit-like tools are available in almost any reasonable programming language.

Choice of supported languages [URL:XPSoftware] lists versions for the following languages and platforms: Ada, Ant, C, C++, Curl, Delphi, Dot-Net, Eiffel, Forte, Gemstone/S, Jade, Java, Java 2 Micro Edition, JavaScript, K-Language, Objective C, Oracle, Palm, Perl, PHP, PowerBuilder, Python, Rebol, Ruby, Smalltalk, Suneido, Visual Basic, and Visual Objects. Notice, however, that both the extent and the quality of these tools are totally different, and sometimes even competing solutions for the same language are offered.

But even for languages not yet supported, the excuse, There is no testing framework! doesn't count. Chapter 5 provided enough insight into the internal parts of JUnit for you to get going in the language of your choice.

Glossary

Abstract class A class that cannot be instantiated, because parts of its implementation are delegated to specific subclasses.

Acceptance test In *Extreme Programming (XP)*, an automated test defined by the customer to check for the extent the software meets the required functionality or the required properties (see also *User story*).

Anticomposition axiom An axiom about object-oriented testing stating that the sum of adequate test suites for segments of a module does not necessarily result in an adequate test suite for the entire module.

Antidecomposition axiom An axiom about object-oriented testing stating that components can contain errors that may not be discovered by testing the system as a whole.

Antiextensionality axiom An axiom about object-oriented testing stating that various implementations of a specification may require different test suites.

AWT Abstract Windowing Toolkit. The original Java GUI library with components whose look and feel depend on the operating system used.

Black–box test A specification-based test that looks at a system or unit exclusively from the outside, that is, over its public interface; see *White-box test*.

Bottom–up An approach used, for example, for testing or design, where a hierarchical problem or system is initially viewed from the finest decomposition step, then works upward to the more general. Opposite: *Top-down*.

Cast A hint for the Java compiler to view an object as an instance of a subclass or interface. Although a cast avoids static typing, it often cannot be avoided because there are no generic types in Java.

Checked Exception A Java exception that isn't being derived from `Runtime-Exception`. Such an exception has to be caught or listed in the `throws` clause.

Class invariant A condition that has to be applicable for each instance of a class at any given time, that is, after execution of an arbitrary public method. See also *Design by contract.*

Code smell The unpleasant feeling you get when you see bad code.

Continuous integration The integration of new code into the overall system several times a day. In contrast to what many developers believe, the integration effort decreases when you integrate more frequently.

CORBA Common Object Request Broker Architecture. An open, language-independent infrastructure for distributed components developed by the Object Management Group (OMG).

CUT Class under test. The class on which a certain test case or test suite focuses. See also *OUT.*

DBC Design by contract. A paradigm stating that each software element (e.g., a method) specifies in a contract the pre-conditions it requires to run, the post-conditions it will ensure upon completion, and which invariants will remain. See also *Class invariant.*

Defensive programming A programming style that attempts to ensure that programming errors occurring in one place cannot cause unexpected results (e.g., program abort) in another place. Practices of defensive programming include mainly the avoidance of problematic language constructs and the definition of coding standards, but also checking of all input parameters of methods.

Delegation An object delegates a task to another object, where the message signature is normally maintained.

Dependency Inversion Principle This principle states that general and abstract program modules should depend only upon abstract modules (interfaces) [Martin02b].

Deployment Delivery and installation of a software product.

Design pattern A ready-to-use solution for a frequent design problem, expressed as partial design, consisting of classes and associations. Each design pattern is embedded in a set of constraints.

DOM Document Object Model. A platform- and programming-language independent API standardized by the World Wide Web Consortium (W3C) for reading and modifying HTML and XML documents.

EJB Enterprise JavaBeans. A component model developed by Sun Microsystems for transactional, distributed, and persistent components.

Equivalence class A set of values handled equally or similarly by a program fragment, so that tests have to use only one representative value from that set.

Error In JUnit lingo an uncaught exception occurring during a test and triggered by the code under test (e.g., a NullPointerException in the application code). Notice the difference to *Failure*.

Factory method A method that returns a newly created object, thus helping to avoid the direct invocation of a constructor.

Failure In JUnit lingo the violation of an assert... in a test case. Notice the difference to *Error*.

Fixture In JUnit lingo a set of objects representing the common initial state for the test cases of a test class.

Garbage collection The automatic collection and removal of objects no longer needed, as all *JVMs* have to do.

GUI Graphical user interface. A graphical (rather than textual) interface consisting of windows, texts, images, buttons, menus, and other graphical elements (widgets). The user interacts with the application by invoking and manipulating those widgets using the keyboard, the mouse, or other input devices.

HTML Hypertext mark-up language. The World Wide Web's standard language for authoring and presenting documents. Despite the word "standard," there exist many different—and partly incompatible—versions of HTML.

IDE Integrated Development Environment. Graphical software tool that simplifies and coordinates the creation of programs and use of a compiler and debugger. Examples include Eclipse, JBuilder, and Visual Studio.

Instance variable A variable of which each instance of a class contains its own instance. The opposite is a class variable or static variable, where all instances of a class share one common variable instance.

Integration test An *interaction test* on a grand scale. The term originates from sequential software process models, where a system is integrated in one single phase after the coding phase.

Interaction test A test that checks for correct interaction between two or more objects.

Interface A Java interface defines a public interface that has to be provided by implementing classes. However, there are also purely descriptive interfaces (e.g., `java.io.Serializable`).

JavaSpaces A technology integrated in *Jini* for transparent distribution of objects in Java.

JDBC Java Database Connectivity. A Java API for access to SQL databases.

JDK Java Development Kit. There are currently the main versions JDK 1.0 through JDK 1.4. Since JDK 1.2, the name was changed to JAVA2 SDK.

Jini Java Intelligent Networking Infrastructure. A simple infrastructure to build virtual networks, consisting of distributed Java-based services.

JSP Java Server Pages. A technology allowing you to embed Java code into HTML pages.

JVM Java Virtual Machine. A program that runs Java applications compiled in bytecode by interpreting or just-in-time compiling of that bytecode.

Law of Demeter A law stating that the dependencies of an object upon the implementation of a "remote" object should be minimized. To achieve this goal, the rule says that, when implementing a method, messages may be sent only to specific objects:

- To the object itself;

- To objects passed as parameters; and

- To instance variables.

In particular, this law prevents message chains, such as `this.getName().getFirstName().equals(...)`.

Liskov Substitution Principle A principle stating that an object of a subtype, and thus also an instance of a subclass, should be able to replace the object of the supertype at any given time [Liskov93].

Mapping tool More exactly, object-relational mapping tool. A library or framework used to map objects to relational databases.

ODBC Open Database Connectivity. Standard interface to access databases.

OODBMS Object-oriented database management system. An OODBMS can directly store objects with their properties, their identity—and sometimes even their implementation. Using an object-oriented database frees developers from explicitly having to translate objects to rows in relational database tables.

OUT Object under test. The object on which the currently running text case executes its operations and asserts. See also *CUT.*

Pair programming An XP practice requiring that each piece of source code to be integrated into the software product should be created by two programmers jointly at one computer.

Persistence A program's ability to persist beyond its runtime. We also speak of *persistent objects,* which are stored to a database or somewhere else for later use.

Polymorphism One of the basic principles of object-orientation allowing an object reference to accept instances from various (sub) classes. A method invocation to the object reference leads to the dynamic execution of the method defined for the references instance.

RDBMS Relational database management system. A system used to create, edit, and manage relational databases.

Refactoring Rebuilding and restructuring code in very small steps without changing the behavior visible from outside.

Reflection A Java mechanism allowing access to class and interface specifications at runtime, defined in the package, `java.lang.reflect`.

RMI Remote Method Invocation. A Java-specific distribution mechanism allowing objects of a *JVM* to invoke methods of objects executed by another *JVM* (e.g., on another computer).

RTTI RunTime Type Information. A standard C++ concept allowing the determination of the type of an object at runtime.

Runtime exception Also called *unchecked exception.* An exception derived from `RuntimeException` (e.g., `NullPointerException`). Such an exception can potentially occur in any statement and thus does not have to be caught or added to the `throws` clause, in contrast to a *checked exception.*

RUP Rational unified process. Commercial software process of Rational.

Servlet A Java technology for dynamic creation of Web contents.

Smoke tests A manageable set of functional test cases that merely check for basic functionality. The term originates from the metaphor, Switch on and wait if smoke escapes.

SOAP Simple object access protocol. A standardized protocol used to call Internet-based services (Web services) by exchanging *XML* messages.

SQL Structured Query Language. A commonly used query language for relational databases.

Swing Since JDK 1.2, Swing is part of the central Java libraries used for platform-independent representation of user interfaces building on *AWT*.

System test A test aimed at checking the entire system.

Task In XP, a task describes a piece of functionality that can be implemented by a developer pair in a few hours.

Test case The specification of a test; it includes the target object, inputs, expected outputs, as well as context and side conditions of that test run.

Test driver A program that runs a series of tests automatically.

Test first Other terms are *test-first programming, test-first design,* or *test-driven development.* A software development approach that specifies the result of a manageably small implementation step in an automated test case before the actual coding takes place.

Test oracle A function or algorithm that uses the input data to create the expected output data, so that a test can use it as expected output data.

Test suite A set of test cases jointly run and viewed.

Thread Also called *execution context* or *lightweight process.* A sequential control flow within a program with its own stack and program counter. Several threads can run in parallel within a program, that is, within the same address space.

Top-down An approach used, for example, for testing or design, where a hierarchical problem or system is initially viewed on the top hierarchical level to then be further decomposed. Opposite *Bottom-up.*

UML Unified Modeling Language. A visual modeling language for object-oriented software models standardized by the Object Management Group (OMG).

Unit test A type of test that, in contrast to a *system test*, refers to a single unit (method, class, component) of a system rather than to the overall system.

Use case The definition of a behavior of the software product based on gradually described interactions between user and system.

User story Informal description of a functional requirement or product property in *XP.* A user story serves as the basis for *acceptance tests* that formally check whether the product complies with the described function or property.

Value semantics An object should be viewed as a *value* when its identity is determined by its invariable state.

Waterfall The simplest sequential software process model, where the analysis, design, coding, and testing phases are done sequentially for the entire system.

White-box test An implementation-based test, in contrast to a specification-based test; see *Black-box test.*

XML Extended Markup Language. A family of technologies allowing one to define so-called markup languages (languages with a structure similar to HTML) and to create, exchange, and edit corresponding documents.

XP Extreme Programming. An agile development process, the origin of test-first development, among other things.

Bibliography and List of References

Bibliography

[Allen01] Eric E. Allen: Diagnosing Java Code: The Liar View bug pattern. *IBM Developers,* April 2001. Available at [URL:DevWorks].

[Alpert98] Sherman R. Alpert, Kyle Brown, and Bobby Woolf: *The Design Patterns Smalltalk Companion.* Boston: Addison-Wesley, 1998.

[Barry96] Douglas K. Barry: *The Object Database Handbook: How to Select, Implement, and Use Object-Oriented Databases.* New York: Wiley, 1996.

[Beck94] Kent Beck: Simple smalltalk testing. *Smalltalk Report,* October 1994.

[Beck98] Kent Beck and Erich Gamma: Test-infected: Programmers love writing tests. *JavaReport,* July 1998.

[Beck99] Kent Beck and Erich Gamma: JUnit: A cook's tour. *JavaReport,* May 1999.

[Beck00a] Kent Beck: *Extreme Programming Explained: Embrace Change.* Boston: Addison-Wesley, 2000.

[Beck00b] Kent Beck and Martin Fowler: *Planning Extreme Programming.* Reading, Mass.: Addison-Wesley, 2000.

[Beck03] Kent Beck: *Test-Driven Development: By Example.* Boston: Addison-Wesley, 2003.

[Binder99] Robert Binder: *Testing Object-Oriented Systems.* Reading, Mass.: Addison-Wesley, 1999.

[Boehm76] B. W. Boehm: Software engineering. *IEEE Transactions on Computers* C-25 (12) 1226–1241, 1976.

[Boehm88] B. W. Boehm: A spiral model of software development and enhancement. *IEEE Computer* (5) 61–72, 1988.

[Boger01] Marko Boger: *Java for Distributed Systems.* New York: Wiley, 2001.

[Brown01] Simon Brown et al.: *Professional JSP,* 2nd edition. Birmingham, UK: Wrox Press, 2001.

[CMU00] Carnegie Mellon University and Software Engineering Institute: *CMMI for Systems Engineering/Software Engineering,* Version 1.02, CMU/SEI-2000-TR-019. Pittsburgh, Pa., November 2000.

[Cockburn97] Alistair Cockburn: Structuring use cases with goals. *Journal of Object-Oriented Programming* September/October, 1997, 35–40, and November/December, 1997, 56–62.

[Cockburn00a] Alistair Cockburn and Laurie Williams: The costs and benefits of pair programming. In Succi, Giancarlo, and Michele Marchesi: *Extreme Programming Examined.* Boston: Addison-Wesley, 2001, Ch. 14.

[Cockburn00b] Alistair Cockburn: *Writing Effective Use Cases.* Boston: Addison-Wesley, 2000.

[Cockburn01] Alistair Cockburn: *Agile Software Development.* Boston: Addison-Wesley, 2001.

[Cohen01] Don Cohen and Laurence Prusak: *In Good Company—How Social Capital Makes Organizations Work.* Boston: Harvard Business School Press, 2001.

[Crispin01] Lisa Crispin: Carefree highway: How an XP tester can drive success. *STQE Magazine,* July/August 2001.

[Darwin01] Ian Darwin: *The Java Cookbook.* O'Reilly, 2001.

[DeMillo78] R. A. DeMillo, R. J. Lipton, and F. G. Sayward: Hints on test data selection: Help for the practicing programmer. *IEEE Computer,* 11(4) 34–41, 1978.

[Deursen00] Arie van Deursen, Tobias Kuipers, and Leon Moonen: Legacy to the extreme. In Succi, Giancarlo, and Michele Marchesi: *Extreme Programming Examined.* Boston: Addison-Wesley, 2001, Ch. 29.

[Dustin99] Elfriede Dustin, Jeff Rashka, and John Paul: *Automated Software Testing.* Boston: Addison-Wesley, 1999.

[Feathers00] Michael Feathers: *Test First Design—Growing an Application One Test at a Time,* 2000–2001. Available at [URL:XProgramming].

[Feathers01a] Michael Feathers: *The 'Self'-Shunt Unit Testing Pattern,* 2001. Available at [URL:OM].

[Feathers01b] Michael Feathers: *The Little Black Book of Test First Design.* Available at [URL:LittleBlackBook].

[Feathers02a] Michael Feathers: *Working Effectively with Legacy Code.* Available at [URL:OM].

[Feathers02b] Michael Feathers: *The Humble Dialog Box.* Available at [URL:OM].

[Fowler99] Martin Fowler: *Refactoring: Improving the Design of Existing Code.* Reading, Mass.: Addison-Wesley, 1999.

[Fowler00] Martin Fowler: Is design dead? In Succi, Giancarlo, and Michele Marchesi: *Extreme Programming Examined.* Boston: Addison-Wesley, 2001, Ch. 1.

[Fowler01] Martin Fowler and Jim Highsmith: The Agile manifesto. *Software Development Online,* August 2001. Available at [URL:SDMagazine].

[Gamma95] Erich Gamma et al.: *Design Patterns.* Boston: Addison-Wesley, 1995.

[Gassmann00] Peter Gassmann: Unit testing in a Java project. In Succi, Giancarlo, and Michele Marchesi: *Extreme Programming Examined.* Boston: Addison-Wesley, 2001, Ch. 15.

[Gilb93] Tom Gilb, Dorothy Graham, and Suzannah Finzi (eds.): *Software Inspection.* Boston: Addison-Wesley, 1993.

[Gomaa93] Hassan Gomaa: *Software Design Methods for Concurrent and Real-Time Systems.* Boston: Addison-Wesley, 1993.

[Hightower01] Richard Hightower and Nicholas Lesiecki: *Java Tools for Extreme Programming.* New York: Wiley, 2001.

[Humphrey95] Watts S. Humphrey: *A Discipline for Software Engineering,* SEI Series. Reading, Mass.: Addison-Wesley, 1995.

[Hunt98] John Hunt and Alex McManus: *Key Java—Advanced Tips and Techniques.* London: Springer-Verlag, 1998.

[Hunter01] Jason Hunter and William Crawford: *Java Servlet Programming,* 2nd edition. Cambridge, Mass.: O'Reilly, 2001.

[Hyde99] Paul Hyde: *Java Thread Programming*. Indianapolis: Sams, 1999.

[Jacobson99] Ivar Jacobson, Grady Booch, and James Rumbaugh: *The Unified Software Development Process*, Object Technology Series. Boston: Addison-Wesley, 1999.

[Jeffries99] Ronald E. Jeffries: eXtreme testing. *STQE-Magazine*, March/April 1999.

[Jeffries00] Ronald E. Jeffries et al.: *Extreme Programming Installed*. Reading, Mass.: Addison-Wesley, 2000.

[Kaltio00] Timo Kaltio and Atte Kinnula: Deploying the defined software process. *Software Process: Improvement and Practice* (5), 2000.

[Kaner93] Cem Kaner, Jack Falk, and Hung Quoc Nguyen: *Testing Computer Software*, 2nd edition. New York: Thomson Computer Press, 1993.

[Kruchten99] Philippe Kruchten: *The Rational Unified Process—An Introduction*, Object Technology Series. Boston: Addison-Wesley, 1999.

[Kruglinski98] David Kruglinski, Scot Wingo, and George Shepherd: *Inside Visual C++ 6.0*. Munich, Germany: Microsoft Press, 1998.

[Langr01] Jeff Langr: *Evolution of Test and Code via Test-First Design*, March 2001. Available at [URL:OM].

[Larman00] Craig Larman and Rhett Guthrie: *Java 2 Performance and Idiom Guide*. Upper Saddle River, N.J.: Prentice Hall, 2000.

[Larman01] Craig Larman, Philippe Kruchten, and Kurt Bittner: *How to Fail with the Rational Unified Process: Seven Steps to Pain and Suffering*. Available at *http://jeffsutherland.org/papers/RUP/Kruchten_Larman_HowToFailWithRUP.pdf*

[Lea00] Doug Lea: *Concurrent Programming in Java*, 2nd edition. Reading, Mass.: Addison-Wesley, 2000.

[Lehman85] M. M. Lehman and L. A. Belady: *Program Evolution: Processes of Software Change*. London: Academic Press, 1985.

[Lewis95] Ted Lewis: *The Art and Science of Smalltalk*. Upper Saddle River, N.J.: Prentice Hall, 1995.

[Liskov93] Barbara H. Liskov and J. M. Wing: A new definition of the subtype relation. *Proc. of ECOOP '93, LNCS 707*, Berlin: Springer-Verlag, 1993.

[Little01] Jim Little: *Up-Front Design versus Evolutionary Design in Denali's Persistence Layer*. XP Universe, 2001. Available at [URL:XPU2001].

[Mackinnon00] Tim Mackinnon, Steve Freeman, and Philip Craig: Endo-Testing: Unit testing with mock objects. In Succi, Giancarlo, and Michele Marchesi: *Extreme Programming Examined.* Boston: Addison-Wesley, 2001, Ch. 17.

[Maier01] Peter Maier: It's GREAT, isn't it? *Proceedings of Net Object Days.* Erfurt, Germany:, 2001.

[Marick00] Brian Marick: *Testing for Programmers.* Available at [URL: Testing].

[Martin96a] Robert C. Martin: The Liskov Substitution Principle. *C++ Report,* March 1996. Available at [URL:OM].

[Martin96b] Robert C. Martin: The Dependency Inversion Principle. *C++ Report,* May 1996. Available at [URL:OM].

[Martin01] Robert C. Martin: *RUP vs. XP.* Available at [URL:OM].

[Martin02a] Robert C. Martin: *Continuous Care vs. Initial Design,* 2002. Available at [URL:OM].

[Martin02b] Robert C. Martin: *Agile Software Development: Principles, Patterns, and Practices.* Upper Saddle River, N.J.: Prentice Hall, 2002.

[McBreen01] Pete McBreen: *Software Craftsmanship.* Boston: Addison-Wesley, 2001.

[McGregor01] John D. McGregor and David A. Sykes: *A Practical Guide to Testing Object-Oriented Software.* Boston: Addison-Wesley, 2001.

[Meade00] Erik Meade: *Design Principles in Test First Programming.* Available at [URL:OM].

[Metsker01] Steven John Metsker: *Building Parsers with Java.* Boston: Addison-Wesley, 2001.

[Meyer97] Betrand Meyer: *Object-Oriented Software Construction,* 2nd edition Upper Saddle River, N.J.: Prentice Hall, 1997.

[Monson01] Richard Monson-Haefel: *Enterprise JavaBeans,* 3rd edition. Cambridge, Mass.: O'Reilly, 2001.

[Newkirk01] James Newkirk and Robert C. Martin: *Extreme Programming in Practice.* Reading, Mass.: Addison-Wesley, 2001.

[Nielsen94] Jacob Nielsen: *Usability Engineering.* San Francisco: Morgan Kaufmann, 1994.

[Nygard00] Michael T. Nygard and Tracie Karsjens: Tests infect your Enterprise JavaBeans. *JavaWorld,* May 2000. Available at [URL:JavaWorld].

[OMG-UML] Object Management Group: *OMG Unified Modeling Language Specification Version 1.3*. Needham, Mass.: Object Management Group, Inc., 2000.

[Peeters01] Vera Peeters: *Simple Design and Unit Testing with Enterprise JavaBeans.*[XP 2001.] Available at [URL:XP2001], Ch. 24.

[Pekowsky00] Larne Pekowsky: *JavaServer Pages*. Reading, Mass.: Addison-Wesley, 2000.

[Pol00] Martin Pol, Tim Koomen, and Andreas Spillner: *Management und Optimierung des Testprozesses*. Heidelberg, Germany: dpunkt.verlag, 2000.

[Rainsberger01] J. B. Rainsberger: *Use Your Singletons Wisely*. IBM DeveloperWorks, 2001. Available at [URL:CoSingle].

[Riel96] Arthur J. Riel: *Object-Oriented Design Heuristics*. Reading, Mass.: Addison-Wesley, 1996.

[Royce70] W. W. Royce: Managing the development of large software systems: Concepts and techniques. *Proceedings IEEE Wescon*, August 1970.

[Royce90] W. E. Royce: TRW's Ada process model for incremental development of large software systems. *Proceedings of the 12th International Conference on Software Engineering (ICSE)*, 1990.

[Rutherford00] Kevin Rutherford: *Retrofitting Unit Tests with JUnit*. XP 2000. In Succi, Giancarlo, and Michele Marchesi: *Extreme Programming Examined*. Boston: Addison-Wesley, 2001, Ch 16.

[Schildt98] Herbert Schildt: *C++: The Complete Reference*, 3rd edition. Berkeley: Osborne McGraw-Hill, 1998.

[Schneider00] Andy Schneider: JUnit best practices. *JavaWorld*, December 2000. Available at [URL:JavaWorld].

[Schuh01] Peter Schuh and Stephanie Punke: *ObjectMother—Easing Test Object Creation in XP*. XP Universe, 2001.

[Seacord01] Robert C. Seacord et al.: *Legacy System Modernization Strategies*, Technical Report, CMU/SEI-2001-TR-025. Available at [URL:SEIPublications].

[Stapleton97] Jennifer Stapleton: *The Dynamic System Development Method*. Boston: Addison-Wesley, 1997.

[Stobie00] Keith Stobie: Testing for exceptions. *STQE*, July/August 2000.

[Subramaniam99] Bala Subramaniam: Effective software defect tracking. *Crosstalk*, April 1999. Available at [URL:Crosstalk].

[Succi01] Giancarlo Succi and Michele Marchesi: *Extreme Programming Examined.* Boston: Addison-Wesley, 2001.

[Wake01] William Wake: *Extreme Programming Explored.* Boston: Addison-Wesley, 2001.

[Weinberg98] Gerald M. Weinberg: *The Psychology of Computer Programming,* Silver Anniversary Edition, New York: Dorset House, 1998.

[Weyuker88] Elaine J. Weyuker: The evaluation of program-based software test data adequacy criteria. *Communications of the ACM* 31(6):668–675, June 1988.

URLs

[URL:Abbot] *http://abbot.sourceforge.net/*

[URL:AgileAlliance] *www.AgileAlliance.org/*

[URL:Ant] *http://ant.apache.org*

[URL:Apache] *www.apache.org/*

[URL:Cactus] *http://jakarta.apache.org/cactus/*

[URL:Cloudscape] *http://www-306.ibm.com/software/data/cloudscape/*

[URL:ConTest] *www.haifa.il.ibm.com/projects/verification/contest/*

[URL:ContIntegration] *www.martinfowler.com/articles/ continuousIntegration.html*

[URL:CoSingle] *www.ibm.com/developerworks/library/co-single.html*

[URL:CppUnit] *http://cppunit.sourceforge.net*

[URL:Crosstalk] *www.stsc.hill.af.mil/CrossTalk/*

[URL:CruiseControl] *http://cruisecontrol.sourceforge.net/*

[URL:Dbunit] *www.dallaway.com/acad/dbunit.html*

[URL:DevWorks] *www.ibm.com/developerworks/*

[URL:EasyMock] *www.easymock.org*

[URL:Eclipse] *www.eclipse.org*

[URL:EJB] *http://java.sun.com/products/ejb/docs.html*

[URL:EJBTutorial] *www.ejbtut.com/*

[URL:ExtremeJava] *www.extreme-java.de/*

[URL:HsqlDb] *http://hsqldb.sourceforge.net/*

[URL:HttpUnit] *www.httpunit.org/*

[URL:IContract] *www.reliable-systems.com/tools/iContract/iContract.htm*

[URL:Jakarta] *http://jakarta.apache.org/*

[URL:JavaWorld] *www.javaworld.com/*

[URL:JContract] *www.parasoft.com/jsp/products/home.jsp?product=Jcontract*

[URL:Jemmy] *http://jemmy.netbeans.org/*

[URL:Jester] *www.jester.sourceforge.net/*

[URL:JFactor] *www.instantiations.com/jfactor*

[URL:JFCUnit] *http://jfcunit.sourceforge.net/*

[URL:Jini] *www.sun.com/software/jini/*

[URL:JProbe] *www.quest.com/jprobe/*

[URL:JsUnit] *http://jsunit.berlios.de/*

[URL:JUnit] *www.junit.org/*

[URL:JUnitEE] *http://junitee.org*

[URL:JUnitExt] *www.junit.org/extensions.htm*

[URL:JUnitFAQ] *http://junit.sourceforge.net/doc/faq/faq.htm*

[URL:JWAM] *www.jwam.de*

[URL:KaCoMa] *http://kacoma.sourceforge.net/*

[URL:LittleBlackBook] *www.mindspring.com/~mfeathers/introduction.htm*

[URL:MockCreator] *www.abstrakt.de/mockcreator.html*

[URL:MockJDBC] *www.mockobjects.com/papers/jdbc_testfirst.html*

[URL:MockMaker] *www.mockmaker.sourceforge.net/*

[URL:MockObjects] *www.mockobjects.com/*

[URL:OM] *www.objectmentor.com/*

[URL:PairProgramming] *www.pairprogramming.com*

[URL:Refactoring] *www.refactoring.com*

[URL:RMITutorial] *http://java.sun.com/docs/books/tutorial/rmi/*

[URL:RupXpPlugin] *www.objectmentor.com/processImprovement/*
  xpRupResourceCenter/index

[URL:SDMagazine] *www.sdmagazine.com*

[URL:SEIPublications] *www.sei.cmu.edu/publications/*

[URL:SFJunit] *http://sourceforge.net/junit*

[URL:Soxabo] *www.soxabo.de*

[URL:STQE] *www.stqemagazine.com*

[URL:Struts] *http://struts.apache.org/*

[URL:StrutsTest] *http://strutstestcase.sourceforge.net/*

[URL:SUnit] *http://ANSI-ST-tests.sourceforge.net/SUnit.html*

[URL:Testing] *www.testing.com*

[URL:TestingAgile] *www.testing.com/agile/*

[URL:TestingCat] *www.testing.com/writings/short-catalog.pdf*

[URL:TestingCoverage] *www.testing.com/writings/coverage.pdf*

[URL:Threadalyzer] *www.quest.com/jprobe/threadalyzer.asp*

[URL:Tomcat] *http://jakarta.apache.org/tomcat/*

[URL:TopLink] *www.oracle.com/technology/products/ias/toplink*

[URL:Turbine] *http://jakarta.apache.org/turbine/*

[URL:UtilConcurrent] *http://gee.cs.oswego.edu/dl/classes/EDU/oswego/cs/*
  dl/util/concurrent/intro.html

[URL:VAJava] *www.ibm.com/software/ad/vajava/*

[URL:WakeAT] *http://users.vnet.net/wwake/xp/xp0105/*

[URL:WakeGUI] *http://users.vnet.net/wwake/xp/xp0001/*

[URL:WATF] *http://watf.sourceforge.net/*

[URL:Webtest] *http://webtest.canoo.com/*

[URL:Westphal] *www.frankwestphal.de/*

[URL:WikiEJB] *www.c2.com/cgi/wiki?EjbUnitTest*

[URL:WikiJWI] *http://c2.com/cgi/wiki?JunitWithIdes*

[URL:WikiMSBP] *http://c2.com/cgi/wiki?MethodsShouldBe-Public*

[URL:WikiRJOMO] *http://c2.com/cgi/wiki?RonJeffriesOnMockObjects*

[URL:WikiSAE] *http://c2.com/cgi/wiki?SingletonsAreEvil*

[URL:WikiTFD] *http://c2.com/cgi/wiki?TestFirstDesign*

[URL:WikiUT] *http://c2.com/cgi/wiki?UnitTests*

[URL:WikiUTATP] *http://c2.com/cgi/wiki?UnitTestingAround-ThirdParties*

[URL:WikiUTFLC] *http://c2.com/cgi/wiki?UnitTestsForLegacy-Code*

[URL:WikiUTNPMF] *http://c2.com/cgi/wiki?UnitTestingNonPublicMember Functions*

[URL:XP2001] *www.xp2001.org/xp2001/conference/papers/*

[URL:XPU2001] *www.agileuniverse.com/2001/xpuPapers.htm*

[URL:XProgramming] *www.xprogramming.com*

[URL:XPSoftware] *www.xprogramming.com/software.htm*

[URL:YahooJUnit] *http://groups.yahoo.com/group/junit*

[URL:YahooXP] *http://groups.yahoo.com/group/ extremeprogramming*

Further Reading

The most difficult thing in giving reading references is surely what to leave out. Therefore, our first recommendation is, Read all books and articles and visit all Web links listed here!

But because this may be difficult for some readers due to a lack of time, the following notes are an attempt to limit our reading suggestions to some highlights of more recent literature.

Extreme Programming

The undisputed cradle of the test-first approach is Extreme Programming. There are currently almost a dozen books about XP. Kent Beck's *Extreme Programming Explained* [Beck00a] is still the seminal work. From the programmer's view, *Extreme Programming Installed* [Jeffries00] is the right continuation, while *Planning Extreme Programming* [Beck00b] offers details about the planning issue for the fledgling XP enthusiast.

Readers interested in the current state of discussion about XP should visit the Yahoo! group "ExtremeProgramming" [URL:YahooXP] and Ron Jeffrie's Web site [URL:XProgramming].

Test-First and JUnit

With his latest work, *Test-Driven Development: By Example* [Beck02], test-first guru Kent Beck has written the undisputed basis for test-driven programming. You will also find an extensive test-first example—using JUnit—in *Extreme Programming in Practice* [Newkirk01]. Shorter examples are found in [Fowler99], [Jeffries00], and [Wake01]. The technical side of JUnit is discussed in several books, including [Hightower01].

Readers looking for advanced material about test-first design will also find them in some Web articles. We particularly recommend the articles of Michael Feathers—[Feathers00, 01a, 01b]—and Jeff Langr [Langr01], because they also discuss less obvious issues.

There is no lack of online JUnit introductions, for example [URL:JUnit], where you will find both the latest version to download and a tutorial, as well as a large number of articles and a list of all JUnit expansions.

Extensive—although unstructured—material is available from Ward Cunningham's Wiki Web site. A good starting-point are the pages "Unit-Tests" [URL:WikiUT] and "TestFirstDesign" [URL:WikiTFD]. Another Yahoo! group [URL:YahooJUnit] is again our first choice for discussions and exchange of experience.

Testing Object-Oriented Software

The seminal work on OO testing is *Testing Object-Oriented Systems* by Rober Binder [99]. This book offers an overwhelming amount of material in 1200 pages such that readers may find it difficult to identify a pragmatic entry. Let's say it in Kent Beck's words: "The biggest problem is that it doesn't balance the cost and benefits of tests."

A Practical Guide to Testing Object-Oriented Software [McGregor01] is a much smaller volume. This book is oriented to practice, easy to read, and it also discusses testing from the developer's perspective.

Of course, there are a great many resources on testing on the Web. One good start is [URL:Testing]. This Web site maintained by Brian Marick includes the test-first approach and can serve as a starting-point for in-depth studies. Starting from here you can also arrive at the home of "Agile Testing" [URL:TestingAgile], which is dedicated to the pragmatic way of testing as needed in agile development.

Miscellaneous

The overall context and the question, "How can I conduct software projects successfully?" is just as important for each developer as in-depth learning of a special field in software development.

Considering that each project is different and no team is identical, there is a need to adapt your approach to each single project. In his latest book entitled, *Agile Software Development* [Cockburn01], Alistair Cockburn carved this out excellently. He managed to represent both the theoretical fundamentals, and to show practitioners what they can immediately change in their projects.

Pete McBreen examines the same problem in *Software Craftsmanship* [McBreen01] and expands Cockburn's thoughts by the aspect of knowledge transfer from the master to the journeyman to the apprentice.

Index

X

Johannes Link has been project manager and software developer for four years at andrena objects ag in Karlsruhe, Germany. He came to andrena after years of practical software engineering research at the German Cancer Research Center and the German ABB Corporate Research Center. Johannes is responsible for andrena's internal and external training activities and has published articles on software testing and software development. He holds a diploma degree in medical computer science from Heidelberg University.

Peter Fröhlich holds an M.S. in computer science from the University of Aachen and a Ph.D. in electrical engineering from the University of Hannover. From 1998 to 2002, he worked for ABB Corporate Research as a developer, process improvement consultant, project manager, and manager of a research group. Since 2002, he has worked for Robert Bosch GmbH as a software architect. His research interests include process improvement, conceptual modeling, software architecture, and testing.

13564882R00229

Made in the USA
Lexington, KY
09 February 2012